The Poet Who
Created Herself

Edith Södergran:
Selected Letters

Some other books from Norvik Press

Jens Bjørneboe: *Moment of Freedom* (translated by Esther Greenleaf Mürer)
Jens Bjørneboe: *Powderhouse* (translated by Esther Greenleaf Mürer)
Jens Bjørneboe: *The Silence* (translated by Esther Greenleaf Mürer)
Kerstin Ekman: *Witches' Rings* (translated by Linda Schenck)
Kerstin Ekman: *The Spring* (translated by Linda Schenck)
Kerstin Ekman: *The Angel House* (translated by Sarah Death)
Kerstin Ekman: *City of Light* (translated by Linda Schenck)
Arne Garborg: *The Making of Daniel Braut* (translated by Marie Wells)
Svava Jakobsdóttir: *Gunnlöth's Tale* (translated by Oliver Watts)
P. C. Jersild: *A Living Soul* (translated by Rika Lesser)
Selma Lagerlöf: *Lord Arne's Silver* (translated by Sarah Death)
Selma Lagerlöf: *The Löwensköld Ring* (translated by Linda Schenck)
Selma Lagerlöf: *The Phantom Carriage* (translated by Peter Graves)
Viivi Luik: *The Beauty of History* (translated by Hildi Hawkins)
Henry Parland: *To Pieces* (translated by Dinah Cannell)
Amalie Skram: *Lucie* (translated by Katherine Hanson and Judith Messick)
Amalie Skram: *Fru Inés* (translated by Katherine Hanson and Judith Messick)
Hjalmar Söderberg: *Martin Birck's Youth* (translated by Tom Ellett)
Hjalmar Söderberg: *Selected Stories* (translated by Carl Lofmark)
August Strindberg: *Tschandala* (translated by Peter Graves)
August Strindberg: *The Red Room* (translated by Peter Graves)
August Strindberg: *The People of Hemsö* (translated by Peter Graves)
August Strindberg: *Strindberg's One-Act Plays* (Translated by Agnes Broomé, Anna Holmwood, John K Mitchinson, Mathelinda Nabugodi, Anna Tebelius and Nichola Smalley)
August Strindberg: *The Defence of a Madman* (translated by Carol Sanders and Janet Garton)
Anton Tammsaare: *The Misadventures of the New Satan* (translated by Olga Shartze and Christopher Moseley)
Kirsten Thorup: *The God of Chance* (translated by Janet Garton)
Elin Wägner: *Penwoman* (translated by Sarah Death)

The Poet Who Created Herself

The Complete Letters of
Edith Södergran to Hagar Olsson
with Hagar Olsson's Commentary
and the
Complete Letters of
Edith Södergran to Elmer
Diktonius

Translated and Edited by
Silvester Mazzarella

Norvik Press
2015

A catalogue record for this book is available from the British Library.

ISBN: 978-1-909408-21-0

First published in 2001 by Norvik Press. This edition 2015.

Norvik Press gratefully acknowledge the financial assistance given by the Finnish Literature Information Centre for the translation of this book.

Norvik Press
Department of Scandinavian Studies
University College London
Gower Street
London WC1E 6BT
United Kingdom
Website: www.norvikpress.com
E-mail address: norvik.press@ucl.ac.uk

Managing editors: Sarah Death, Helena Forsås-Scott, Janet Garton, C. Claire Thomson.
Editorial Assistant: Elettra Carbone
Production Assistant: Marita Fraser

Cover design: Marita Fraser
Cover photograph: Edith Södergran, Self Portrait.

Södergran
Starcatcher! -
your net glitterfull
of thundering gods
and rustling dead flowers.
Unborn you saw it all;
Sick you cured the well.
None bred poems like you did:
so full of life,
sucking blood.

- Elmer Diktonius

Achnowledgements

In putting this book together I am deeply indebted to the published research of Agneta Rahikainen, George Schoolfield, Roger Holmström, Clas Zilliacus, Holger Lillqvist and others. I am also very grateful for invaluable assistance of various kinds from Alan Beardon, David Heald, Merete Mazzarella, Agneta Rahikainen in her capacity as archivist of Svenska litteratursällskapet i Finland, Laurie Thompson, Robert Vilain, the secretary and librarian of the Anthroposophical Society of Great Britain (Susanna Mainzer and Margaret Jonas) and staff at Helsinki University Library and the Library of the University of Kent at Canterbury.

Silvester Mazzarella

Contents

Photographs

1 ES with 'Totti', 1917.

2 ES contemplates the world from her sickbed.

3 Hagar Olsson at her parents' home, Räisälä, c.1920.

4 The Södergran's 'ramshackle' villa at Raivola, which Edith and her mother had abandoned in favour of a small cottage in the grounds by the time Hagar Olsson came into their lives. Troops were later billeted there.
Photo by ES

5 The 'little cottage' by the Orthodox church in Raivola, where Edith lived with her mother during the years of her correspondence with Hagar Olsson.

6 R. R. Eklund.

7 View of Lake Onkamo and Raivola. Helen Södergran and her dog Martii out walking. The Södergrans' house can be glimpsed on the right.

8 Elmer Diktonius.

Cover: Edith Södergran, Self Portrait, Davos 1912-14.

The publishers are grateful to Agneta Rahikainen and Svenska litteratursällskapet i Finland for permission to reproduce these photographs here.

General Introduction

This book brings together three pioneers of modernism in Nordic literature: Edith Södergran, Hagar Olsson and Elmer Diktonius. Edith Södergran was born an only child in April 1892 in St Petersburg, then capital of Russia. Her father was an engineer and businessman and both parents came from Swedish-speaking areas of Finland.[1] When she was three months old the family moved about sixty kilometres westwards across the Finnish border to Raivola, a small country village on the Karelian isthmus[2] where they settled in a large wooden villa next door to a Russian-Orthodox church. She spent six years at a high-class German school in St Petersburg where she was strongly influenced by a French teacher she idolised. When she was fifteen her father died of pulmonary tuberculosis. A year later she developed the disease herself and left school, settling with her mother at Raivola apart from some miserable periods in the Nummela sanatorium near Helsinki where her father had been unsuccessfully treated. She read everything she could lay hands on including Schiller, Kant, Schopenhauer and Nietzsche, and began writing poetry, mainly in German. A favourite hobby was taking photographs of the family's domestic life, including its many cats, and of the village with its surrounding lakes and forests. During a period of remission from her illness she prepared for matriculation at a school in Helsinki (or 'Helsingfors' to give it the Swedish name by which she always knew it). Between 1911 and 1914 she and her mother spent three winters in Switzerland where she was treated more happily at a sanatorium in Davos; the two women even managed a short trip to Italy. At Davos she was able to read, among other things literature in English at the sanatorium library, including Shakespeare, the Border ballads, Dickens, Swinburne and Whitman but nothing more modern. She also developed a crush on her doctor and wrote a description of him as an English exercise.[3] For a while after her return to Raivola things went well enough; her health was reasonable, she had a secret romance with a married Russian doctor from the

9

neighbouring seaside resort of Terijoki and she began writing poetry in Swedish, the language she had always spoken at home even if she insisted all her life that German was her 'best language'. Her Swedish was idiosyncratic; Clas Zilliacus has written:

> She created a new language, a meta-language. The words are reminiscent of Swedish words but the similarity is deceptive. It is safer to regard them as Æolian and look them up in a dictionary, and the dictionary to look them up in is her poetry. Very many words in her poems are charged with colour deriving from her inner world rather than the outer world. They bear little relation to the spectrum but form part of an absolute poetic idiom. They derive their significance from relationships within that idiom, not from the colours of outer reality.[4]

By 1915 she was confident enough to show some of her poems to various cultural figures in Helsinki, and felt sufficiently encouraged to approach the publisher Holger Schildt, who brought out her first collection, *Dikter* (Poems), in 1916. On the strength of the welcome this received from the critics she visited Helsinki again in 1917 and called on a number of writers, both of her own generation and older. At the same time she had her portrait taken in a photographer's studio, a hat decorated with a bird's wing on her head and her eyes burning with intensity. This is probably the last time she was photographed. The Russian revolution of 1917 brought the loss of the family's investments in Russian and Ukrainian stocks, and grinding poverty was added to increasing ill-health. There was no more money for medicine, trips to Helsinki or film for her camera and scarcely enough for food. One consequence is that we do not know exactly what she looked like during the years she wrote the letters in this volume (1919-23). But she continued to distil her experience of life into poetry. The second collection she persuaded her rather casual publishers to bring out was *Septemberlyran* (The September Lyre), product of a sudden burst of inspiration in the early autumn of 1918. This book was noticed by a young journalist who had recently joined the Helsinki Swedish-language evening paper *Dagens Press* which, as it happened, was regularly read by the two isolated women at Raivola, almost their only link with the world of the capital.

The young journalist was Hagar Olsson, born in September 1893 at Kustavi (Swedish name 'Gustafs'), a small island town just off the south-west coast of Finland. She was the fourth child and only daughter of a

Lutheran pastor. Like Södergran, she too made a short journey westward to a new home when only a few months old, in her case to Föglö, a parish in the Swedish-speaking Åland Islands (in Finnish 'Ahvenanmaa') which have remained politically a part of Finland though geographically they are nearer to Sweden. Here she passed most of her childhood, going to school on the mainland at the nearest large town of Turku (Swedish 'Åbo') where her mother had grown up. When she was twelve the family moved from the extreme west of Finland to the extreme east, her father becoming pastor of the parish of Räisälä on the Karelian isthmus about sixty kilometres north of Edith Södergran's home at Raivola. She finished her schooling at the nearest large town, Viipuri, and when twenty moved to Helsinki to train for a commercial career. But showing more aptitude for languages than accountancy, she enrolled at Helsinki University to spend two years reading literature and philology. She too was busy writing, and like Södergran made her debut in 1916, in her case with the short novel *Lars Thorman och döden* (Lars Thorman and Death). Like Södergran's Poems, this book attracted some interest without generating any great excitement, no one at the time realising that these two slim volumes by unknown young women were the first stirrings of a literary revolution. In 1917 came her second book, a 27-page collection of narrative prose-poems to which she gave the title *Själarnas ansikten* (Soul Faces), Then in September 1918, just as Södergran was writing the poems that would form the core of her breakthrough volume *The September Lyre*, Olsson started her first full-time job as editorial assistant (or maid-of-all-work) on *Dagens Press*.

Elmer Diktonius was born in Helsinki in 1896, the youngest of four children in a Swedish-speaking family at a time when the city was almost equally divided between Finnish-speakers and Swedish-speakers. But the family regularly spent long summer holidays in the Finnish-speaking district of Nurmijärvi just north of Helsinki where Diktonius' mother's family owned a farm, and when he was put through the Helsinki Finnish-language school system rather than the Swedish he became bilingual, unusual if not unique among Swedish-language writers of his generation in Finland. He left school at sixteen and began a lifetime's voracious, if undisciplined, reading. He also began to compose music and studied the violin, playing one of his own compositions at a charity concert in aid of the prevention of cruelty to animals. Such compositions led to the award of a place at the Helsinki Music Institute (now the Sibelius Academy), and during his time there made two very different friends who became influential figures in his life. One was the Institute's director, the composer Erkki Melartin; the other, also an older man, happened to answer an advertisement Diktonius placed in the left-wing press in 1915 in a search of pupils to whom he might give lessons in musical theory. This was Otto Wille (or Ville) Kuusinen, future henchman of Stalin and Khrushchev and quisling-in-waiting when in 1939-40 Stalin attempted to take over Finland by force. In April 1918 Kuusinen would be forced to flee to Russia in danger of his life after the defeat of the 'Reds' by the 'Whites' in the bitter four-month civil war that followed Finland's unilateral declaration of independence. But in 1915 he was simply a leader of the Finnish left with a passion for philosophy and political theory, and in return for his music lessons he gave the receptive Diktonius instruction in Marxist theory and offered criticism of the poetry the young musician was beginning to write. In 1918-19 Diktonius spent a year on compulsory military service (which he unexpectedly found he enjoyed) in what during the civil war had been the 'White' army. His serious musical ambitions ended with a disastrous recital of his songs in Helsinki in May 1920 (though a fairly recent recording of his music exists).[5] Kuusinen, still planning revolution, risked his life again by returning to Finland incognito. Diktonius, in contact with other figures of the left and under police surveillance, managed to meet him from time to time. Kuusinen evaded the police and left the country and Diktonius, at a loose end, began to feel he should do the same.

But when he finally did leave, in November 1920, it was as much for romantic as political reasons; he had fallen in love with Salme Pekkala, a young woman prominent on the Finnish political left whose marriage was beginning to fall apart. Salme had gone to England whose workers were supposed to be the key to world revolution. On his way to London Diktonius met Kuusinen and others in Stockholm where he arranged for a few poems padded out with aphorisms[6] to be vetted by Kuusinen before being published by a small left-wing firm under the title *Min dikt* (My Poem). From Stockholm he went to Paris to meet Lidia Stahl, a glamorous international revolutionary figure who had had some contact with Finland. She introduced him to several avant-garde thinkers and writers including Henri Barbusse and Ivan Goll. But London, when he finally got there, proved a disappointment: Salme met him at Victoria Station with 'Why have you come? I don't love you any more'. Then, lending him the keys of her flat and handing him over to her English friend Mary Rhodes Moorhouse (who was later to marry Salme's husband), she departed for the conference of the Third International in Moscow. Mary Moorhouse supplied the destitute Diktonius with money, hired him a violin and took him to Cornwall to spend seven weeks as a guest in the cottage at St Merryn near Padstow that she shared with her friend Eva Hubback. All this: Paris, being jilted by Salme, being moved on from a London park bench at night by a bobby, thrilling to the violence of the Atlantic and responding to the affection of Hubback's six-year-old daughter, supplied his poetic muse with plenty of material. Returning to Finland late in 1921, he went with his friend Lauri Salava[7] to introduce himself to Hagar Olsson in her newspaper office and ask her to join the editorial board of a new review he had planned, to be called *Ultra*. Many years later she recalled her first impressions:

> A short gentleman in a racy tie with an unmistakably continental air put in an appearance in Helsinki around New Year 1922. It was as if he had dropped from the sky - just what he wanted you to think. I knew nothing of him, where he'd come from or what sort of person he was. He called himself a composer and, grasping in his fist a book from some unheard-of small publisher in Sweden, said his name was Diktonius.[8]

He thrust the book into her hands. It was a good move; she read it, admired it, and persuaded the prestigious journal *Nya Argus* to let her review it. Sensing a new ally in her battle against the stuffy Helsinki literary establishment, she packed the author off to make the acquaintance of the ailing Edith Södergran in Raivola.

This is not the place for any detailed discussion of the works of Södergran, Olsson and Diktonius, but it may be worth asking why modernism in poetry reached a distant fringe of the Nordic world before it made headway in its major centres. The word 'modernism', over the years, has meant any number of different things to different people and it isn't a word these three writers used at the time. Even so, it is not difficult to see what they were trying to do: they wanted to discard what they thought artificial for what they felt was natural. Such 'back to basics' renewals happen from time to time in all cultures; an example from English literature being the sudden breakthrough of romanticism with the publication of Wordsworth and Coleridge's *Lyrical Ballads* in 1798. Södergran, Olsson, and Diktonius wanted to get away from rhyme and strict rhythms and outworn 'poetic' diction and imagery that no longer seemed to have any relevance to contemporary life. No subject however shocking should be excluded from poetry, and the poet had a duty to try to make the world a better place for generations to come; like all art, poetry was considered a potential force for reconciliation and unity. In much Nordic modernism there was also what Clas Zilliacus has called a 'Franciscan streak': modernists elsewhere were happy to be drawn to the bright lights of the city, but Nordic modernists tended to condemn this as a betrayal of nature.[9] In Finland the poets who blazed the trail were Södergran and Diktonius. Södergran, not much interested in the superficial details of external 'reality', was the more expressionist of the two, as Zilliacus implies when he writes about her 'Æolian' language. The difference between her and Diktonius was not unlike the difference the English romantic poet Keats saw between himself and his contemporary Byron: 'He describes what he sees - I describe what I imagine - Mine is the hardest task.'[10] Olsson published no poetry (unless we include her early expressionist prose-poems) but became the herald and standard-bearer of the new movement as it fought for space in the literary world. As early as 1917 she had recorded in a notebook:

> Something new has penetrated the consciousness of humanity during these cursed and blessed times in which the whole world is on the verge of collapse. Some great nameless bird is trying out its wings before flying up out of a ring of isolation, a great huge bird from the heart of human consciousness.[11]

Soon after Edith Södergran's death, others were to build on the work of these three pioneers, among them the Finland-Swedish poets Rabbe Enckell, Gunnar Björling, Kerstin Söderholm and Henry Parland. But of course some Finland-Swedish poets were never converted. Arvid Mörne, leading light of the previous generation, initially welcomed Edith Södergran's work but was less enthusiastic as her talent developed while Jarl Hemmer, contemporary of Södergran, Olsson and Diktonius, irritated them by pouring out successful volumes of verse in the old style. But why was it isolated Finland that pioneered this literary breakthrough and why in particular its Swedish-speaking minority, not more than a few hundred thousand people? Hagar Olsson later tried to explain this in a newspaper article in which she rejected the conventional academic view that this sudden new 'vision and rhythm of life in our little out-of-the-way corner of the world' with its displacement of traditional cultural values had been the result of an accidental coming-together of talented writers:

> There is no way we can ignore two absolutely decisive factors, i.e. that the time was revolutionary not merely in the political sense but in a deeply spiritual sense with all that implies in the way of prophetic presentiments and a passionate longing for liberation, and that our country as a border land was more exposed to sudden volcanic eruptions and changes of direction in the wind than more sheltered countries like Sweden.[12]

So it was a question of time and place. The First World War caused the collapse of established empires and revolution in Russia. To be young at this time in central and eastern Europe was to have a world in need of reconstruction at your feet. The major centres of Nordic culture had escaped direct involvement in the war but Finland had been part of the Russian empire. Even so Helsinki was relatively sheltered, but at either end of the Karelian isthmus, in Viipuri and St Petersburg where Olsson and Södergran spent formative years, things looked very different. The Viipuri of Hagar Olsson's school days where speakers of Finnish and Swedish rubbed shoulders with Russians, Germans and Balts was the most cosmopolitan town in Finland and Petersburg was one of the most cosmopolitan capitals in Europe. This shared outlook was one of the things that brought Södergran and Olsson together and set them apart from the parochial and conservative Helsinki intelligentsia of the newly independent Finland of 1918. As for Diktonius, he had come in touch with international currents through Kuusinen and post-war Paris (he made no literary contacts in London). And Södergran had been persuaded by Nietzsche that if you wanted something done you should get up and do it: will was power. Thus it was that the first breeze that ruffled the calm waters of Nordic poetry in the years following the First World War came from a small section of a small community to the east, the Finland Swedes. This is the story told by the letters in this book together with Olsson's much later commentary. Unfortunately, all the letters Olsson and Diktonius wrote to Södergran have been lost, probably deliberately destroyed by their recipient near the end of her life.

Diktonius' revolutionary fervour mellowed considerably in the years after Södergran's death. He continued to write but aged rapidly, both in body and spirit and spent the last four years before his death in 1961 in a home; from the Kremlin the octogenarian Kuusinen sent flowers to his funeral. In the late twenties Hagar Olsson became Finland's first modernist playwright and continued until the 1960s to publish novels, stories and essays, but her main contribution to the cause remained her aggressive polemical journalism. She liked to think of Edith Södergran's legacy as her own private property[13] which brought her into conflict with Diktonius who also saw himself as principal guardian of the shrine, though they did manage to co-operate to the extent of bringing together Södergran's major uncollected poetry in *Landet som icke är* (1925, The Land That Is Not). Olsson allowed her sense of guilt at not having done more for Södergran when she was alive to dominate her life and inhibit her own writing. A series of other women with whom she had intense relationships also died young of tuberculosis. Kylli Siegberg, at one time Södergran's rival for Olsson's attention and affection,[14] emigrated heartbroken to the USA when Olsson ended their relationship, then returned to die in Helsinki in 1931, aged thirty-six; Olsson, who had had no contact with her for years, wrote a brief appreciation in the press. When another intimate friend, the artist Ella Frelander, or 'Ka', died at thirty-nine, in 1948, Olsson was again predictably assailed by feelings of guilt. But none of these premature deaths touched her more deeply than that of Toya Dahlgren. Olsson first met Toya at a hotel in eastern Finland when both were on holiday in the summer of 1928. Olsson was nearly thirty-five and famous, while Toya at eighteen had just completed a year's treatment for tuberculosis in Nummela sanatorium - the very place where both Södergran and her father had been unsuccessfully treated for the same disease, and which Södergran had come to fear and loathe. Surviving letters and diaries make clear that the relationship between Olsson and Toya was passionate and deeply satisfying to both, and when Toya died aged only twenty-two all Olsson's largely self-inflicted Södergran wounds opened once more. Throughout her life Olsson with her guilty conscience continued to fight in her books and in the press for the liberal and spiritual values she and Södergran had shared. Having long done battle in an attempt to open Finland's windows to the rest of the world (to use a Diktonius expression), she lived to see many of her illusions shattered by the rise of Nazism and the Second World War and in old age became a reclusive hypochondriac, afraid to set foot outside her little Helsinki flat for fear of draughts. By the time she died in 1978 all that most young people knew of her was that she had once been Edith Södergran's friend. In recent years some of her writing has been reprinted, and an afterword to the 1987 edition of one of her major essays describes her temperament and style as 'an improbable combination of Jan Myrdal and John Lennon'.[15] The indefatigable Roger Holmström has researched her life for a two-volume biography whose titles tell their own tale: *Den öppna horisonten 1920-1945* (The Open Horizon), and *Den växande melankolin 1945-1978* (Growing Melancholy).

In her later years the Finland-Swedish writer and film maker Jörn Donner came to know her well and in his introduction to a 1963 reprint of her three earliest books offered his own version of what happened in those heady years around 1920:

> Though every writer's path is determined by his or her own individual temperament, modernism can be summed up in a single phrase: a freer and richer relationship with reality. Facing life without blinkers. Accepting nothing as self-evident. Thus the artistically radical element in modernism

was often taken for political radicalism, and the new Soviet state at first openly encouraged this new approach to art. Disillusion came later but in the early twenties it was still reasonable for people to believe future generations would be able to live and think more freely.

Finland-Swedish modernism remains a paradox if we insist on isolating it from its European context. If there had been no gifted people with a powerful need to say what they wanted to say there would never have been any revolt against the establishment. But we can see now that modernism had its roots in the changes Europe's spiritual climate was undergoing at the time. Psychoanalysis was leading to a clearer understanding of our instinctive urges, the pace of life was increasing, technological discoveries were revolutionising the world and beliefs long accepted as self-evident were being questioned. We humans are creatures of habit who need time to adjust ourselves to change. It was a situation in which writers became catalysts of unrest and yardsticks of change.[16]

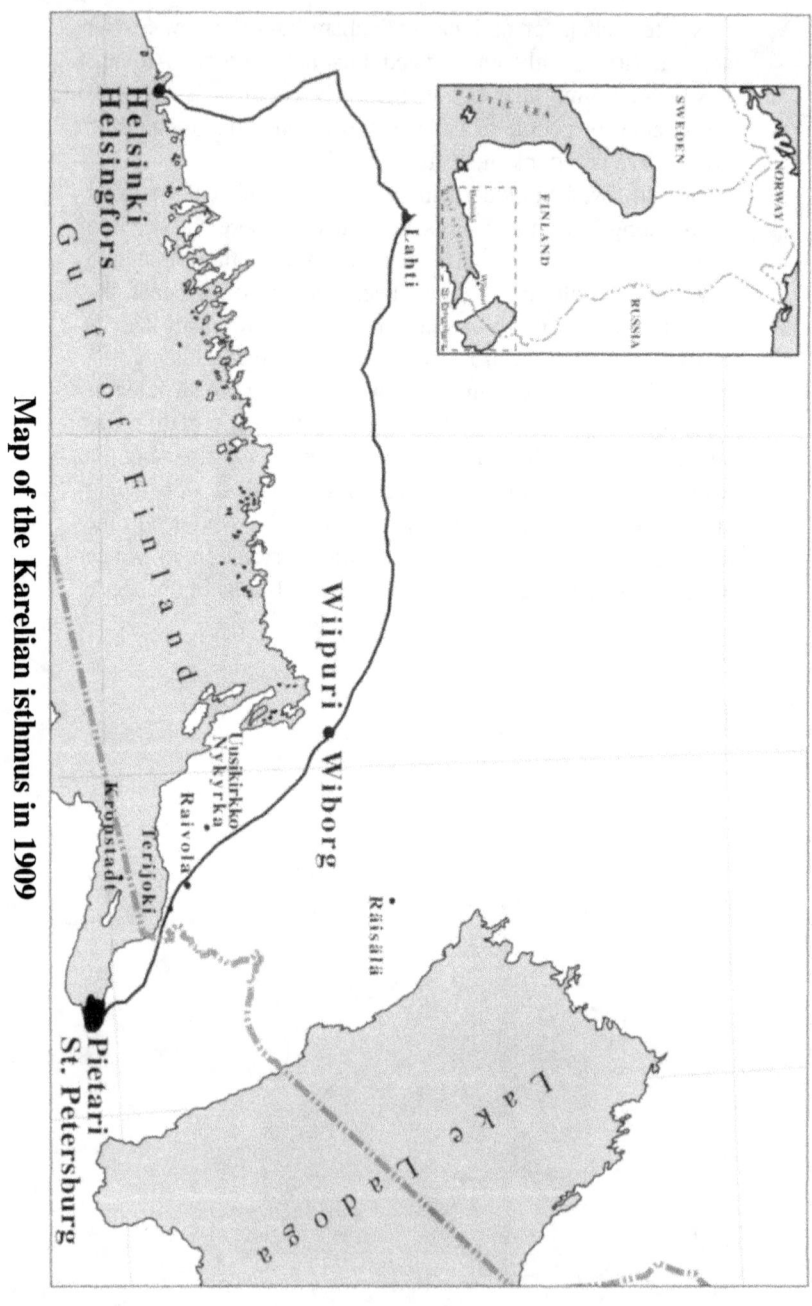

Map of the Karelian isthmus in 1909

Hagar Olsson

Introduction to Edith Södergran's Letters to Hagar Olsson (1955)

I was in a hotel room in Bandol[1] when the news of Edith's death reached me. I shall never forget that beautiful room, its balcony doors wide open to the sparkling Mediterranean. It was the first time I had travelled south, and for one who came like me from the plain grey north everything was new and intoxicating: hot dark evenings, gaudy crowds swarming the cafés and narrow streets, velvet-smooth sun-warm peaches fresh picked from some dark-skinned old woman's trees and real palms that made my heart leap when I saw them in magical moonlight on my arrival, fronds rustling softly of faraway shores.

I remember I stood in the middle of the room holding the telegram while everything round me ceased to exist. I'm not sure what happened next. I only know that when I came back to life I was another person. Now a permanent sense of leave-taking weighed on me; life had put on a veil of mourning and turned away leaving nothing but a feeling of guilt. It was as if I had been condemned under some incomprehensible law for setting out on this journey so eagerly and expectantly, and so carelessly that I hadn't even said goodbye to my friend. It never crossed my mind that I might not see her again. She had been ill all the time I had known her, but had shown a remarkable capacity to rise above her infirmity in times of crisis. It's easy for others to take a long-term illness like hers for granted, easy to see it as a natural and permanent condition. Her characteristically exuberant feeling for life also helped lull me into a false sense of security, and I was only too willing to let myself be distracted by all the 'new' things life offers so liberally when one is young. Thus I deprived my friend of the last fragment of pleasure I might have given her, and myself of my last chance to be with someone who was about to leave me for ever.

I'm sure this has affected the whole of the rest of my life. It has become in a strange way an integral part of my destiny and I have never since been able to avoid feeling painfully and perhaps unnaturally sensitive to that feeling of guilt which lies at the very foundation of our lives and which death activates every time he comes near us. But even if the circumstances of our own lives form part of the guilt we feel when someone close to us dies unexpectedly, this guilt still remains puzzling, inexplicable, a massive shadow we can never assimilate. Perhaps when all's said and done it's simply the inevitable guilt of the living before the dead, a burden we shall never shed until we too leave life behind us.

This analysis of my own reaction to Edith's death may seem superfluous, even inappropriate, in relation to the publication of her letters. But I'm only trying to explain why I've never written a book about her when so many people seem to have expected one from me and why I've let her letters lie hidden in a desk drawer for a quarter of a century without ever re-reading them. I buried them on purpose. I was determined to seal away the bitterest experience of my youth and do all I could to avoid reviving the pain that lay deep inside me.

But I did sometimes write about Edith, of course, and I did what I could to keep her memory alive in the dark years after her death. That was inevitable, given the way things were. But what I wrote was as it were written from outside myself. I couldn't face doing anything that might bring her back to life. I couldn't even bring myself to glance through her letters. I hid them as if afraid they might burn me, and for long periods even managed to 'forget' their very existence. Later, if I needed to look at one to check a quotation or confirm some piece of information, I would do it as quickly as possible since every word I read was deeply painful to me, while even more painful were the memories brought back by her childish, clumsy, slapdash but extremely expressive handwriting. I would hurry to put the letter back in its place in the large envelope in which I kept the collection, and I would hide this envelope under piles of papers so that I could never come on it by accident.

And there the letters would certainly have remained undisturbed and unseen till death took the responsibility for them from me, had not Gunnar Tideström come one day to tell me he was preparing a monograph on Edith Södergran and that he couldn't do the job properly without studying the letters she had written me.[2]

It is perhaps understandable that I objected strongly. Even the thought of taking out the letters, of breaking the carefully preserved peace in which they lay, disturbed me. And if I was to hand them over to a stranger I would naturally first have to read them myself, page by page and line by line. I would be able to evade nothing, leave nothing in oblivion; everything would be revealed and all the time that telegram would be there at the back of my mind. Letter by letter as I read I would be conscious of the telegram approaching until in the end I would be forced to accept it, back once more in that beautiful, terrible room in Bandol.

It seemed too much to expose myself to such anguish just to help an academic researcher. My whole being rebelled against the idea that what for me was still full-blooded living reality should be considered legitimate material for a professional literary historian. Worse still, I was being asked to betray my dead friend's trust and expose her most intimate secrets to the public. What she had written spontaneously in the closest confidence, what had inspired her passionate heart in moments of loneliness, doubt, recklessness and despair, what she had whispered in the ear of her only confidante, would lie open on the table to be examined and picked over by a professional researcher who would then present his work to the public as a fine example of his own diligence.

I once saw a heart operation on film. The secret muscle lay quivering and trembling in its open ribcage, naked on its bleeding bed. Something, perhaps its terrible clarity in close-up, made it almost unbearable to watch as I listened with awful fascination to the mechanical thumping of the pulsing rhythm of life.

This was roughly how I felt when this literary-historical researcher held out his hand for Edith's letters.

I've always distrusted literary research and its methods. I consider it amateurish in its analysis of literary context (usually based more on the researcher's reading than the poet's) and unscrupulous in its treatment of intimate biographical detail. It's often hard to distinguish the material the researcher has collected from mere gossip. Lack of respect for the basic human right of privacy seems to be considered a virtue when the subject is a poet, that most defenceless of human beings. One isn't supposed to ask questions about the assumptions the literary biographer brings to his work or about the hidden psychological motives that may form the basis for his interpretations. One must simply approve what he produces as the 'result of research' without pointing out that his interpretation of intimate material cannot help being coloured by his own psychological make-up and limited by his particular spiritual horizons.

All this now became particularly painful reality for me. Like all creative people Edith had instinctively detested the intrusive rooting about in personal matters that is so important to researchers and done all she could to protect herself from it. Towards the end she methodically destroyed her personal papers and other unique material and made me promise to destroy anything that survived her. She was determined to leave nothing for the worms that infest dead bodies, as she put it. She never exacted specific promises from me about her letters or even mentioned them, perhaps because she took it for granted that I'd always destroyed them as soon as I'd read them. I can't be certain of this, but it seems likely from what she wrote on one of the Swiss picture-postcards she used to send me when she urged me in passing not to burn it as it had sentimental value for her since Nietzsche had lived in the area shown in the picture. Whatever the truth of the matter, there can be no doubt that her letters were the sort of material she would have shuddered to see in the hands of a literary academic.

I defended myself as best I could but in the end allowed myself to be persuaded. The problem was a complicated one - the simplest and most extreme course would have been to destroy the letters, but how could I do that? I never had time to gather my thoughts and think the matter through. I was caught off guard. Tideström maintained that the letters were the most important Södergran source-material for the period in which they were written, and that he would have to finish his monograph even if I refused access to them, in which case it would be my fault if the vitally important first full-length monograph written on Edith Södergran was unsatisfactory. That tipped the balance for me. So much had been written on Edith that was misleading or wrong because it was based on ignorance that I couldn't allow myself to be an accomplice in allowing new fantasies about her to be published in a work likely to have lasting influence.[3]

I've come to think since that this argument was irrelevant and that I might easily have spared myself the conflict with my conscience I suffered when I acted against my deepest convictions. In the long run it matters so little what a biography contains; most of it is nothing but speculation and cannot be otherwise, no matter how many footnotes there are. It is as the poet herself wrote: the 'unknown person' will reveal herself - to anyone capable of the art of reading her work.

But what's done cannot be undone, and once the cat was out of the bag I decided the right thing to do was to publish the letters in full myself, with my own commentary. They needed to be seen in their living context so they could speak for themselves. They would have been published eventually in any case, and I felt that if Edith had had to choose between two evils, she would have preferred an edition with my commentary to a dry academic one. But I hesitated for a long time. It was as if an invisible barrier blocked me every time I tried to get to grips with the job. I know this barrier was in my own heart. It's only now that I've worked right through the letters and lived through my experience again to the end that I've come to feel that I may have done the right thing.[4]

There have been moments during these years of doubt when I've felt a strong compulsion to destroy the letters despite everything. It seemed a duty, taking into account the trust Edith had shown in writing them and what I knew of her feelings about such things. If she hadn't trusted me absolutely she would never have exposed her vulnerability to me in the way she did. But I couldn't bring myself to commit what seemed an act of vandalism; I don't know whether this was right or wrong, probably both. It would have been the same if I'd destroyed the poems she sometimes left with me. I see the letters not only as an irreplaceable complement to the poems but as an integral part of her writing as a whole so that they belong not to her or to me but to everyone. They radiate a spiritual power and an enduring passion that rise above what is ephemeral and time-bound in them. With their extraordinary spontaneity they invite the reader to share in big things and small at a personal level, offering an intimacy rare in literature and building up from fragments a portrait of a 'whole person'. The ability to offer a glimpse of this kind of portrait is an eternally fresh element in all literature that has the power to survive.

It was with this in mind and to preserve Edith's spontaneity in all its freshness that I decided not to alter anything in the letters but to let them go to press exactly as they'd been written. One might argue that her erratic spelling should have been corrected and that a number of indiscretions could profitably have been taken out. But if you start changing a text where do you stop? And what yardstick do you use? As I understand it her misspellings, abbreviations and incomplete sentences tell their own story of an impulsive and changeable nature and of exhaustion and physical weakness. And if the letters contain indiscretions and hasty or emotionally charged judgments, why should that be any different from the same thing in private conversation? To take out elements of this kind would be to deprive the letters of some of their spontaneity, while the knowledge that things had been taken out would inflict on the reader that disturbing sense of insecurity which is always a consequence of arbitrary censorship.

Unfortunately a good many of the letters have been lost. But when I think how adept I am at losing things, it astonishes me that most of them were still in existence when Edith died.

The dates given are postmark dates. Edith never dated letters herself and often continued to write the same letter over a period of several days.

In my commentary I've tried to recreate the contemporary background to the letters and put them in their personal context. Thus I haven't hesitated to say a good deal about myself, noting my reactions whenever I can remember them. I've always thought editions of letters unsatisfactory that give no information about the recipient or matters alluded to in the text; when this happens many nuances are lost and the letters seem to hang in the air. In any case, letters form part of a dialogue in which each voice gains colour from the other and is most expressive in its natural context.

The best I can do in giving Edith's letters to the world is to ask the reader to remember they are confidential messages, a substitute for the conversations Edith and I were so seldom able to have. This is what gives them their character. They are not literary letters and nothing in them has been corrected by the author or even carefully calculated; they were written spontaneously about this and that, big things and small, and they were written in a variety of moods. Anyone can see how defenceless they are. The writer is making no attempt to be cautious or protect herself, or to dress her words in literary clothing. All is open and naked and entirely without any thought of discretion. Take what is ephemeral in them for what it is: the fleeting, glistening spray that leaps into the air when a heavy wave strikes a rock.

On Thursday, 19 December 1918, *Dagens Press*[5] carried a routine advertisement for new books. Three were listed, two of them about the civil war.[6] The third, *Septemberlyran* [The September Lyre], was cheaper than the other two, being priced at five Finnish marks. I had joined the paper's editorial staff that autumn and published my first literary review on 12 October. I was now asked to review The September Lyre. There was no hurry with reviews in those days, especially when the writer was someone like Edith Södergran who was unknown to most readers, even though she had already published her first book *Dikter* [Poems] two years earlier. But before I or anyone else could get round to reviewing her new book we received a statement from the poet herself. This was published on the last day of the year, on the Letters to the Editor page, and read as follows:

I would be very grateful if you could find room for the following in your paper:

INDIVIDUAL ART

A few words in connection with my book *The September Lyre*.

This book is not intended for the general public, still less for exalted intellectual circles, but only for those few individuals who stand closest to the frontier of the future.

It so happened that I was unable to be present at the final selection of the poems, nor did I get a chance to read the proofs. As a result several important poems have been left out and some superfluous ones put in. This adds an extra touch of worthlessness to a book which already has a casual air and is really nothing more than a private rough draft.

Even the dating has been left out and poems have been juxtaposed between which lies a gulf as great as that between my first collection and this one. What gives value to many of these poems is that they have been produced by a new type of individual. 'Solbrandsfärgade toppar' [Sunflame-coloured Peaks], 'Vanvettets virvel' [The Whirlpool of Madness] and 'Världen badar i blod' [The World is Bathing in Blood] are transitional poems. What is new can be clearly seen in 'Är jag en lögnare' [If I Am a Liar], 'Framtidens tåg' [The Trains of the Future] and the fragment at the end. From these poems streams a higher fire, a more powerful passion, than from what I have written in the past. I cannot help anyone who is unable to recognize that the wild blood of the future is pulsing in these poems.

Inner fire is the most important thing we possess. The earth belongs to those who have the highest music in them. I turn to these rare individuals and urge them to heighten their inner music, which is the same as building the future.

I myself offer up every atom of my strength to my lofty purpose; I live the life of a saint, I steep myself in the highest creations of the human spirit, I avoid all influences of a lower kind. I regard the old society as the mother cell, which must be sustained until the individuals it produces can raise the new world. I urge these individuals to work only for immortality (though this is not the right word), to develop themselves to the highest possible point - to put themselves at the service of the future.

My book will not have failed in its purpose if one single person is able to grasp what it is about this art that is tremendous and unprecedented. I am happy to have written these poems, and there is no way I can overestimate the huge service the publishers have done me in publishing them. A new age is at hand. What Hemmer[7] foreshadows in his poem 'Pelaren' [The Pillar] is about to become reality. I hope I shall not find myself alone with the great thing I have to bring forward.

Edith Södergran

No one had heard anything like this before. Here was the consciousness of modern humanity suddenly exploding into Finland's provincial cultural milieu which, despite world war and civil war, was still completely anchored in the past and imagined that it still retained unchallenged possession of its territory. It is both tragic and comic to remember how totally incapable readers were of understanding such language at the time. Here was a poet who took it for granted that she was partly responsible for the future development of the human race, but who saw her poems not as evidence of personal talent - in this respect, like most great artists, Edith Södergran was humble - but as an independent spiritual phenomenon, something which grew and became reality in her subconscious, a gift she had received from the gods and was fortunate to be able to pass on. In the eyes of the philistine bourgeoisie such a poet must have seemed either unbelievably comic or unhinged by delusions of grandeur, if not simply a victim of serious mental illness. The result was the notorious and outrageous controversy that became known as the *September Lyre* 'feud' and which gave brutal evidence, from the very first, of what early Finland-Swedish modernism could expect from the establishment. As usual it was genius that took the sharpest thrusts. And also as usual it was thick-skinned stupidity that first attacked the forerunner and ended up proclaiming in its own malignant way the birth of a new consciousness in the world.

Such was the dramatic prelude to my correspondence with Edith Södergran.

It has been claimed that it was through me that Edith was able to make contact with the Finland-Swedish literary world. But I lived in no literary world except the one I was gradually creating for myself. In fact, at the beginning of our relationship I was as isolated and homeless in my own country as she was, even if I did have the columns of one of the capital's newspapers at my disposal. The empty room I worked in was just as lacking in echoes as the one in which Edith was writing her poems and letters-to-editors. I was able to write freely and air new ideas and revaluations only because Dagens Press happened to have a sophisticated liberal editorial policy that supported me. It's important to stress how much this paper's tolerant attitude helped the breakthrough of modernist poetry in Finland. This fact has generally been underplayed, perhaps in an attempt to protect the reputation of the principal Helsinki Swedish-language daily, *Hufvudstadsbladet*. It was *Hufvudstadsbladet* that did most to establish received opinion, setting up a barrier of barbaric ignorance hostile to anything that was new or betrayed any influence from abroad. This was where the popular and influential columnist 'Jumbo'[8] whirled his reactionary flail; he was the first to use the stupid but effective term 'literary Bolshevism' in an attempt to crush the new poetry. To judge by the brief obituary notice they allowed her, even when Edith died a few years later the *Hufvudstadsbladet* editorial staff still knew virtually nothing about Finland's greatest lyric poet of modern times. After listing the published volumes of her poetry they ventured an assessment: 'Possibly her greatest achievement lay in her depiction of her native (!)[9] city Petersburg as it appeared in its days of prosperity.' Not a word more. A statement which is a classic of its kind and deserves to be as widely famous as the pronouncements of the Holy Fool.

Such was the barren cultural milieu in which the most richly colourful figure in Finland-Swedish poetry, a passionate, proud and hotblooded being, was compelled to produce her life's work.

Edith first got in touch with me after reading my review of *The September Lyre*, which appeared in *Dagens Press* on 11 January 1919. The controversy she had stirred up was at its height; some of the lampoonists had already been exercising their wit and Ragnar Ekelund[10] had come forward in her defence, though he, too, thought her letter to the editor of *Dagens Press* had 'invited ridicule'. During the autumn Edith had been reading my articles and undoubtedly saw me as a potential ally, but now she rightly considered herself insulted. My review was the most bombastic and intolerably censorious I had ever written, and I had written in this way out of exasperation. I had immediately recognized the poet, then unknown to me, as one of those 'Kinder der Zukunft'[11] I was so passionately determined to welcome. Here at last was one of the chosen who would throw out the old enfeebled vocabulary and speak the new language of a new age and a new universal consciousness: for me that was what mattered, that was 'it'. And then came her defiant letter to the paper, not to mention her Foreword to *The September Lyre* in which she had made the dubious claim that she had 'found her dimensions'.[12] She could not have done more to damage her cause and expose the new poetry from the start to cold and heartless ridicule. The intellectually arrogant attitude of her letter particularly irritated me. Hence my sharply critical tone, and young and pompous as I was I didn't mince my words: 'She has come before the public not as one steeped in the pathos of things - though this does give some of her poems purity and fire - but as one of those cheap purveyors of worthless glitter whose purpose is self-advertisement.'

Naturally I had failed to grasp the deep, burning significance in Edith's words. I knew nothing of the hard-won victory she had achieved over the forces of destruction ranged against her, a victory which must have given her spiritual confidence and a sense of power. I was only aware that she had allowed a thoughtlessly impulsive statement thrust on a public too immature to understand it to damage not only herself but the cause we both believed in.

I also criticized a tendency towards commonplace effects in the poems, the 'risky finery' to which Edith herself drew attention in her notes on the Hyacintha motif[13] - but despite my reservations, I made it clear that *The September Lyre* was close to my heart. I called the book a 'glorious find', talked about 'uncommonly rich and creative intuition' and 'no less uncommon intellect', and drew the reader's attention to passages marked with a 'seriousness and responsibility of perception' which seemed to me outstanding. It was only because I was so exasperated that I did not express my enthusiasm in a much less reserved manner.

And then came Edith's first letter.

1919

1/90   [Raivola, after 11 Jan 1919][1]

Hagar Olsson,
You charge me unfairly with cheap motives for my public statement.

(Between you and me) This is how my intervention came about. I had asked for a selection to be published. The publishers took out a good many of the best poems (thereby robbing the book of its substance), had it printed without more ado using wide-spaced type 'as light and merry as armed devils', crowned the whole thing with a devil[2] and sent it out into the world. When I discovered from the newspaper that this disaster had happened I wrote to the paper to put things right. I would never have allowed the book to rush out into the world in such a condition if I'd had a chance to read the proofs.

~~Among the poems left out were the following~~.[3]

Write with abbreviations, casually, don't give yourself too much trouble. Let me know what you think of the poems I've enclosed. I grant you there's nothing original in the following: 'Jungfruns död' [The Maiden's Death], 'Till en ung kvinna' [To a Young Woman], 'Vad är i morgon' [What is Tomorrow], 'Skymning' [Dusk], 'Triumf att finnas till' [Triumph of Being], 'Starka Hyacinter' [Strong Hyacinths] and 'Trädet i skogen' [The Tree in the Forest]. This is because they belong to the period of my first book. I had dated the poems but the publisher left the dates out. I mentioned this in my letter to the paper.

I see nothing wrong with the spirit of the other more recent poems (except 'Månens hemlighet' [The Moon's Secret] with its furtive lust for the smell of dead bodies though this should make it popular with readers.)

If you have any comments about the spirit in these poems please let me know ~~if it isn't too much trouble to you~~. In this way whether I agree or disagree you will be helping me find the right path. Poets cannot be their own critics.

Pansartåget[4] - The Armoured Train
I sent you fifty wagonfuls of hopes, America
Home they come empty... Freight of disappointment
Now I send armoured trains, hard masks in watchful gun-slits
Wagons of fulfilment in thousands come home.

Rosenaltaret - The Rose Altar
I dissociate myself from you -
for I am more than you are.

I am at nightfall
a temple priestess, consecrated,
guarding the fire of the future,
I come out to you
with a happy message:
God's kingdom's beginning.
Not the fading empire
of Christ,
No; higher brighter
human forms
are nearing the altar
bearing heaven-scented gratitude
overpowering the senses.
The altar stands there
like a sigh from God's breast;
crown it with roses
till all you see
is a mountain of beauty.[5]
Lightly shall sit on it
the spirit of the hour
drinking a toast
from fragile golden glass
to the hour.

Mina sagoslott - My Fairy Castles
I looked into the philosopher's house (Lichtenberg)[6]
and saw he was happy.
But my fairy castles
stand on fragile pillars, indescribable,
O my fairy castles
they fall down, fall down,
turn to golden rubble...
I love you too much: die!
I'll build you up again
trembling
in order to kill you - you are too beautiful,
my fairy castles -
you shall one day stand on Earth...
then gloomily I'll drop both hammer and chisel...
The end of the world for me?

Gryningen - Dawn
I kindle my light across all the Atlantic...
Unknown lands, shores steeped in night,
wake to me!
I am cold dawn
I am the merciless goddess of day
~~clad~~ in mist-grey veils
and a brief gleam from morning's helmet...
Lightly, lightly leap my winds over the sea.
My loud horn hangs by my side, I ~~have~~
~~I do not wait~~ do not blow the command to break camp...
I wait still! Is a god lost in dreams?
Morning rises red from the ocean

Från dödens marmorbädd... - From Death's Marble Bed...
The Earth is is has been turned to a heap of ashes.
In penitent clothes
I sit lightly on it and dream.
My dreams are so full of sunlight! ~~beautiful~~
I am strong -
for I have risen from death's marble bed.
Death - I looked you in the face, I tilted the scales against you!
Death - I am not cold in your arms
I am myself the fire...
Who is God? What has he done to us?
Don't blaspheme - he's near
- - -

From silver cups I pour delight over the Earth
against it Aphrodite's dreams pale...

Lidandets kalk - The Cup of Suffering
Let weaker hands grasp the cup of suffering,
Lifting it to paler lips
My conquering lips still do not need it...
But - no.
Giants with dark faces still sit in my heart,
stone hands pressed together...
They will emerge one day from their shadows
They will call to you - pain

Give me a hammer to strike sparks - from the stone image,
Hew out my soul!
So my soul may find words that never sat on human tongues

    I don't know if in the next poem I managed to find all the right words for the music I heard, the greatest I've ever heard.

<u>Fragment</u>
O gods, gods!
In all my weakness I find mighty words -
words for you.
Is not the world beyond words
now you've touched things with enchanted hands?
- - -
No one has yet seen the world
you veil it   the covering
A ray of light has touched my wretched path

Nietzsche says: Ich ging zu allen, aber kam zu niemand.[7] Will it happen to me now to find someone? Could we reach out our hands to one another? You are now the object of my offensive, I want you to see me as I really am and show yourself to me as you really are. Could we become divine companions, so that all barriers fall away? I am still speaking to you in a tentative and humiliating foreign language. Nietzsche is the only human being before whom I would not be afraid to open my mouth. Are you that sea of fire I want to dive into? If you <u>laugh</u> you are my own. If you don't <u>laugh</u> you must even so be mature enough to achieve the highest form of friendship Nietzsche in his wisdom warns his own people against.
<u>I enclose a new letter I've written to the paper. If you think it could be a great help to the cause please let them have it or write and tell me to send it to them.</u>
Address: Raivola   Edith Södergran

HAGAR OLSSON COMMENTS: I cannot describe the joy I felt when I received this letter. It was a joy which reached deep inside me to where I felt most lonely. I understood at once that I was being approached by a sister-spirit. In his Södergran monograph Tideström makes some rather far-fetched attempts to explain why Edith called me 'sister' and what this could have meant. To a woman nothing could be easier to understand. I felt we were 'sisters' as soon as I read Edith's first letter. A 'sister' is someone who speaks the same language as you do, who understands things implied but not stated, and for whom you feel intimate affinity regardless of whether or not the two of you otherwise share views and feelings.

In those days I was a sociable person; life bustled around me as it does when you're young, and I was full of activity. But I never opened my inner self to anyone. I felt other people spoke a different language, that even my friends were on a different wave-length. I longed for sister-language. I thought it must be possible for people to understand one another intimately and know they shared one heart and soul. Not just couples but many together, a group or large family. I constantly dreamed of this. It may have been because in childhood I'd never had the opportunity to experience close family intimacy but grew up under psychological pressure:[1] this kind of thing generates a hunger that can hardly ever be satisfied. But I also felt people were too dull and sluggish in their thinking and reactions and in their relationships. It seemed to me my own psychological make-up and consciousness were unlike those around me, and that I lived on two separate planes: one plane where I was surrounded by friends and one where I was alone and unable to share my intimate life with anyone.

On top of this I suffered from a psychological condition that terrified me and added to my feeling of isolation. At any time - and it happened often - I might fall into a state of mind in which not only the room I happened to be in but my whole physical existence would dissolve into unreality, and without the least protection of any kind I would be jerked as if by a spasm into eternity. It was a terrifying experience, and when it hit me without warning I felt I would not be able to endure it for a moment without going out of my mind. The only way I could re-establish contact with reality was by banging my head wildly against a wall. I suppose it's possible I have an innate disposition for the 'inner eye' which lies at the heart of occultism and can only be endured and further developed through conscious training. But I've never taken any interest in that kind of thing and fortunately the experience has become less intense with time.

I mention this because it may have some connection with what Edith came to find in me and with the paths by which we reached one another, and may help to explain why, when I read Edith's first letter, I knew immediately that here was someone who was conscious not only superficially but also deep inside, someone I'd be able to approach on the plane where I'd always been completely alone. She wrote in this first letter of 'the highest form of friendship' and asked 'could we become divine companions?' This was music in my ears. I opened myself at once and wrote an answer from my heart.

I didn't give much thought to the practical implications of the poems she'd copied out with her letter, and which so clearly reflected the tense and tragic conditions in which she lived. Usually when one reads poetry one doesn't imagine that a poet who writes that she has 'risen from death's marble bed' has done precisely that, and one doesn't visualize such terrible realities as starvation, lung haemorrhages, critical illness and total destitution as being literally part of the poet's game of balancing the scales against death. I remember the poem 'The Armoured Train' seemed to me extremely strange and obscure. There was indeed at the time a great shortage of food throughout Finland and during the civil war period I certainly didn't get enough to eat myself, but even so I had no idea of the degree of famine that prevailed in the frontier region of the Karelian isthmus or of what it could mean to someone there if America didn't send food. But for Edith these were concrete facts that affected her life and the life of her whole environment. She sent out her wagons loaded with hope and got in return a 'freight of disappointment'. And her reaction to this was straightforward: to toughen herself so the blows of fate couldn't hurt her. But I thought the other poems extremely good and wrote and told her so. I also said a lot of rude things about her publishers and about Runar Schildt - in those days he was literary adviser to the Holger Schildt publishing house - for turning down poems of this quality and excluding them from her book. I also asked her why the book was called *The September Lyre*.

Only one thing bothered me - the new letter she had written for the paper. What ought I to do about that? I was sure no one would understand it. I didn't altogether understand it myself. I didn't want to pass it on to the paper. But on the other hand, I had already burnt my fingers on the subject of letters-to-the-editor and didn't want to be guilty again of criticising and misinterpreting what Edith was evidently trying to say. My feelings towards her were now quite different from when I wrote my review. Just thinking about her was enough to warm my heart. I don't believe I told her what I thought of her new letter-to-the-editor. If I remember rightly I just wrote that it would be best if she sent it in herself. She took this to mean that I hoped she would do this, whereas of course it was intended as a tactful suggestion to rethink the whole matter.

2/91   [Raivola, 26 Jan 1919]

My delightful young thing! Can't come. Insomnia, TB, empty cashbox. (I live by selling furniture and household utensils. Capital tied up in Ukrainian and Russian bonds, salvation depends on fall of Bolshevism). If I can manage to sleep a bit better I'll try and come in a few months, but I can't be sure. I've found what I need now: your objective eye, and your brain is big enough for both of us. May one ask? Do you work for the cause in a general sense or are you anxious to meet particular individuals? Give me a list. There are several souls I'd like to capture: Hemmer for instance to sing for the cause and Grotenfelt to sing or rasp away.[1] Ragnar Ekelund doesn't come into my calculations. I share <u>Severyanin's</u>[2] view that if a talent is a trifle dull it isn't brilliant enough. Igor Severyanin is Russia's greatest lyric poet of the present day. I've seen him at a poetry reading, never talked to him. But I've felt confidence in him the way I feel confidence in you. <u>He's a very powerful force and bound to be receptive to our ideas</u>. But first we'll have to train him properly, he has trashy manners and doesn't know how to look after himself. He can be our bridge to Russia, through him we'll get the best of Russia on the move. How about Sweden? Will it work there? We'll reach the rest of Europe one fine day. Do you speak to individuals? Is that something you plan to do? You should read Severyanin's best poems, it would refresh you even though he's obsessed with the boudoir and so far hasn't aspired to our heights.

I was born again last September, hence 'September Lyre'. I suddenly felt with utter certainty that a stronger hand had grasped my painter's brush.

How old are you? Health? Nerves? I want you well and strong. Send me a short CV! Mrs or Miss? Level of education? As for me: residence: Raivola, educated at Petrischüle,[3] TB at 16, sanatoria at Nummela and Davos, induced pneumothorax,[4] waiting for someone to discover a cure for TB.

We'll be ruthless with one another and sharp as diamonds.

It's horrible for me to address you in this virtual journalese, I want to use only beautiful words, our real mutual language, but in any case who wants to waste hard-won strength on letters? We have a beautiful dilapidated old place like something in a fairy-tale.[5] Come in summer (for several days at least) if we haven't already been forced to sell it by then. We could lie on the grass and sunbathe and talk and gossip. We have a great ancient ramshackle house, uninhabitable in winter but in summer it would make a fabulous meeting place for our people from Finland and Russia, we could have a heavenly party with drunken speeches. I once spent an evening with Hemmer and Grotenfelt and it's one of my happiest memories.[6] I long to have congenial company now and then. We could run riot here just as they do in Gösta Berlings saga,[7] just think what a blessed place this is - hard to get hold of a copy of H:bladet[8] and our nextdoor neighbours have only just discovered that I can even write.

Only half the poems I sent belonged to 'The September Lyre'.
Runar S.[9] must have been confused by them and misunderstood them completely. It's not really his fault.

Oh, it'd be such fun to come to you, I'd rush up the stairs.

I have a sister and I've never heard her wonderful voice - I'm <u>determined to see</u> deep down inside <u>you, you holiest person of all</u>.

It warms my heart that the old men came forward to defend me.

I shall write my love-letters to you,[10] Hagar, when I'm in the mood. Now I've got someone of my own, for the rest of my life. Two years ago I wrote a poem. Each stanza began 'I want a playmate' (of course I was thinking of a male one) and it ended 'I want a playmate who can break forth from dead granite and defy eternity'. Now I have my happy playmate, after waiting two years.

The doctor alarms me, things could be getting rough. D'you know the fellow, or how do you know what he's getting at? If you see him and get the chance to put in a cunning word to ward him off, then do just that.

I've kissed your letter countless times. I do so desperately want to come. I've been sleeping better at night, it'll give me the courage to become 'reisefähig'.[11]

OLSSON: Edith asks whether I 'work for the cause in general'. That's exactly what I was doing, and I was often disconcerted when she demanded precise tasks from me as if we were taking part in a carefully planned and organised operation. Edith loved a concrete, hands-on approach. During the autumn I'd written a good deal in my articles about the 'cause' (she must have got the word from there) and living 'for the sake of the cause'. This simply meant not being egocentric, having nothing to do with art for art's sake, and keeping an elevated concept of humanity in view in all one's activities. To live for the 'cause' was to fight for a higher consciousness, and to appeal in all circumstances to the free creative spirit which alone is capable of raising us to a level where true fellowship can become a reality. It was in this spirit that in one of my first articles I cited Nietzsche's words, 'Man is something that must be conquered'. Edith was on the same wavelength, which is why she talks about the 'cause' and 'our ideas' as though they were to be taken for granted.

Those who are young now[1] may find it difficult to imagine the excitement we felt. Nowadays we are rushed round so fast on a merry-go-round of change that it's difficult for us to grasp what's happening to us. But in the First World War period, when these ideas first took root, it really was possible to understand what was going on if one had one's ear to the ground. We took a deep breath and realised the world was being turned upside down and that the future lay before us like virgin earth so that all we needed to do was sow seed. And who better to do the sowing but young poets and artists who had repudiated the old contaminated values and who carried within themselves an inspired vision of a new humanity, something higher and more sensitively organised and conscious of its mission. That's how we felt, Edith and I; each of us had reached this point independently by her own route which is why we were so happy when we found one another. Out in Europe and Russia there were many who felt the same way, and it was Edith's constant dream that one day we would make contact with our soulmates in the great world. She was to sacrifice much of her strength for this dream, only to see her hopes bitterly dashed.

Of course this was not a question of 'ideas' developed by theoretical thinking so much as a spiritual impulse which was in the air at the time. It was something one was instinctively aware of, a longing or cry in one's nerves and blood that was constantly in one's thoughts as a tremendous opportunity. When one reads the view of learned literary historians that Edith's 'commonwealth of the future' was 'a metaphysical, even religious idea' and other such grandiloquent stuff, one can't help being reminded of Faust's words to his assistant Wagner, that prototypical academic pedant: 'You'll never understand what you haven't experienced'.

Edith writes that with Severyanin we'll be able to get the 'best of Russia' on the move. By this she means quite simply the best spiritual forces in Russia and not at all, as Tideström claims, the old Russian ruling class. One can do a writer no greater injustice than load her words with opinions and judgments that can't possibly have been relevant at the time her words were written. It was a time when no one knew what would eventually become of Russia or what form Russia's relations with Finland would take in the future. Everything was still in a state of flux. In his monograph, Tideström is anxious at all costs to detect a hostile attitude to revolutionary Russia in Edith's words. This is because he's looking at the situation through his own eyes and those of his own backward-looking generation, and not through Edith's eyes, which were forward-looking and hungry for the future. 'The letters are evidence of how strongly her feelings were engaged in the struggle against Communist Russia,' he states flatly. But there's no evidence to support this assertion, quite apart from the fact that this and other equally unambiguous statements savour much more of Tideström than Södergran. She hadn't committed herself either for or against anything definite. To her the whole course of events was a process of creation like childbirth; beyond this, like the keenly aware person she was, she thought it best to wait and see. When she writes as she does in this letter, 'salvation depends on fall of Bolshevism', she's clearly not expressing a carefully thought-out political attitude. She's just explaining why she and her mother are now destitute, and giving her opinion that if Bolshevism were to fall they might get their money back. She wasn't one to let her personal economic problems influence her political views. I've never known anyone so completely indifferent to horrible circumstances in their own life as she was.

The 'old men' who came forward to defend her were Hjalmar Procopé, Arvid Mörne, Bertel Gripenberg, Sven Lidman and Runar Schildt.[2] These well-known and generally admired writers had published a letter dated 20 January 1919[3] in *Hufvudstadsbladet* in which they protested against what they considered the unworthy treatment of a colleague and stated that they had no hesitation in wanting to join 'the troop of lunatics who see evidence of a deeply committed artist in Edith Södergran's poetry and who have found there traces of great and distinctive beauty'. I don't know who took the initiative but my guess would be Hjalmar Procopé, who was a decent man with a warm heart, or Arvid Mörne, who had a high opinion of Edith's early poetry, even if he was critical of *Septemberlyran* and her later collections. Gripenberg must have been on the list almost by accident. Much later, when Edith was dead, he wrote a disagreeable article about her - in *Svenska Dagbladet*[4] I think - bringing in nonsense typical of him about Bolshevism and the like and doing all he could to damage Edith's reputation in Sweden. But the letter from the 'old men' was very important for Edith at the time it was published. It was the only encouragement she ever got from the establishment.

The 'doctor' who might come up with something rough was the neurologist Dr H. Fabritius.[5] I had warned her in my letter to expect him to contribute to the debate. His piece carried the alarming subtitle 'Prophetess or Swindler?' but turned out to be innocuous, even offering some useful interpretatory analysis of the poems.

Edith's second letter to *Dagens Press* was published on 29 January:

OPEN LETTER TO REVIEWERS AND KNIGHTS

Among the poems excluded from 'Septemberlyran' was the following:

Gudarna skratta [The Gods Laugh]

People don't know themselves well,
they think they're as poor as they seem in life,
they don't know gods live in their breasts unrecognised.
The gods laugh. Life is theirs.
They drive the chariot with fiery horses, etc.

In this poem (and in many others) I have given expression to that exalted laughter of which Nietzsche says: 'I found no one else today strong enough for that.

'No longer a shepherd, no longer a human being, but one transformed, one glorified, who laughed. Never before had anyone in the world laughed as he laughed!

'O my brethren, I heard laughter, which was not human laughter - - - and now I am consumed by a thirst, by a longing which never rests. My longing for that laughter consumes me: how could I bear to die now.' (Zarathustra).

Supported by Nietzsche's authority I repeat that I am an individual of a new kind. It is not the content of my art that is unprecedented, but its <u>character</u>. My art can only be understood from that viewpoint, and from that viewpoint what I have to say will not seem exaggerated and naïve. I appeal to Hagar Olsson's perceptive conscience and beg her to confirm that what I say is right, and at the same time for the sake of the cause I beg Ragnar Ekelund (and other potential knights) to withdraw their hasty judgment of my previous letter. I should also be grateful if Hagar Olsson were prepared to comment on whether she was being serious when she attributed cheap motives to me for my initiative, thereby besmirching the representative of an important cause.

This should solve the problem and settle the matter. The first legitimate heir to Zarathustra's doctrines has been forced to take instruction from many sides...

Edith Södergran

3/92   [Raivola, 2 Feb 1919]

My nestling,
Come here, if you can tear yourself away from your work. But let me know in good time if and which train and when, I'll meet you at the station with the horse.

Just got your card. Economic reasons prevented me writing at once. Our little housekeeping machine has come to a stop, when it gets going again I'll be ready to receive you. But I hope you're going to answer my letter to the paper. If the final sentence was too much you can certainly intercept the blow, which was aimed at you. You must have something to say, or is it possible that Hagar could be a traitor?

It's so beautiful out on the ice in the sunshine, we could go for walks there so long as the snow doesn't get too deep. Yesterday there was such a beautiful starry evening, thought of you, the sky was such an unbelievable dark blue. It makes more sense for you to come here to a home where you'll find everything ready for you than for me to go hunting for food and rooms in Helsinki and most of the time my health hangs by a thread. But if it's altogether too big a step for you don't do it. Maybe in a few years there'll be so many people expecting you to go and visit them that you'll laugh to think you once came to Raivola. There's so much I want to talk about. My name is what it is. Anyone who believes in Frk Sörensen[1] is welcome to do so, but I prefer 'l'obscurité ou les dieux nous cachent'.[2] Darling, wait for my next letter before you decide to come. The way isn't clear yet.

Edith

OLSSON: If Edith had come straight to the point and said 'we've no food in the house and I haven't had enough money for a stamp' I would have been shocked into grasping how things really were. But that wasn't her way. She always alluded indirectly to embarrassing difficulties with such delicate tact that it was easy to miss the stark implications.

As it was, I was much more disturbed by her unfortunate letter to the paper, which was already casting a shadow over this latest delightful letter to me. All I could do was let things take their course. Since I knew nothing of the spiritual circumstances that lay behind these laconic insinuations and couldn't remember the episode in Nietzsche she alluded to - about a young shepherd who manages to laugh after he has been forced to bite off the head of a repulsive black snake which has crept into his mouth - I missed its moving significance. I understood her to mean by divine 'laughter' nothing more than a general expression of superior independence. In any case, one could hardly realise how much every word in this literary letter to the editor of a newspaper had cost its author, or that she had been hinting at a hard-won victory over suffering and ruin in conditions where the very foundations necessary for life to continue at all seemed to be giving way under her, and that she had laid bare her innermost being to the public in this badly composed communication disfigured by grotesque printing errors. I was sure any contribution on my part to the debate would merely give rise to further attacks and ridicule, and the last thing I wanted was to prolong the painful dispute. So I decided it would be best to keep quiet. I was also annoyed that in her letter to the paper Edith demanded a direct answer from me and insisted I take back what I'd said in my review. I didn't think this was right, though at the same time it was precisely this demand and the criticism of me implied in it that had prevented me asking her not to publish the letter. I must have written back with some irritation that I had no intention of saying anything at all.

Her reaction was violent.

4/93   [Raivola, 5 Feb 1919]

You[1] have stuck me in the public pillory. I asked you if you thought this letter to the paper could be of great help to the cause. This was naturally on the assumption <u>that you would answer, not intended in any way as a criticism of you</u>. No one has treated me like this before.

The worst thing for me is that I've lost a sister who had begun to play a wonderful part in my poetry. I can't come to you because of my health. <u>If you can tear yourself away for 4 days or so I'm ready now to see you at any time whatsoever</u>. If you won't do this I shall break with you for ever, since I am <u>a</u>

person whose decisions are final. You have no idea what you have inflicted on me and what a beautiful world has been spoilt. Send back all my letters - if you want to break with me. No matter what fate has in store, I've never wavered once I've made up my mind. But I shall grieve terribly over this loss.

Don't forget this letter is a letter of destiny. I don't trust letters - I insist you[2] come here as proof of your integrity. I'm not prepared to spend several months negotiating and waiting for someone I don't trust: that's how I am - I can't be any different.

I demand you now pay for our friendship by making this journey - if you don't it'll be quite clear to me that I'm alone. Let me have my way, Hagar, and you'll find something more beautiful than any love and we'll be able to experience the most wonderful things.

OLSSON: When I saw how Edith was taking things I realised I must act at once. Her distressed letter moved me deeply. I wasn't hurt by its harsh tone; on the contrary, the despair that spoke through it brought out all my warmest feelings. Naturally it frightened me too, but one could read between the lines. I wrote warmly that I would come as quickly as I could, and immediately pulled myself together to write something I hoped would put an end to the shabby debate and spoil the fun of the over-clever as they quoted what to them was mad-house verse. This I did. My piece appeared in *Dagens Press* on 8 February and proved to be the last word in the public 'feud'. I wrote what I felt at that moment. Above all, I tried to make it clear to everyone that a poet of Edith Södergran's type spoke in the name of the spirit, in the name of the god who dwells in the breast of each one of us, and not in her own name. And that to accuse her of arrogance was as tasteless and stupid as similar accusations aimed at the great mystics who felt close to the almighty in their souls. And finally I suggested that the cultural outlook in Finland was depressingly narrow, and made a not very hopeful gesture towards the outer world:

'Edith Södergran in no way stands alone in our time. You have only to think of the young lyric poets of present-day Germany, that Germany which has suffered so much. And Pär Lagerkvist[1] in Sweden. But who in Finland has heard of any of them...'

5/94   [Raivola, 7 Feb 1919]

Now I've had 24 hours to think about it I've realised for the first time that you may have genuinely misunderstood what I was trying to do. So I take back the

40

demands I made in my last letter to you. But if my letter to the paper really did nothing to help the cause, if all it was likely to do was to prolong the 'S. affair'[1] why on earth did you suggest I send it in? 'Perceptive conscience' is not an attack on your 'honour as a critic' but a compliment (you are the only person whose conscience sees) and I wanted you to be a witness to my statement and I also wanted Ekelund to take back what he said about the letter. Don't speak against me in public - if you have no intention of speaking for me in public, which I had understood you did want to do. I hope the matter can now be regarded as settled. If you're not furiously angry with me, write. If you'd like to come it's best to take the night train; you'll be able to have a complete rest here.

6/95   [Raivola, 9 Feb 1919]

Dear Sister!

Welcome to Raivola. I'll be at the station and from there it's 2 kilometres to our place. My mother's very happy you're coming. Cat Nonno and dog Martti will also be very pleased to see you, as will our Punikki Aino.

The night before your malheur-letter[1] came I dreamed a magnificent black horse broke loose and rushed at me. The night before my S. letter[2] to the paper I dreamed a herd of cows came after me with clanging bells and I also dreamed I was walking in the street in a red cap, and a pedantic person I know nodded to me from the church tower - which you will see.

Just got your travel-letter. In my letter I said nothing except that after 24 hours I'd come to see there could have been a misunderstanding so I retracted my harsh offended letter. But surely you've already had that letter, or has there been some muddle? Bring a piece of soap with you. Come but be careful, don't jump off the train! Don't hurt yourself.

OLSSON: The whole family was waiting to welcome me, even the cat and dog, a sign that even these high authorities presumably approved of my coming. 'Our Punikki Aino' was a maid who slept in the kitchen. 'Punikki' is derived from the Finnish word for red and has long been used as a traditional and honourable name for cows though during the civil war it gained political overtones as a term for the Reds. But in the present context it is of course teasingly affectionate. Edith met me from the train with horse and sleigh as she had promised but I have no visual memory of our first meeting. I can no longer see her in my mind's eye standing as she must have done in deep snow on the station platform at Raivola that cold February day thirty-six years ago, watching out for me with her characteristic half-cheerful and half-melancholy but always expectant smile. I was much too deeply affected by the dramatic aspects of the situation to take in any external details. I was also shy and perhaps a little afraid. The only thing I can be certain of is that from the first moment I was drawn into a field of energy that made quite different demands on my inner resources from anything I'd experienced before. And no one should be under any illusion that I'd found favour through writing nice things about Edith in a newspaper! She made it absolutely clear from the first that she was no sort of mystic medium but a realist of the most uncompromising nature, indeed a pagan. I felt pretty crushed and realised there would be no point in trying to get her to understand that it was necessary for tactical reasons to emphasize the elevated passages in her work in an attempt to neutralise the effect on the general public of the vulgar ridicule she'd been subjected to.

I was able to stay only a few days; naturally I had to get back to my editorial work on the paper, and the long journey from Helsinki almost to the Russian border, involving a change of trains at Viipuri, took time. But it was a rare experience. The word 'fairytale' springs to mind when I think of it: the little low-roofed wooden cottage where the Södergrans lived near the Orthodox church with its cheerful bells, the two delightful women in their old-fashioned clothes - one with the bold profile of a young hawk and the other with her rosy cheeks the image of a beaming little mother troll - their merry mutual banter, their eccentric manners and wonderful capacity to accept whatever life might bring them quite independently, it seemed, of the material side of existence over which they had no control; all this contributed to the impression that they were living in a fairytale, far from the familiar realities of everyday life. This impression was reinforced by the spell that bound Edith to me. I can't use any other word: it was simply a magic spell that held us in its power, creating an atmosphere in which one felt everything was possible and anything could happen. The future burned in us, making us long for the tempting but terrible crown we expected it eventually to bring. As we sat at dusk in the little old-fashioned living-room with its view of snowbound garden and lake, chattering of this and that, reading poems to each other, daydreaming and looking through Edith's many delightful albums full of pictures of cats, this was the predominant atmosphere and it filled everything with implicit significance.

'Did we not live in a fairytale, where all impossible things become possible -'

Today's young people may perhaps find it difficult to understand the magic power the future held over us then. We were poor and unknown and lived in a distant corner of the world yet we felt like royalty. Our wealth was buried in hopes which hovered like the hands of angels over a shattered world pointing the way to a new human society. At that time the elite of Europe still had the self-confidence to dream a great dream, that it would become possible for every individual human being to share in one single spiritual community. Being young, we felt we had been given a tremendous opportunity on the threshold of a new world.

This mix of emotional intoxication, intellectual delight and secret excitement together with our impulsive girlish enthusiasm made of our being together a celebration as gentle and full of dreams as spring itself.

Naturally there were many difficulties too. Edith was unusually sensitive, touchingly considerate of others, as tender-hearted towards all living creatures as St Francis. But she was also full of suppressed passion, a pent-up emotional power that charged the atmosphere. She burned to go into action. She wasn't the sort of poet who is content to shape words into patterns to please literary people; she wanted to mould and transform life itself, engage herself in the development of humanity. But her illness and the extreme poverty thrust on her by political upheavals tied her to an inactive, impotent existence, cut off from outside contacts and intellectual company. The life of a writer in our civilisation is at best an unsatisfying half-life, but Edith's life was more savagely restricted than most while her fury was the fury of genius. It was a fury that sometimes flashed forth and made me tremble. There were moments when it seemed nothing could hold her back: 'My iron heart must sing its song'. This was a different Edith from the one who was to leave me several years later after following the terrible path of self-mastery to the very end and sacrificing the last drop of her life-blood in conquering the materialistic[1] elements in her nature to win celestial peace.

Edith also came to believe the psychological relief she gained from contact with me would free her from her isolation and that together we would be able to 'conquer the world'. I became necessary to her, not just as an intimate friend and kindred spirit but as a sort of idol, a source of the inspiration she needed for her imaginative life and a living guarantee that everything she dreamed of for herself would actually come true. These expectations brought me under pressure from a despotic creative will, making it difficult for me to continue being myself.

I did not always understand Edith's violent reactions which could contribute to making me feel insecure. At that time I had a close relationship with R. R. Eklund[2] and had brought with me the MSS of some prose-poems he had written; they later appeared in his first book *Jordaltaret* (The Earth Altar).[3] I read them aloud to Edith, and it became obvious while I was reading that she was deeply impressed. But suddenly she became violently upset, got up and went to her bedroom. I couldn't understand what had happened. When she didn't come back I had no idea what to do. In the end her mother came to my rescue. She knew Edith's reactions better than anyone and was always ready to give warm and understanding support. In the discreet way that was typical of her she hinted that hearing fine things others had written might make a writer feel her own work was no good. It then occured to one of us, I can't remember which, that Edith might go so far as to burn her own poems. I felt very uncomfortable but didn't dare intervene.

Naturally the dark cloud lifted and the sun shone again. Edith was a sun-child, her whole being was sun. She herself wrote 'I know of nothing but the sun'. One could sense this when one was near her, and it was the greatest experience imaginable. She was capable of irradiating her surroundings so powerfully with vibrant life that it seemed she actually carried a physical sun inside her. She overflowed with happiness, graceful playfulness and merry extravagance as if strewing basketfuls of roses about her. If anyone seemed created to be happy it was she, and it was remarkable how strongly she herself felt the contrast between the warm vitality of her nature and the pale chill of her illness. She looked on her illness as some kind of moral failing. Though she regularly rested on her daybed out on the little veranda even while I was in the house, I was never allowed to see her in this 'humiliating condition'.

7/96   [Raivola, 20 Feb 1919]

Dear darling Hagar,
thanks for the letter and the parcel. But why did you send me the polluted Lagerkvist? People of his sort profane the temple of art. As does the starchild too.

Never saddle me with transcendental books, it destroys my inspiration. Now for several days I haven't been able to write, the contamination needs time to dissipate. Don't hamper my creative work!!! Nietzsche and your lad's inspiring poems, that's something else, I want that!!

You must submit to my will. If you can sing now without it being transcendental, you will walk alone. But if it's transcendental then your book can have nothing to do with me and I hope it stays unwritten. You know perfectly well that no one is allowed to bring such gifts to the rose altar. I want you to go all the way to the gods. 'One does not look back on one's way to the gods'. If it's in my power I shall save your art from the transcendental. If that's impossible, I hope at least not to see the transcendental in you, because if I do I won't be able to write poems about you, and it's a source of power for my art to have a living model. I want to see in my sister a mermaid to hold me captive; I want to spend many years contemplating the god in her,[1] but not the medium. My darling, darling Hagar, forgive me for speaking like this if the transcendental can't be mitigated.

Here's a poem to annoy you, Hagar.[2]

The alien preacher - was she my sister?
Do I now have transcendental folk and gypsies for sisters?
Oh well, here's my hand, you voice from heaven.
Ancient she-cat, delinquent child, image of a god dreaming in tears...
Hyacintha, Hyacintha! Heaven's sent you a sister.
If there's a cathedral where angels' voices rise high
I shall hurry to the altar, heavy with thanksgiving.
Darling Gypsy-girl! depths reprieved by blonde hair
from a sea in your gaze.

Mamma says thank you for your nice letter.

OLSSON: I can't remember which of Pär Lagerkvist's books I'd sent Edith; I had every one that had so far come out. *Ångest* [Anguish] must have been among them. At her request I'd also sent my own book *Själarnas ansikten* [Soul Faces], which had been published in 1917; it contained 'Sagan om Stjärnebarnet' [The Story of the Starchild], against which Edith reacted as strongly as she did against the Lagerkvist material. Besides, it had as epigraph a quotation from Lagerkvist's play *Sista mänskan* [The Last Person].

The book I was writing, and which Edith was already treating in advance with the greatest suspicion, was *Kvinnan och nåden* [Woman and Grace]. It came out at Christmas the same year and was received enthusiastically at Raivola by a very changed reader who now longed for a message of 'grace' more than anything else. 'Your lad' refers both here and later to R. R. Eklund to whom I was engaged at the time. Our relationship had a very romantic beginning when he wrote me a letter in response to an article on van Gogh I had written in *Studentbladet*.[1] He was editor of *Vasabladet*[2] until I got him a job on *Dagens Press* when he came to Helsinki.

I was hurt when Edith so brusquely dismissed both my own work and Lagerkvist's books, which I thought would interest her as an example of the latest poetry from Sweden. In fact it was the first time I felt offended by her harsh tone. I wrote to her coldly to send the books back if they were so detestable. At the time neither I nor Edith herself understood that her violent reaction against the 'transcendental' exposed a sore point in herself, and that this would be the beginning of a harrowing spiritual conflict within her, which would not be resolved until death was near, and that this conflict, added to her physical suffering, would do more than anything else to use up her strength during the last years of her life.

8/97   [Raivola, 22 Feb 1919]

Here are the Lagerkvists. I can't send your book back because I've cut out the starchild and burnt it and I'd like to keep the rest. My loathing for this spook-literature is so strong because everything that has to do with you makes such a strong impression on me. <u>I will not look in through that door</u>. I'm telling you nothing you don't know. If any way can be found to deliver you from it - let me be your doctor.

Hagar kissed me once. That kiss meant more than words can express, in it lay the distressing story of an illness. If you insist on driving away one who has your wellbeing as much at heart as I have - that's up to you. Again last night I dreamed that a horse rushed after me. Greetings from Raivola.

9/98   [Raivola, 26 Feb 1919]

Dear darling Hagar! It hurts me so terribly to have done you harm. Your article's magnificent, in it you stand like a pillar of fire in the night. Don't say you belong to another race. You are as we are. But you've received a double-edged gift. And you've let yourself be infected when like me you ought to be fighting against the insidious horror of ghost-stories.

Hagar, you're a sick child. Come to my arms as you would to a mother's. I feel I have the strength to overcome your enemy, let me take control of you - surrender yourself to my will, to the sun, to the life-force, to prana.[1] Let life fight all the way as it always does in nature. The awful path you are taking is not the path of humanity. I've been created to help you, for I've become bliss and light itself.

There are powers in me that want to break out, my will-power will take care of you. You're still a little child and I know what will be good for you. There are two things I want: 1) that you shall feel spiritual relief (your kiss, painfully burning itself into my blood, told me you're suffering) and 2) that if at all possible your art shall be protected from this pollution. Nietzsche calls mysticism <u>Aufschiessen in Unkraut</u>.[2]

I myself needed a different sort of relief right up to the moment when I became capable of creating from the fullness of my heart. For you the moment of relief will come when you are able to bring the love you already have to your own real creative work and, above all, when you can see your own dangerous talent differently, essential if you are to become a really happy human being.

My words are gold, take them and keep them in your heart. Sit down and think it all out as nicely as you usually do.

It was hellish the paper came two days late, that pains me.

Will you still edit my book? And will you send me those poems which are closer to a religious service than my own?

The sweet Hagar who lay under the red hide coverlet must not be her sister's enemy. I see how dangerous your path is and I want to run after you and snatch you back from the darkness. Because the air there is joyless.

I will send my living store of energy streaming out over you. Don't push your sister away. I am life, happy life!

OLSSON: The article to which Edith refers appeared in *Dagens Press* on 22 February [1919]; in it I discussed Fröding's[1] journalism and letters which had been published in three volumes. My reviews could generally be read as personal statements and Edith often rightly read them as letters to herself. Here she directly takes up a point in the article and answers it. I had quoted from a letter Fröding had written to his sister, reproducing it and commenting on it with the unmistakable frantic bitterness of personal experience:

> Fröding delineates his situation without beating about the bush: 'It's certainly true, as you say, that I am myself to blame for my isolation, though sometimes I long for the company of others and try to be like them, which usually doesn't work. We come of different races and do not understand one another.[2] I have sometimes thought it had to do with a difference in talent - that sometimes I am superior and sometimes they are - but it's not that, it's a difference of kind which has nothing to do with superiority and inferiority. I am from the moon or Jupiter and have come by mistake to this place where I am treated like a changeling, and that is what I feel myself to be.'
>
> Not a word can be taken from or added to this confession. The marked one has spoken.
>
> Naturally one should not talk about such things. In real life people don't like ghost stories. It is altogether too gruesome to suggest that spooks might be at large among us, spooks that long to mingle with our human blood. Clearly no civilised person's nerves would stand such a thing. Though fortunately it would be easy to murder such a changeling. Changelings are only too vulnerable and of course they're outcasts.

This was a brew that was fermenting inside me too. But the situation of being different and treated as an outcast was also relevant to Edith, it was our common lot in the bourgeois world in which we lived. And much else in the article was put in precisely with Edith and the treatment she had experienced in mind, as for example the triumphant reference to how Fröding in an article on Ibsen demolishes the 'pet saying of the philistines' that what is obscurely said must also be obscurely thought.

Edith asks if I'm still prepared to edit her book. This refers to *Rosenaltaret* [The Rose Altar]. I had promised to check the poems because she was so anxious for me to do so. The poems 'closer to a religious service than my own' were by R. R. Eklund; she hopes to see more of his work after what I read to her at Raivola.

10/99   [Raivola, 4 Mar 1919]

Dear Hagar, when I used the word 'polluted' I didn't mean unclean in the usual sense but sick. I want you and your lad to know that. I know as well as anyone that the starchild is the most beautiful poem in Soul Faces, but it's also true that a very great talent has no business being sick. I'm the last person to call in question your creative power, I know on what a monumental and magnificent scale you work. Got your second letter now. We're beginning to understand one another. I used the term 'to profane' with deliberate cruelty because I wanted to give you a sharp shock to wrench you out of something that doesn't exist. You can't believe what a relief it is to me that you're ready to burn all your boats, it's as if something dreadfully sombre, a weight, had fallen from my heart. I shout for joy that the piece in Schildt is no accident but that you're going to go on like that, I hunger so for the tower.[1] I've read your lad's poems aloud to Mamma, she found them terribly beautiful, they're the sort of thing that could be read out in churches - a divine service for the future. At night before I go to sleep and in the morning when I wake I read that passage in 'Skapelsens dag står upp' [The Day of Creation Dawns]. That poem really is 'dew' to exhausted senses.[2] I prophesy that everyone who possesses a spark of soul is going to love his poems and thirst for them. Humanity will find it easier to understand an art capable of slaking the great thirst of the soul than any other art that has so far existed. I believe many souls long for real edification, something humanity is now beginning to receive for the first time. I can't wait for the book to come out.

Sat yesterday in front of the kitchen fire and let a piece of wood burn between my fingers till it became red and transparent as if transformed by spiritual inspiration. I thought about the three of us,[3] it was so wonderful.

Mamma and I have voted.[4] Rotteli[5] is behaving well at home, has now become more presentable, pity you saw him in poor condition. Don't like writing letters. If you happen to pass Akademiska,[6] be an angel and ask if the Nietzsche has come in and what it costs, I've already written to ask them so many times I feel too embarrassed to do it again. As soon as I know it's in I'll write to them and order it. Thanks for the chocolate and the cakes. Darling Hagar must not be so generous to devilish murderers etc. You will write again before we meet, won't you. What's Proco up to? How are Lucas and A.E.? Mamma asks to be remembered.

I've thought up a fine letter for you but it'll have to stay unwritten.[7]

OLSSON: I was working on my third book *Woman and Grace* and the 'piece in Schildt' was the first chapter of it, which Holger Schildt had sent out with the firm's 1918 Christmas List.[1]

The passage Edith refers to from one of R. R. Eklund's prose poems runs in its entirety like this:

> The power of their hands makes of us discoverers, the first people: around us Earth lies new and what seemed unthinkable flourishes at our feet. The day of creation dawns. It arches its spotless vault over the earliest runner after Time's quivering horses, and the first morning drips dew on exhausted senses. We see things a thousand years old, and we see them for the first time.
>
> Thus do our thanks go up as if from the wide trembling gaze of children. Thus do our lips whisper great and wondrous words: Creator, Giver, Restorer and Rehabilitator.

'Rotteli', also called Trotteli, Råttikus and most often Totti, was Edith's beloved cat.[2] His 'official' name was Nonno and he had contributed in his own way to ensuring my stay with the Södergrans was anything but the 'complete rest' Edith had so optimistically promised me.[3] He spent much of his time out about his own business and when he came home bore evidence of terrible battles. Edith's agitation knew no bounds. I shall never forget my first night in the little anteroom where I slept. I was woken in the middle of the night by Edith, hair all over the place and completely beside herself, dashing from her room and out of the house. I was terrified, sure that something dreadful was about to happen. It later transpired that Edith had thought she heard the cat howling and jumped to the conclusion that someone was doing him harm. As later became apparent, there was more sense in her agitation than I could have imagined at the time.

'Proco' was the kindly poet Hjalmar Procopé, one of Edith's favourites.

'Lucas'was Max Hanemann, a leading liberal journalist and influential columnist on *Dagens Press*, and 'A.E.' was Artur Eklund who wrote in the same paper, a brilliant writer but deep-dyed reactionary and early forerunner of fascism who would one day write Edith a gruesome obituary.[4]

11/100   [Raivola, 11 Mar 1919]

Hagar, my love! I saw T.f. in the paper today, are you ill?[1] I've got a long letter I've written you but I'm not going to post it. I don't know whether what I wrote in it is accurate or not. It dawned on me like a shower of shooting stars, I've seen so much but I want to check it first. If I can't sing Dionysus[2] I'm the unhappiest being ever created. The letter I've written you was a sorcerer's letter, a Lenten letter, a talisman specially for you. It was the great letter, the rose letter, the sunshine letter. Write, I'm worried about you. We've had letters from Pburg, the situation there is frightening.[3] Several days later. Again no Hgr[4] in the paper, I'm worried about you. Write! I can't write poetry any more. The Dionysiac claims my whole soul, but I can't sing it. When are you coming here. When are you coming to Raivola? tell me. I'm not happy with the Dionysiac.

12/101   [Raivola, 19 Mar 1919]

Dear darling Hagar! It's nice you had a trip to Stockholm but be careful, it's so easy to catch cold after Spanish flu. I'm worried you may have got TB from me judging by your cough. There are 1000 things I want to talk to you about. I've become an arch-fanatic, doomed. And so wild travel-plans rule, to stay in Albergo Stella d'Italia at San Momette.[1] Sometime we must travel together. Don't forget to ask Ellen K.[2] what it was like being N's mistress!!! Have a good look at everything so you can tell me later how it was. Copying out my poems now, it makes me so angry to have to do it, I don't want to sleep a single second, I want to be sunk in ecstasy. Get Nietzsche's 'Morgenröte' or 'Menschliches, Allzumenschliches' or 'Wille zur Macht', or 'Geburt des Tragödie'.[3]

Mamma sends kindest regards and says you must take care and not travel if you haven't fully recovered. Send a few lines from Sweden. Just get one Nietzsche if they're very expensive. The magic's still working!

OLSSON: The expression 'arch-fanatic' seems a bit dubious, as if Edith had already been influenced by the terminology in my *Soul Faces* where the word 'fanatic' is used in a sense far removed from its usual meaning and refers to those who (beyond 'truth' which is but a brother's lie and 'faith' which is but a brother's prison) seek in a sort of ecstasy of thought the only absolute, that 'which is not'.

I had an invitation to call on Ellen Key in Stockholm, and Edith as usual was enormously keen to hear full details of my trip ('Have a good look at everything'). 'N's mistress' was probably a figment of Edith's imagination like many of her racier ideas. What she meant by it was as much a riddle to me when I got her letter as it is now.[1] I was so used to Edith's strange fancies that I tended to pass them over with no more than a smile for comment.

That you couldn't get Nietzsche's works in Helsinki says a good deal about how shut off we were from contact with world culture. I'd offered to get the books for her in Stockholm, hardly the last time we in Finland have had to turn to Sweden for essential spiritual nourishment no less than for bodily nourishment.

13/103[1]   [Raivola, 26 Mar 1919]

Hagar dear,

It's so strange when you write so seldom, it's as if we were immensely far from each other. I lie in bed, Spanish in mood.[2] I've read your brave article. Take care, don't go to Stockholm if you aren't quite well. You'd be better off here enjoying a rest-cure lying beside me on the veranda, but this damned having to depend on the Bolsheviks!!! I've got so much to say to you, a path of delight, but I'm forced to keep silent. I've developed a wild hunger for work. And a hunger for knowledge. I feel as if flames were bursting out of me, I long for storm suffering and pregnancy. I speak to all the Germans I meet in the street or in shops and ask them if they have any of Nietzsche's books. Will do all I can to get him. It's so wonderful to write to you. At the same time I loathe any kind of writing.

We have a terrible day's work ahead of us. We have no time to lose. I wish I could be really well and that I had double the amount of talent and that suffering were more accessible to me. I wonder if we shall tread the path to the Dionysiac or whether that was for Nietzsche alone. This is now what I want most, O you who gild my life, but perhaps it's unattainable. I've copied out my poems into an exercise book and will send it to you in the hope you'll edit them. If not, send it back to me. I loathe these poems.

I long for something totally different. Write at once and tell me what you think of them. I'm so tired. If you manage to see Selma,[3] look really carefully at everything, what it looks like, Selma's home and everything connected with it, it interests me. What a long way we still have to go, what a whirlwind of heavy serious work. What a glorious thing our life is! I'm not sure if I can manage to send my poems to reach you before you leave. You write to me so seldom. Have you forgotten me already? Are you neglecting me? Perhaps a wave of Bolshevism will sweep in and I'll never be able to see you again. I wish you could be here instead of in that damned Stockholm. I know much more than I did when we last met and you wouldn't be able to keep me down now. We should be like real sisters who know each other really well. Write. Mamma and Trotteli say hello.

OLSSON: My 'brave article' was so far as I can judge 'Spökteknikens genombrott i dramat' [The Breakthrough of Spook-technique in Drama], published on 20 March.[1] It deals with Strindberg's final dramatic works[2] and, without discussing their form at all, seems to concentrate its attack on the surreal next-world atmosphere Strindberg so brilliantly created, suggesting a link between his *Toten-insel* [The Isle of the Dead] and Lagerkvists's *Den svåra stunden* [The Difficult Hour]. Clearly I wasn't prepared to have anything to do with such spookery which was not the genuine mystic experience then forcing its way into literature with 'visionary force', and that Lagerkvist could hail this spookery as the way of the future was 'evidence that his blood had grown remarkably thin'. It can be seen that this was the very debate on the transcendental then in full swing between Edith and myself. I was trying to make clear that I wasn't interested in perspectives from the next world, but in a dimension of life itself, a perspective rooted in reality which had been hidden but had now manifested itself again in human consciousness: 'the gods turn back'.

Naturally I hadn't even dreamed of calling on Selma Lagerlöf, but to Edith it seemed natural that I should do so. She was very anxious to know about Selma's home life and to see all the details for herself, and this desire with its tinge of romantic longing for the past had come over her at the very moment when she was gripped by thoughts of the heavy daily labour which lay before those of us who were to bear the future on our shoulders.

Edith complains bitterly that I write so seldom, a complaint that will recur regularly together with disappointment over visits that never happened. This is what I found most painful when I re-read the letters, and it cuts me to the heart now to think of it. She might have been more understanding if she'd had some idea of the furious pace at which I had to work in those days in conditions which were far from ideal. I had to keep writing night and day just to earn enough to break even. My days were spent on routine jobs at the newspaper office and my evenings on reading and reviewing new books, and on top of that there was my own personal writing. When I eventually gave up my job as the paper's maid-of-all-work I took up translation, continuing at the same time as a literary critic and taking on theatre criticism as well, all for a pittance. It wasn't easy for Edith living her sequestered life at Raivola to imagine how things might be for me, and the last thing I wanted was to burden her with my personal difficulties. At the most I might have whispered them in Trotteli's ear, but he and I met so seldom we never got on close enough terms for that.

I comfort myself with the thought that if Edith hadn't had me she would have had no one and that would have been a really bad thing.

14/104   [Raivola, 30 Mar 1919]

I've sent off the manuscript.[1] Why don't you write? Am I no longer in fashion? It's getting to the time you should be coming here again and renewing our acquaintanceship. Come as quickly as possible, but by no means for less than 4 days. Too short visits have no meaning. Write what you think of the book of poems, and advise me if you will what to leave out. If you have to go to St.holm[2] immediately better send the manuscript back to me so it won't be lying about for weeks. I'm deeply hurt you forget me so.

15/105   [Raivola, 4 April 1919]

Good you wrote, suspected you were fed up with me and had abandoned me. How odd, just the same poems I'd thought to leave out. It'll be no loss if your trip comes to nothing in this cold-catching weather. When the bird-cherries bloom on Skansen,[1] that's when Stockholm's alluring.

'Syster, min syster, du är ännu liten' [Sister, my Sister, you are still little] seems rather feeble to me, I'm not enthusiastic about including it. It can seem stronger if one reads it the way Sonia reads the gospel to Raskolnikov[2] (in Dostoevsky, I've read him now) but I don't like the idea of that. Don't say anything to Schildt about royalties. I'd like to add a few poems at once to replace those cut out, but I feel profoundly lazy.

I've nothing against it if you think it won't give rise to knowing remarks, but I'm sure Runar Schildt has taken it into his head that I'm referring to myself with 'queen so glorious'[3] and the thought of this disturbs me so much I can't bear it. The comment on Lichtenberg must stay in,[4] I've always liked Lichtenberg. Trotteli's come home with a bloody nose, he wages war at night. Come here when they bombard Kronstadt,[5] that's going to be interesting. What d'you think of spontaneous poetry, is that a brand-new idea, yet old Goethe[6] says: 'Jedes Gedicht ist ein Gelegenheitsgedicht.'[7]

My brain's been hard at work and I'm utterly exhausted. I would certainly have included 'Brev från min syster' [Letters from my Sister][8] in the collection if I'd been satisfied with its beginning and ending.

It's occurred to me the sister cycle could be named 'Fantastique'. Would you be happy with that? Thanks for all the trouble you've taken over the book.

I hope no one'll suspect who the sister is. Be cunning, don't give the Schildts a chance to suspect anything.

The change you suggested for 'Scherzo' is excellent, I'm happy about it.[9]

Follow your instinct: if 'Sister, my Sister' seems weak, leave it out. I've begun copying out poems, among them 'Faller ej håret lätt' [Does not your hair fall lightly][10] but I'm so tired, so boundlessly listless and lazy, it's barometric pressure and Trotteli too is so tired.

OLSSON: The warning not to mention royalties to the publisher is characteristic. This over-sensitive pride always got in the way whenever I tried to find some way of getting Edith financial assistance. It needed every ounce of one's cunning even to dare to try.

I really thought it childish of Edith to worry that people might guess who the sister in the little cycle of poems was. As if anyone in the tiny Finland-Swedish arts world would have cared! And even if they had, there can be no doubt I would have been the last person they would have thought of. Some people can live invisible in their milieu and I was and am one of them, no matter how visible I may have been as a writer. Endless nonsense was later written about the sister poems, just as it was about much else that Edith wrote. In the final analysis what delights literary people is structures invented by themselves; real life is too simple for them. I'm happy to leave them to it.

16/106   [Raivola, 4 April 1919]

The following poems can be left out: 'Eros'[1] 'Pansartåget'[2] 'Aftonstämning'[3] 'Blå rök'.[4]

The order of the poems doesn't matter. The sister poems should be brought together as a cycle starting with 'Vårmysterium' [Spring Mystery] and ending with 'Gudabarnet' [The Child of God].

In 'I mörkret' [In the Darkness] the following changes could be made. 'Skälvande gick jag' [Quaking I walked], 'Höstliga nätter' [Autumn nights] Jag fann en syster [I found a sister].

The poem No! No! No! must be given the title '<u>Alla ekon i skogen</u>' [All the Echoes in the Forest] and No, no, no must be written without exclamation marks.

In 'Sången om oceanen' [The Song of the Ocean] the last bit beginning at 'uppe i norden' [up in the north] can be cut.

In 'Scherzo' delete the line 'vakna: Besinning. Syster Fantasia stig ned på jorden' [wake up: Take notice. Sister Fantasia has come down to earth].

In '<u>Det fasansfulla tåget</u>' [The Terrible Procession] delete 'stackars magra ben lunka med' [poor thin legs jog along too].

The poem 'Till de starka' [To the Strong] can be retained if you approve.

The poem 'Syster, min syster, du är ännu liten' [Sister, my Sister, you are still little][5] can perhaps be included in the cycle but there can be no harm in calling this in question. It isn't strong and could weaken the cycle.

OLSSON: My much-discussed trip to Stockholm became reality between this letter and the next. I stayed all week there with Ellen Key at Strand and I shall never forget her, a kind little old lady who met me off the train in a homespun costume with a wicker basket on her arm. This is the simplicity of all really great people, I told myself, and all my nervousness disappeared. At their home her companion Malin welcomed me and said a few politely appreciative words about *Soul Faces* which she and Ellen - 'we', said Malin - had read with great interest. And then came liverwort and crocuses and Easter eggs with rhymes and an ageing warrior's incredible delight in the young.

Edith knew I was home again when she saw 'Rachel' in the paper - a pen-name I used for my more feminine jobs such as reporting on lace exhibitions and the like.

17/109   [Raivola, 3 May 1919]

Saw 'Rachel' in the paper, expecting a letter from you. How was it? Write! Spring work has started. The lake is so blue, soon it'll begin to be 'specially for you', the minute there's a sign of leaves and a little velvet-grass and small forget-me-nots and buttercups. I wonder how you'd like it here then. Send the earth altar![1] I'm so listless and tired, have been all month. Here we're waiting for pleasant events.[2] Have you got Nietzsche with you?[3] I'm very curious about everything that happened to you on the trip. Write! Love. Who are 'we all'?[4] I've had an invitation to join the Society of Authors[5] but have left it unanswered for economic reasons. I've reached an agreement with Schildt, but I've no idea when the book'll come out.

18/111 [Raivola, 7 May 1919]

Darling Hagar

Thanks for your incredible enormous kindness. That you were able to get me Nietzsche - you've no idea how I've waited and fretted for the old books. But why haven't you written? What experiences did you have in Stockholm? And congratulations on being attacked by Jumbo!![1] I'm sure something awful's going to happen to me. Last night I dreamed Mannerheim[2] took me in his arms and his caresses were more heady and seductive than those of anyone else in the world. It was such a terribly vivid dream and he was incredibly attractive. If in real life he's like he was in the dream I'd be desperately in love with him. Tell me, what is he like? I really think it's time you came here, if you yourself really want to, shan't nag at you. But soon the bird-cherry will begin flowering, in 10 days I think. I want you to see Raivola then.

I treat The Earth Altar as a delicacy, only read a few poems a day for fear of overindulging. What do they say about it? Rotteli has a great bald patch on his head, nearly always bloody, he has the quickest-healing skin I've ever seen 'given him by providence because he's so good', but the wicked 'cat-thedrals' rip it open again. What did Nietzsche cost? Write to me about Stockholm and how 'The Earth Altar' is doing! Does anyone understand what it's about? If the old ladies[3] have written to you about interesting things please send me something from their letters, be an angel! If I find the time I'll get some people here to read 'The Earth Altar' without telling them beforehand how brilliant it is, I want to find out exactly how it affects different individuals, I want to study them. Mamma says hello and looks forward to seeing you again.

OLSSON: That Edith was so excited about how *The Earth Altar* would be received and even wanted to try the book's effect on different people is clear proof not only that she loved the book but also that she saw it as a dove released from the ark of the new poetry. Would it return with a fresh olive-leaf in its beak? If so she would take it as a good omen for all our efforts and not least for her own poetry.

19/112 [Raivola, 11 May 1919]

Why don't you write? World events are making me think strange thoughts, I wonder if when you were in Stockholm you stumbled on <u>the same thought</u>. It would be useful to meet. The garden will soon be ripe for your coming.

I've realised I've now managed to draft the book better, tried to improve this and that.

It's strange you're keeping the results of your trip from me and that I may not know who 'we all' are. The Earth Altar is the first thirst-quenching collection of poems I've come across, the book appeals to me more than I can say.

We really could have a lot to talk to each other about. My own collection begins and ends gracefully, and 'Fantastique' in the middle is a gracefully woven garland, it comes over me like a fragrant white veil, there's something in it that's painful and burns. The first part of the book is even and strong apart from the invocation, though this is characteristic of one side of my nature, a side perhaps seen most clearly in my latest poems, which are otherwise brown and dull and coloured by their subject-matter, they are nearly all about planets and stars.

I can't claim I was favoured with inspiration in April, and this is why my newest poems are dull, and why this letter too is deathly dull.

Perhaps now all the old things are falling apart at the same time, it looks as if everything is rolling forward. Everything that is healthy and full-grown. We are an atom in the heart of the young and immature and have no name.

Vårmysterium [Spring Mystery] isn't a powerful poem but part of the whole, it has the fragrance of violets and grace and the same delicious burning atmosphere.

I understand now, that if one says:

My sister

comes like a etc (this line is not complete)

So I've put: You come. But then 'my sister' becomes superfluous and loses its power again.

The Schildts have taken out 'the diamonds on your toes'. I wrote on the proofs that I wanted it left in, unless they were implacably opposed to it, since the second section deliberately leads into it.[1]

Perhaps you've been writing something? Finished your book? Or has your correspondence been all to do with Stockholm. Has 'The Earth Altar' already been reviewed somewhere.

WRITE! Who are 'we all'?

OLSSON: The 'world events' which had intervened so decisively in Edith's life are still vivid to me. The war of intervention in Russia had flared up again with redoubled strength during the spring. Fighting raged in many areas including the south side of the Gulf of Finland, and Kronstadt was so near Raivola that with binoculars one could see the 'news' from Suomenkylä hill. In Finland too activist sentiments were gaining ground: an expeditionary force had been prepared to help east Karelia break away from Russia and many expected the government to

57

abandon its wait-and-see position. Edith, keenly vigilant, listens to the 'storm' which 'comes up from dark ravines of night to dance/ alone his ghostly dance above the earth'.¹ What will fall apart, what will be spared? It is a time of uncertainty and tension; Edith's new poems take on the 'colour of their subject matter' (they were later included in *Framtidens skugga* [The Shadow of the Future] in the cycle 'Planeterna stiga' [The Planets are Rising]) and she feels new upheavals are near to bringing undreamed-of opportunities for all who do not bear the soul's sword in vain.

In her isolation Edith imagines I am withholding from her remarkable experiences I had in the great city of Stockholm and presses me to tell her exactly who 'we all' are. What I meant by this phrase was our sister souls around the world - the young, those coming into their own; I was certain they existed and was happy to point to them to keep up both Edith's spirits and my own. But Edith was never satisfied with oracular hints: she demanded facts. She would have been depressed if I'd told her how heavy the shadow of the past still lay over the literary life of Stockholm; I preferred to conceal my own disappointment in pregnant silence, allowing her to believe what she liked.

20/113   [Raivola, 16 June 1919]

Come. It's not dangerous here, so far the Bolsheviks haven't eaten us up. The only way we can talk properly together is out on the grass in summer. I've been waiting so long for you. (If it's absolutely impossible, I can't demand you plunge yourself into ruin.) The lilacs are in flower now, I hope you'll stay till the roses. I'm thinking out the walks we'll take together. From Suomenkylä hill you can see the sea and the news through binoculars. I'll clip Martti in honour of your coming and do a bit of raking here and there. It's so vital that you come. If you can't, which I couldn't bear to hear, you owe me a long letter.

Write to say when you're coming. Mamma's looking forward to seeing you.

Give your own family at home my regards if they know of me and if my regards would mean anything to them.¹

21/114   [Raivola, 22 June 1919]

Still shaking with rage over Mörne's review of 'The Earth Altar'. Is that the way to welcome genius? There's Mörne for you. I've spent a long time thinking out reviews of him, I mean R.E.¹ Oh if only I could presume to write one!

Thanks for your letter. I'm very happy you're coming. I'm thinking out which walks to show you. It'll be lovely to lie together on the grass and talk. When everything's green with summer is exactly the time I long so terribly to have you with me. Seeing how indecently banal Mörne can be, I begin to think that in Sweden you must have run into nothing but idiots.

I wonder what strong impressions Sweden made on you? And what you can be despairing of after such enviable experiences?

My blood runs warmer when I think of you coming. You shall sit on the sauna-logs by the lakeside and lie at the southern bathing-place and sit in the sun on the sauna steps and on the bench on the north side. Bring an old dress with you.

Germany's misfortune causes me such pain. Why does nobody in Finland protest against the peace terms? If I could write an appeal to help collect protest signatures I'd do it.

Mörne's a pig. It's easy to see he knows what's involved. O Hagar what do you think of that review? 'Kniven' [The Knife] is the best bit[2] in my opinion, it's incomparable. It shows his intelligent profile in such an interesting light. And 'Tystnadens hed' [The Heath of Silence] is Mamma's favourite, and I particularly like it from 'our fabled fire has burnt low' onwards.

I'm upset about the review. Want to write a blazing rebuttal in my own natural style. Is no one going to say anything about it, must this wonderful book lie hidden by dust until one day it's discovered. How has it been with the other reviews. Has no one understood it better? What has Hemmer's reaction been? What do people say in general. Write. I can approve if you want to save the cost of a stamp and if you don't want to tire yourself with writing that's something I can understand and I've every sympathy. I'm writing to you in this slapdash fashion because I don't want to tire myself out and waste my chance to be out in the lovely greenery. You aren't offended, are you? I like writing to you. O Hagar just imagine, you could come here into the womb of nature and forget the city and everything in it. I think they've all become terrified of us. How icy cold Mörne's review is.

That business with the Germans gives me no peace. I've written an article: Shall we look on in silence while a whole nation is hammered into chains? Can't send it you, it isn't finished, but I wonder what you'll think of it. <u>Can't you write something for the Germans</u>? I don't know how I can swallow this. Goodbye. Send your Räisälä address. When you come, bring a picture of yourself and if you've got one to show me, one of your lad. My article about the Germans is very down-to-earth and not at all like my letters to the paper. If I had any talent whatever for writing articles, and if my aversion from doing so were not just as unbounded as my enthusiasm, I really think I'd be able to achieve something or other by this means. Come.

OLSSON: It may be of interest to look more closely at the review by Arvid Mörne (20 May) which upset Edith so deeply. He starts with an excerpt which he seems to have chosen with a negative ulterior motive in mind and goes on:

> This excerpt will perhaps give the reader some idea of the character and style of this profound little collection of meditations which a new writer, Ragnar Rudolf Eklund, has published under the title *The Earth Altar*. It would not be fair to dwell on its great debt in both form and language to Pär Lagerkvist and Nietzsche and other more remote models and its lack of originality from the point of view of content, because if we did we should discover a considerable negative balance, particularly if we take into account the fact that the author has not made the most of the extensive atmospheric richness inherent in the basic poetic material relating to Man and the Earth that he clearly has at his disposal.
>
> But if we take this slim volume as an experiment, it is from any point of view a remarkable work. It shows courage. Ragnar Eklund makes it clear he has no fear of the derision and mockery his metaphorical language is bound to evoke from nine-tenths of his readers. Anyone so utterly alien to the aspirations of our younger writers as to feel nothing but scorn for Edith Södergran's poetry will stop only to greet *The Earth Altar* with an equally contemptuous guffaw. But what I most value in Eklund's writing are his many purely poetic stylistic felicities: delicate little details, as for example when the windows of his dwelling are bathed in streams of light or, to take another example, the richly atmospheric wordplay in his prose-poem about an old knife.
>
> But having said this, it is a serious failing that Ragnar Eklund's prose so lacks the spark of spontaneity, even if we must remember that spontaneity will always be inhibited in a stylistically pioneering work whose aim is to get some new and risky project off the ground. We should not take *The Earth Altar* into account in assessing how far this writer is likely to go as a poet.

That Edith could take this kind of criticism so hard and be so impatient for someone to 'react' merely shows how difficult it was for her to adjust to a chilly cultural climate. She also felt a certain disappointment that it was Mörne of all people, from whom she had expected something better, who was so unenthusiastic.

22/115   [Raivola, 27 June 1919]

Waiting impatiently for you. Here everything's calm and still. Come as quick as you can. Have you had my card? Why don't you answer, I'm worried. Is it enough to put 'Räisälä' as an address? I've had two cards from you and this is the second I've sent. The loveliest time is exactly now, come quickly. We're all waiting. There are a few minor problems with the pass,[1] but nothing that can't be dealt with. Hagar come!

OLSSON: 'There are a few minor problems with the pass'; I can almost see Edith's crafty smile as she writes this. She knew perfectly well the problems weren't minor ones, but her impatience to have me come would brook no further obstacles. The fighting in Russia was very near the Finnish border and the military authorities[1] had closed the border area on the Karelian isthmus, which in any case might at any moment become the front. My parents weren't at all keen on me going there.

23/116   [Raivola, 1 July 1919]

Very happy you felt the necessity, I do very much. It's extremely important that you come. You must apply to the second division or to General Thesleff's[1] office. If anyone in that world knows you I'm sure they'd vouch for you. You should be able to get as far as Uusikirkko[2] without difficulty, the pass is only needed from there. But the young commandant at Uusikirkko seems nice and friendly, if you can find someone to vouch for you there, all will be well. Go forward with the energy and audacity of genius, make it clear that you're a poet who must visit a poet, that you've worked on Dagens Press. I believe in my innocence this will get you through. Here everything's fine. We know the local administrator.[3] The tiger Råttikus may not be aware he's doing it, but he says hello. We ought to go down this Zügenstrasse one day.

OLSSON: Edith had a large collection of old postcards she had bought on her travels, mostly in Switzerland. Some were mounted in an album. She often sent me cards of this kind. This particular one is beautifully coloured and shows 'Zügenstrasse beim Bärentritt'.

24/117   [Raivola, 1 July 1919]

They've told me going to the local military authorities and trying to put pressure
on them won't help, but I want at least to ask them what the possibilities are.
Dreamed about you last night. Martti is now in his summer suit, clipped and
scrubbed. We are in the process of felling a great dead birch. The roses are in full
bloom. We've already started bathing. The little maple-tree and the harebells and
the garden are waiting for Hagar, <u>they've been waiting for her for many years</u>.
Don't burn the Zügenstrasse card, Nietzsche lived round there and if there's any
justice in this world we should stroll there together one day. Oh how I love
[- - -][1] generally speaking. Say hello from me to your family.

   Bring a piece of soap with you again, we have no toilet soap. And an old
dress too, but perhaps it's best you travel light. Make all necessary enquiries
before you start out, I don't want to inflict a difficult and pointless journey on
you. Mamma says hello.

   I'm rather pleased with the appearance of 'The Rose Altar' despite the
plainness of the blue paper, it's the only one of my books I can bear to look at.[2]

25/118   [Raivola, 5 July 1919]

I've managed to find out that it would be a good idea if your father, as a pastor,
could certify that your journey is necessary or - more to the point - that you are
harmless. The more documents the better. I've also heard that controls at
Uusikirkko will be strict. It'll be such a bore if you don't come. Try to get here,
but without causing yourself too much bother.

26/119   [Raivola, 22 July 1919]

Traitress.
4 cards and no answer. I was about to write you a letter full of bitter reproaches,
but refrained when I heard that someone we know who has furniture in our old
house and was on the way to fetch it was turned back at Uusikirkko. And we
have been presented with the prospect of having 160 men billeted on us, our land
to become a sort of barrack-yard, but so far nothing has happened.[1] It's beautiful
on the north side of the garden. I sat there early one morning watching the light
percolate through the lime-trees and wished you were here. You'd never believe
how lovely the sun-trap on the south side is, snug among its bushes, warm as a
nest, a little paradise. And to sit on the old logs by the waterside and walk the

merry path to the lake. That's all I long for, it would be sweet and wonderful to have you here. That's all I ask of reality this summer. If you're suffering from some kind of depression I shall know how to cure it. I've kept everything I never sent in that so-called magic letter.[2] I want the two of us between us to put this thing into words before either of us leaves this world. Just now writing to you depresses me, it's like talking to a wall. I've an idea your keel could cut deeper here than in Stockholm, but that's something we can only sort out when I get a chance to let you know what's in my 'golden letter'. I once told you you'd laugh to think you'd ever come to Raivola. You must be laughing already, you must have met people more brilliant than me. Is that so? I can't bear not having you here. I face the future with unimaginable courage. You can have no idea how much courage there is in me, I don't know where it comes from. What's the point of keeping from me the interesting experiences you've had? Cast a beam of light into the dark cage where I sit like an animal that knows nothing of the world outside. During the time I've been writing this letter a few things have changed in our garden: the fence is down, bits of it have been thrown into the river and soon we may not be able to get down to the waterside without ripping our clothes at least five times. I write to you as to an abstract idea, deep inside I'm so bitter and vengeful that I doubt this letter will ever reach you. Autumn with its red berries is on the way, the weather here is still beautiful, you and I have a thousand things to discuss. I hope you've been hit by some depression or sorrow, so I can have a chance to get you 'ins Geleise'.[3] Are you being creative or thinking or what are you doing? I haven't written a single poem this June and July. I have no inspiration, I hear wonderful music deep inside me but don't know how to get it out. Last time you were here I hadn't matured to the situation and didn't know how to make the most of my opportunity; I would if you were here now. You muted me. You are mine and there's a lot more I want to do for you. Are you forgetting, is there no constancy in you? Sometimes you've been so irritable in your letters, is it me you're irritated with? Maybe I write too much, it could be dangerous to spoil you. I want you to grow together with me and with this place so that nothing can separate us, so that you will not be able to detach yourself. They say the future casts a shadow, is that true, you who know the darkness?

A dagger is thrust into me every day the post comes without bringing anything from you. I suffer silently, cruelly, deep inside. Are you made of stone or have you become deaf and dumb?

OLSSON: I hope I told Edith I was both 'creating' and 'thinking', for I was in fact doing both quite intensively. I was working on my own book so it would be ready for the autumn and simultaneously toiling away at translation jobs which tired and irritated me dreadfully as I had no inclination for that kind of work. I had to do a great many other things as well, but naturally Edith could have no idea of what being the only daughter of a country pastor could involve. In summer I had to be ready at all times to receive callers, both people I knew and strangers, not to mention all the calls I was expected to make myself. On top of this I was responsible for the horse which meant constantly running to fetch it from the pasture, hitching it to the trap and acting as driver for all sorts of people, or taking my father out into the parish to services made interminable by long-winded hymns and endless coffee-drinking. The days flew by and before you knew where you were you had a huge pile of letters to answer. Edith was ill and time stood still for her, but for me it rushed by and this was why my letters were always delayed, and my visits too. How well I understand this now that I myself have become the one who sits still while everyone else is rushing about in a hurry to get the most they can out of life!

27/120   [Raivola, 30 July 1919]

I've now got definite information. Two people from Viipuri have been here to take away their furniture, also a third who came to pay us a visit. All you need is a travel-pass from your local authorities. If you take the early morning train from Räisälä you'll reach Viipuri in time to collect your permit from the offices of the Second Division (in Aleksanterinkatu)[1] between 10 and 12. The 3.20 from Viipuri will get you to Raivola by half-past five. Here all's peaceful, no thought of war, in fact it's always been quiet and not at all as the papers at one time wanted us to believe. You can tell your parents that. The person who worked out your travel plan is a most uncommon human being, a pearl of reliability and consideration for others and a railway specialist to boot. Our cash box is in very poor shape, but if the worst comes to the worst I could come to Räisälä to fetch you, we can afford the price of a ticket to Räisälä and back.

Mamma has just been to see the commandant,[2] who is the big boss in Raivola, and he promised his regiment won't be quartered on us. At the same time she asked him if it would be all right for you to come here. He said there should be no problem getting permission from Divisional staff HQ opposite Alfa.[3]

As far as good summer weather goes, it's still not too late. If the lieutenant gets over-suspicious a note from your father should do the trick; the only reason our acquaintance gave for coming to see us was 'urgent private business'. It's a good idea to have a white lie ready, or some convincing way of giving the impression that your journey's essential. We're all waiting for you.

OLSSON: Edith's stream of imaginative suggestions intended to help me charm the authorities gave me a good deal of amusement, but nothing was more wildly comic than the idea that she should come to Räisälä to fetch me; if you aren't up to coping with reality, you might as well turn everything on its head!

Well, for once no one was kept waiting in vain at Raivola. I set off on my journey and no lieutenants sprang forward to put obstacles in my way. But one did realise one was entering a restricted zone and approaching an unsettled frontier. The further one went the more desolate the atmosphere on the train became. I sat alone in my compartment; there was no sign of any other human being anywhere and an extraordinary sense of unreality stole over me, chilling me despite the heat.

But I felt deeply happy when I finally left the train for the open road which was sun-warm and cheerful and as delightful as every Karelian summer road I have known. I felt a strong sense of spiritual contentment in this countryside with its old Russian dachas which lay embedded in luxuriant greenery as if mysteriously sunk in a kind of blossoming decay, their decorative curlicues so loved by the birds. This was Edith's land, that was obvious in summer. She herself was waiting for me in front of her house, and I had the feeling that everything else there had been waiting for something too: the wonderful tall trees, the chaotic garden where a few yellow raspberries and clusters of red-currants gleamed brightly among the weeds, the sun-trap nestling among the bushes, and the great deserted villa itself guarded by its mighty larch, a haunted castle no longer fit for human habitation. What was the old place waiting for, what dreams was it dreaming? It was so closely bound up with Edith's poetry that when you walked on the grass under the catkins that hung from the birches you couldn't help hearing her poems in your head, and it seemed her own dreams for the future and spirits connected with them must be wandering merrily but restlessly behind closed doors in the empty rotting house.

This time I stayed a little longer. Perhaps this was why I got so upset at the terrible shortage of food in the Södergran household. There was no escaping it, things had got worse. Edith and her mother might be able to lay their hands on a little flour, but the good Fru Södergran was more at home with world literature than the art of baking bread. Still worse, they had to bake in a tiresome old oven which burned sticks and twigs that had to be gathered by hand and were often green. I found it hard to sit down at table. I could barely hold back my tears, aware that this meagre food was all a sick and physically very weak person had to depend on for nourishment. But tact required that one never let escape any sign that might cause distress or be misinterpreted. The best thing was the milk they were able to get on credit from their nearest neighbours the Galkins, but Edith absolutely refused to touch it. She had made up her mind that the Galkins were putting the evil eye on her beloved pet cat Totti or Råttikus, which meant that the milk that came from them must be 'evil'. Her mother appealed to me and I did all I could to change Edith's mind, which I found almost as heartbreaking as seeing her leave the milk untouched, so genuine and emotionally deep-rooted was her aversion to it. This helped me understand clearly for the first time that, in the last resort, whether or not food can nourish us is determined by psychological factors.

28/121   [Raivola, 30 August 1919]

Little Sister! Thanks for the letter. I've enclosed two copies with no dedications in them because I think you will be able to make better use of them than I will, for instance if you make a trip to Stockholm it might be a good idea for you to have a few copies with you for giving to people.[1]

I've taken my books and written in them, listening to my heart and chosing my words accordingly. Hence Selma[2] and Severyanin,[3] and then Vilhelm Ekelund.[4] I haven't posted a single one.

All this time I've been feeling an almost unbearable infernal <u>electric current</u>.[5] As if I were lying all the time in the arms of Eros himself. I feel myself the most blessed creature ever to have risen from the foundations of existence. Now if ever is the time I need to capture the mood. I've written some poems, but this is not yet a period of inspiration. I need someone to plant a dagger in my breast. And there's no one I respect sufficiently to entrust my suffering to. You have to wound me, Hagar! If I could create now, it would show up everything I've done so far as rubbish. For the first time it would be me . But still rubbish for the most part, in this life one is never allowed to strike a really rich vein. I'm much amused by Brun's reference to 'ethereal' sister poems.[6] He talks like Leonora with the princess in Tasso.[7] He hasn't the faintest idea of the laws of poetry.

Råtte has caught a bird, but I detached Totti[8] from it and it saved itself. I'll have a book out for Christmas on 'The Mysteries of the Flesh', a counterblast to horror mysteries. Schildt will gape and the general reader with him. Eros holding a service in his temple. Eros is 'Wille zur Macht'.[9] Now I've told you a fable. I've read three tales by Poe,[10] and been gripped by horror so prolonged that it stayed with me for several days. I've taken the book up to the attic, can't bear to hold it in my hand. R.R.E.'s portrait is even more impressive than his poems. I wonder what he'll be creating in, say, 5 years. Life is so utterly wonderful, so much to experience if only one had inspiration. If the three of us could create fully after our hearts' desire, what would we not have accomplished after 10 years?!!!

It must be wonderful to be able to live in Swedish-speaking areas. There was no comfort for you here, it was quixotic to invite you to stay with a family of proletarian beggars like us. I mean, Mamma has been going round with 35 pence[11] in her pocket for several days now, two nights I've gone to bed half-hungry, and no buyer has so far appeared.[12] It's like this all the time on and off and this is the reason I'm so weak and can find no strength. I had to lie down for several days after I took you to the station, I was dead tired.

Nothing comes of nothing, and to write poems about you all I need is a lock of your hair, I'm like Böcklin not Zorn.[13] Mörne understood better.[14]

[It serves no purpose at all to mention it and it can't be helped now, but I must tell you how much it hurt me and still hurts me, dear Hagar, that during what was in any case such a Spartan visit, you also had to do without the most essential things. And that this should have happened to someone we would have liked to entertain with genuine generosity! -

I wish you a happy journey, good spirits and good work. There will certainly come a time for those who have the future ahead of them. Keep well!

H.Södergran.][15]

By 'most essential things' Mamma actually means 'guardsman'. That's what I was talking to her about but she misunderstood the word 'guardsman' and put an extra blanket on your bed instead.[16]

OLSSON: It looks as if the first copies of *The Rose Altar* didn't reach Edith until August, or she would have sent me the books earlier, or given them to me when I was with her. Bearing in mind the incredibly casual way her publishers always treated her, this wouldn't have been surprising.

The Arvid Mörne review Edith draws attention to had appeared in *Dagens Press* on 27 June. Even if he held a considerable number of reservations, especially about 'preaching', he nonetheless granted her a degree of recognition none of the other older establishment figures would have dreamed of: 'Her poems avoid metre and rhyme and depend on a development of visual expression which has already passed far beyond the boundaries set for today's "valid" poetry in Finland and Scandinavia. Her poetry is quite simply among the most powerful written in Swedish in recent times, which can allow only one judgment of her method.' Mörne was himself a genuine poet and, in contrast with the æsthetes and literary historians who over the years developed their 'ethereal' theme, he understood instantly what sort of voice was speaking in the sister poems: 'The second section, Fantastique, is dominated by a passionately powerful tone, a human voice that does not declaim but speaks in rich deep notes.'

The 'Brun' who amused Edith so much can only have been Karl Bruhn, though I have been unable to find the review referred to here. He had published one in *Nya Argus* on 16 July under the title 'Our Homegrown Literary Expressionists' which dealt with Edith and myself but concerned itself mainly with my pronouncements in *Soul Faces* and only touched briefly on *The Rose Altar* without mentioning the sister-poems at all.[1]

'To be able to live in Swedish-speaking areas': I had just been staying in the place where I spent my childhood, Föglö parish in the Åland Islands.[2]

Fru Södergran's courtly apology and Edith's 'explanatory' comment are a charming illustration of the dignified, not to say prim, tone that prevailed in the Södergran home: neither of them could bring herself to name the prosaic object in question![3]

29/122   [Raivola, 20 November 1919]

Sometimes one lets slip the chance to say how delighted one is with someone. It happened to me with Muralt, for example. But it won't happen this time. I can't tell you how much your book means to me.[1] Within me there is now a wonderful fragrance of hyacinths, lilies of the valley and young birch leaves. You have drawn round yourself a ring of greatness which makes one want to worship you. All misunderstanding loses its power before your greatness. It would never be possible for me to feel any anger against you or interpret your words as malevolent. You raise the whole age we live in to a higher and more secure plane. The mere existence of such a person should be enough to remove misgiving from all humanity. Even horror is powerless before the triumph of this sacred greatness. You have given to me from the fullness of life. To me this book is the most precious object I possess. How glorious you are, and only now have I become aware of the music in your past. I expected something wonderful but I couldn't have imagined this. There is no one, no one in the world I admire as much as I do my darling Hagar. And if you aren't already on the path to full deliverance I shan't let go of you until you are. Nature has answered me:

One must not ask whether God exists or doesn't exist, one must simply lay one's tiny intelligence aside[2] know and believe are not suitable words for relationships with God. God's law is simpler than all else. Whether physically or morally, one can breathe only in absolutely pure air. The knowledge of God has a very powerful effect on one's lungs and heart. It's as though one's breathing permeated one's whole body. I feel myself before God to be above all a creature of nature. You certainly know all this better than I do. I go entirely free in this confidence without asking. It is not taste that has driven me in this direction but the truth I sensed behind it. I have had to fight my strong aversion to mysticism, religion and Christianity. I have proceeded soberly on my way and my healthy natural inner instinct has brought me to mysticism, which is only a sickness when one denies God and doesn't tread the right path. Don't laugh at me, I've freed myself from prejudices.

Dreamed of you the night before last. You were sitting in the rocking-chair and your face got bigger and bigger, immeasurably large, but shadowed as in the mountains where the sun cannot reach. The same shadow that lay across your face also lay on your hair, which hung down in locks on one side.

Last night I dreamed you are to become a prophet. I want the ring you once thought beautiful to be yours. The sister-ring, it comes in one of the poems I've written this autumn in another connection.[3]

What you've given me with this book is more than I can say. I'm happy our cause is going so well. I worship you now. To call you sister would be presumptuous. Nor would I now be afraid to open my innermost self to you. I want to study the occult at an academy for mysticism, the <u>Goetheanum</u> at Dornach in Switzerland.[4] I want to go there <u>with you</u>. Steiner[5] shall cure your terror, if you have any left. I've caught small glimpses of the astral plane[6] and had a small revelation. Goethe's been granted the status of initiate,[7] but you know that, don't you? I want to leave behind everything worldly and prepare myself in secrecy.

You're a permanently running spring. The whole of life has gained in value through this book, you don't know what it means to me. You shall recover from your terrors and become a saint. Every day brings experiences as heavy as chunks of rock. How will my body be able to bear it all? And that's me living here in tranquillity. What have you not experienced?

For me there can be no doubt. I've asked God and he's given me a half-answer, which will do. My book has grown so out-of-date for me. Am tired, can't write any more. Write.

I've discovered that the Swiss painter Hodler[8] reminds me a bit of R.R.E. and of Giotto.[9]

OLSSON: This last letter was written nearly three months after the one before, a sure sign that a bundle of letters has been lost. Much has happened during these three months and a serious crisis has eased. There's no longer any question of writing a book with the challenging title 'Mysteries of the Flesh' to settle accounts with mysticism. Edith has given up her opposition and announces her intention of studying occultism at the anthroposophical college and has already committed herself to preparatory occult exercises (clearly under the guidance of Steiner's *The Way of Initiation*).[1]

When one reads the Eros poems in *The Shadow of the Future* - they would undoubtedly have gone into the projected book about the 'mysteries of the flesh' - one has the feeling one is dangerously near a breaking-point and that overheated sensuous ecstasy could not have been driven further without inspiration overbalancing into its opposite, meaninglessness. This tendency towards meaninglessness is also alarmingly clear in such poems as 'Materialism' and 'Hamlet'. The closing lines of 'Hamlet' are evidence that the poet had already accepted mysticism or the 'transcendental', the very thing she had previously hated and feared, as a way to the truth, but that she had only achieved this against strong opposition from inside herself. The poem ends with several sombre appeals which give an impression of painful self-denial:

> Truth, truth, do you dwell in mortuaries among worms and dust
> Truth, do you dwell there where is everything I hate?
> Truth, do sorrowful lanterns light your way?[2]

This poem came last in the original manuscript of <u>The Shadow of the Future</u> which Edith had by now sent to the publisher. Later she added a lot of new poems in which tranquillity and triumph again have a place. Among these is the captivating spring-fresh 'Hyacinten' [The Hyacinth], one of the most moving celebrations in existence of the irrepressible nature of life . In the printed volume these two poems, the gloomy and the bright, stand side by side.[3]

Olof Enckell,[4] who has thoroughly investigated the significance of the 'Hamlet crisis' and managed to shed more light on it than anyone else so far,[5] argues convincingly at the end of his book *Den unga Hagar Olsson* [The Young Hagar Olsson] that it was reading *Woman and Grace* that changed Edith's mood and restored the faith in life which is reflected in 'The Hyacinth'. Enckell maintains that *Woman and Grace* had 'the power of a revelation' for her in her deep spiritual distress. The hyacinth poem carries echoes of the mood she expresses in this letter: 'within me there is a wonderful fragrance of hyacinths, lilies of the valley and young birch leaves'.

Woman and Grace says nothing about lilies of the valley or hyacinths, but talks of the 'flowers' of grace, and of how the heart will wake and rise from its grave. It talks of the woman condemned to give birth to her child alone in the wilderness, of her agony and depression, of the increasing weight of her pregnancy and of her cries for help which are lost in the wastes of the universe; but also of her happy relationship with the unborn child, the new life which will 'break the silence of the revolving moon with its dreaming cry to God' - and of the wonder that will reach fulfilment in her soul when her belly contracts in labour. The 'messenger' and 'grace' are central symbols in the book and Edith was to return to them often, just as despite her first strongly negative reaction she returned to the 'horror' and 'what is not' in *Soul Faces*. Now she was deriving comfort and solace from the concept of grace; it was as if she'd needed something to temper the abstract severity of the studies she'd devoted herself to, something to spread a soft living shimmer over the path leading to what still lay hidden.

'It is true: when night is past new hearts will rise from our graves. Like flowers they will sprout from the heap of ashes we have left and one day like flowers they will speak of grace.'

These were the final words of *Woman and Grace*.

Dr Ludwig von Muralt had been Edith's doctor in Davos, a man of strong and unusual personality for whom Edith felt a bond of deep feeling all her life. She kept his portrait on the wall by her bed.[6]

30/123   [Raivola, 25 November 1919]

Hagar dear! It seems you've abandoned me, but I'll send you a greeting just the same. A Fröken Kanerva[1] has been to see me on your behalf, she brought me greetings from you and talked about you in such a lively way she was like a medium through whom I could reach you. I often dream about you and you are so lovable in the dream, have you really forgotten me?

There's been a review of The Rose Altar in some Finnish-language periodical but I haven't been able to get to the local administrator's to see it, apparently it makes some comparison with a Ragnar Eklund or Ekelund, they don't know which.[2]

I plan to publish a collection of poems 'The Shadow of the Future' by Christmas if possible. O Hagar if you knew what sweet pain, what a measureless scream I carry inside me. If you knew what a sense of having been abandoned that represents, you would write to me.

I've brought myself to the point of longing for something new. I believe I've been doing mysticism an injustice. But I don't want what is not but what is. The only thing wrong with your mysticism is that it's sick, you scoop up water from nature's fresh spring and think you're drinking mist, you don't let your heart penetrate your brain. You must understand me, you mustn't undervalue my confession. I want a less constricted life, which only mysticism can give, but it must consist of what actually exists. My heart is expanding and longs for what is beyond measuring, and I want that, of which we know nothing. Don't scoff at me, don't laugh, don't say anything to anyone about it, but I go for evening walks and look up at the moon and stars and demand that <u>nature answer</u> my thoughts. If you knew how the moon solemnly and - oh it's all the same, I can't give any idea of how I feel. It's best you keep silent about all this rather than <u>scoff at it</u>. I realise I did <u>something terrible when I wronged mysticism</u>. Have you already found redemption? Goethe as mystic thrills me now. He was sound. Maeterlinck[3] is half-sick because he doesn't know enough. Goethe knows more. Why don't you go down paths like Goethe's?

31/124   [Raivola, 28 December 1919]

Dear darling Hagar!
Now Totti's dead. What I was afraid of that night has happened.[1] Our little sunbeam has gone. Now we're just two solemn humans, Mamma and me. I've had the idea of working as village photographer in the spring. There's no pleasure in earning a living when your child is gone.

    <u>Tell me which</u> occultist you're planning to go to and for what <u>reason</u>. I've been thinking about Steiner. I'm studying his 'Occult Science'[2] and 'The Way of Initiation'. He has been director of the Goethe archive.[3] He's said to be about 55 years old now, at twenty he met his master-for-life.[4] He's incomparably the most profound and down-to-earth of those who appear in public. But if you've found someone else <u>I want to know</u> about him. I want to <u>choose</u> before I commit myself. <u>Write about this at once</u>. Because I'm thinking of turning to Steiner very soon.

    Thanks for your Christmas greetings.

    Here's a half-poem I've just written.

O mighty one, you are in all things. In the tree and in me.
My dust will sink to nothing, when I sense you behind these shadows
O mighty one, clear mirror of all things.
We shudder when we raise our eyes to you.
our feeble earthly ~~hands~~ arms[5] cannot cling to you
fear grips us.
Grieving dust, we see across innumerable empty worlds
You are everywhere, with hands of fire upholding all things
It's human dust's sad joy to uphold the Eternal
Where our dust dwells night's perpetual and you wander
Through the star-world, cloaked in darkness
But we know you bear light's lantern in your breast
- - -

I feel so unblissful today. In the evenings sad about Totti. There's a wound in my soul. The first real wound. Mamma has completely lost heart. She doesn't think Schildt will send the 500 marks for 'Motley Observations';[6] my only reason for publishing it was to make a little money. My new collection of poems was ready, but Schildt wanted to publish this supplement on its own and put off the poems till next year.

Grief for Totti has penetrated deep inside me. I'm not capable of feeling happy and wouldn't allow myself to feel happy if I were capable of it. The love we had for Totti is homeless, it doesn't know where to go. There are little secrets and not all creatures are made to respond to so much love as he was.

In the October or November 'Aika' there was a review of 'The Earth Altar'.[7] Not profound, but showing incomparably greater understanding than Mörne's. Is Ellen Key a Goethe disciple in the esoteric sense? Is R.R.E. also with us? And Anna Lenah?[8] It's dreadful I wasted the two wonderful occasions you were here. Once you started saying such marvellous things 'Do you know where I live?'. That's what it is to be unprepared.

What's Proco's address? Let me have it, I want to send him a book, because he was so specially nice to me when we met. And in general how can one find out writers' addresses in e.g. Sweden? Would one ask Schildt? I've a copy of The Rose Altar set aside for Vilhelm Ekelund.

I'd very much like to write to the two Frenchmen, the bellicists.[10] We ought to be in contact with them, they are certainly of our sort. Send answers to my main questions. I wish you and your family a happy Christmas holiday and for you a rich and fruitful New Year.

Sometimes I have such beautiful dreams at night, like symbolic visions from another world. Oh if only you could tell me about grace. How shall I get the happy little ring to you which will set a seal on the Rose Altar story? I haven't dared entrust it to the post.

OLSSON: The killing of the cat was such a meaningless and brutal act that it makes one wonder what really lies at the root of human nature. Edith's next-door neighbours must have known how deeply attached she was to this creature which she saw as an inviolable personality that in an unsentimental and graceful way accepted and even reciprocated her affection.

Edith asks which occultist I'm planning to go to; we must take this as an example of her amusing habit of ascribing to me purposes which were her own or which she had imagined for me. I've never in my life 'planned to go' to any occultist, but since my earliest youth I've studied what are generally known as the great questions of life, initially with the German philosophers (it was certainly hard work for a schoolgirl to plod through their voluminous writings in the library at Viipuri), and later with every mystic or teacher of wisdom I could lay my hands on who, I thought, might be able to suggest a solution to the problem of eternity, which never left me in peace. I've always found it depressingly easy to slip out of the reality of time and space and lose all sense of the limitations of time, which made it difficult for me to feel any sense of security so long as I could achieve no synthesis of these two worlds which seemed to slip into and out of one another within myself. I searched for this synthesis. Edith perceived more clearly than most people this slipping 'across the border' in me (a secret that caused me both ecstasy and pain) and got it into her head that I possessed God knows what occult insights and had been through God knows what occult experiences. Unfortunately I possessed nothing of the kind as my search was conducted on purely intellectual lines, but I was deeply interested in finding out more about what she had discovered in the 'secret science' she was now devoting herself to.

Edith had chosen a lonely path for herself and was desperate for concrete evidence that a circle of like-minded people existed among intellectuals. With touching eagerness she tried one name after another among those she had come to take an interest in through me and wondered whether they could be counted as members of the esoteric ring. She knew little about Anna Lenah Elgström but was not prepared to rule out the possibility that even she might be an occultist!

The review of *The Earth Altar* in the periodical *Aika* was written by Rafael Koskimies.[1]

1920

32/126   [Raivola, 6 January 1920]

Dear darling Hagar!
I've never before felt such eagerness, such a need to write to you in a hurry, and
wrongly, since as an apprentice occultist I should control myself and keep all
extreme feelings in check. I shall go in for occultism and I see this as my life's
greatest throw of the dice. I can't send you Steiner now, he doesn't belong to me
and his owner lies in wait for me to take him back. I see you don't know what's
involved or what I'm up to. My bliss is so great it's bursting out of me. I can't
even cry. When I first had Steiner in my hands I looked on him with great
suspicion. I did this for a really long time. (You know better than anyone how
much I loathe the transcendental). But now I've fought through to the belief that
this is truth. So far as I understand you are a mystic who has developed only <u>one
part of your occult senses</u> like Maeterlinck, Lagerkvist, probably Agelus Silesius[1]
and Eckehardt[2] etc. But occultists like Goethe and Christ are real scientists,
<u>initiated</u> in the fullest meaning of the word, who know everything, without
imagining or guessing. All you need is to entrust yourself to the hands of an
<u>initiate</u>, and with your great and mature aptitude for occultism you will very soon
attain everything. I'm ready to entrust myself with full confidence to Steiner's
hands. And I know of no more pleasant adventure than to study occultism with
a real teacher. In such a case the teaching is naturally done in the language of the
mysteries, and I long to have the chance to teach myself that language. It would
be too much to hope that you already understand what I want. Three months ago
I would myself have dismissed what I'm now telling you as drivel if you had
presented it to me. And it'll be very sad if once again we aren't going to be able
to understand one another fully when we meet. If only I had your talent for the
occult and you were on the path I'm now on: what's coming now is the kingdom
of God, literally. And today one can't achieve anything big without being a full-
blown occultist. One day we shall take power in our hands and then we (talented
artists and spiritual workers) could form an alliance together with occultism - the
pure religion. Only in this way will we get everything into our hands. We must
come exalted, pure, masters of ourselves and in possession of knowledge. We
must come with God and Nietzsche. (It's possible Steiner doesn't understand
Nietzsche at all).[3] My reverence for Nietzsche grows daily, I'm constantly
discovering him again for the first time (even if he's lost a large part of his
significance). Darling Hagar, I believe we need one another. And we should stick

close together with <u>everyone</u> who is <u>of our kind</u> and pass on to them our secrets. (This when we have ourselves reached a high level, which you will easily be able to do.) I also understand now why I so hated the Starchild and Lagerkvist, I am myself soaked in the same thing and could have been in danger. I've had a go at doing <u>Rosicrucian</u> exercises[4] and discovered something in myself. But with me a process of excavation is necessary. I wrestle horribly with my character. I want to keep every thought and the movement of my spirit under control. And inside myself I carry an intensely choleric element - a woman of action, capable of murder at any moment. But I've overcome the worst, I haven't murdered Totti's murderers.[5] I haven't even hated them for a second. Our poor little child!

Everything I write is unnecessary, just playing about and wasting time. We can only talk of delightful things face to face and even then misunderstanding could be possible.

I long to come into my master's hands, whoever he may turn out to be. I'm sick of this letter, I'd like to tear it to bits. Not everything I want to say can be said.

It's terrible that so many valuable people don't know the truth. And among them people like you, who actually hold it in their hands.

Ruin's review was excellent. Ekelund[6] has always been synonymous with tedium as far as I'm concerned.

Schildt hasn't sent the 500 marks, if you can sort the matter out we'll be grateful.

What does Anna Lenah say about the 'Woman'?[7] It'll be nice if you come. I only ask for one thing: victory over myself.

We can talk about the bellicists Pierre Drieu de la Rochelle and Joachim Gasquet when we meet. There was something in Pressen about them.[8] I want to go to Dornach in the autumn to study at the university of 'Spiritual Science'.[9] I can't think of anything that would be more fun. Don't be ill, you're Totti's deputy and heir. But that's just my fantasy.

Don't know Överland,[10] haven't any of his books or any acquaintance with him. And I certainly know nothing of Sallinen, Rissanen, Collin and Churberg.[11]

May we find one another some day, may your next visit here be blessed. I'm not allowing myself any ~~unnecessary~~ hasty illusions about Steiner, but he's an expert and has what I need. At the worst he's a very good teacher of the occult, at the best he brings the highest form of spiritual nourishment that exists in our time. His conception of Christ should interest you, it's so exalted that all human ideals look like platitudes in comparison. What's coming now is not the poor kingdom of mankind, but the kingdom of God in the most basic and sober sense of the term. And who is there to bring this about if not <u>us</u>.

You do need a permit to come here, but it's easy to get one now. Mamma says hello. We're waiting. You can get Rudolf Steiner at the Academic Bookshop. 'Outline of Occult Science'.

OLSSON: The person who lent Steiner's writings to Edith and woke her interest in anthroposophy was Dagmar von Schantz, a retired teacher who had recently moved to Raivola.[1] Edith had very little to do with her socially, as will be seen all too clearly from outspoken comments she makes later, but as an intermediary between Steiner's writings and Edith she was destined to have a fateful influence on Edith's life. Who can say whether this was good or bad, but Edith was now thrown into a spiritual conflict of the most harrowing kind. She was torn between incompatible elements in her own nature and faced with having to make a choice without being capable of choosing ('we should go with God and Nietzsche,' what an impossible task!). As was bound to happen, this all-consuming inner strife made it impossible for her to write poetry. It was only when death was very near that she managed to sing again, once she had freed herself from the 'false prophets' and opened herself in a childlike way to nature and the gospel of Christ. And what a song it was to be! But it must be admitted that had she not first trodden the difficult path through the prophets' fire, it's not likely she would have become capable, as she did become, of expressing, with such purity and gentle radiance, in poetry what could not be said in any other way.

'Ruin's review' presumably refers to Hans Ruin's understanding review of *Woman and Grace* in *Dagens Press* (17 December).

33/127   [Raivola, 20 January 1920]

[Dearest Hagar.[1] Thank you for the letter, Edith was very happy with it. She's got over the Spanish flu now, but she's extremely weak and it's going to take time for her to get her strength back. How is everyone at your home? It was Aino who got it first and then me very soon afterwards. At that time Edith was the healthiest but then she got it worse than any of us. The whole village here is affected by this plague.]

Hello, - Write something about the worlds you are experiencing, I'm dying to hear something about them. I've still got a high temperature and I'm wondering how I'm going to get through this.

34/129   [Raivola, 3 February 1920]

Dear darling Hagar! I'm sending you the book now, today's my big day for sending things off, a Rose Altar to Proco and one to Vilh.Ekelund.[1] How are you?

Have you had the Spanish flu! I've been a bit worried.[2] Still in bed, dead-tired, it was a horrible Spanish flu. Schildt has sent the money, I dunned him.[3] If work could be found for me writing modest reviews for Pressen,[4] I would do it as simply and conscientiously as I could, in fact I could write several as samples. I have to begin earning something, though I don't know how I shall manage it, I'm so tired. But you'd be doing me an enormous service if you could send me work of this kind, it needn't be very many reviews. I must turn my hand to something. ~~It's heartbreaking to watch Mamma wasting her strength on drudgery.~~ Goodbye, I'm not up to writing any more. My love to you, tell me something about the higher worlds, about your own worlds which you know.[5]

Regards to your family.

OLSSON: Things were in a bad way now, and I knew something had to be done. Edith was utterly exhausted after her severe illness and her high temperature was reluctant to return to normal; these were bad signs. Added to which there was no money in the house and no hope of earning any. All she got for her collection of aphorisms was a paltry five hundred marks, and she didn't even get that without pleading for it and drawing attention to her extreme poverty, which for her was a humiliation. I continued to stay with my parents in the country toiling away at my translation of Sillanpää's *Hurskas kurjuus*. I myself had no money at the time. The worst of it was that even if I had been able to scrape a little together I wouldn't have been able to send the money to Edith just like that. It wasn't so simple. I would have had to invent some source for it. Anyone who has all he or she needs for the bare necessities of life can have no idea how sensitive those who are less fortunate can become, how difficult it is for most people to accept that they are an object of charity. Once or twice I did very secretly collect money for Edith and I don't know which was worse, people's incredible unwillingness (and the richest were usually the worst) to help in such a situation, or having to fob off Edith's suspicious questions by telling her fabricated stories as innocently as I could, terrified all the while that she might see through the whole thing and send the money back.

I decided that as soon as I got back to Helsinki I would talk to the Society of Authors and the publishers in the hope that some way might be found to provide for Edith in a way that would not offend her. I prepared her for what I was about to do as carefully as I could and tried to make her understand that her poems were a unique gift to the world and that the least the world owed her in return was financial support.

It was quite clear to me that her idea of writing reviews was pure desperation. Quite apart from anything the editorial staff might have to say to the proposal, she was now so weak it seemed impossible she would be able to cope with a type of work she was not used to and had no aptitude for whatever.

35/131   [Raivola, 9 March 1920]

It was a pity you didn't come, I'd hoped you could in some way devote a little of yourself to me, so that simply through the contact I should have had with you you might have brought me closer to the higher worlds. A boundless adoration has burst forth in me, I want to leave everything, even art, because it's unholy. This is very difficult because the illusion of life thrusts itself on me from every side. I feel that for me it's a crime now, something morally reprehensible, to live on earth, I must turn completely away.

So it was a scoundrel who robbed you, like Totti being taken by his murderer, couldn't he have found himself some war profiteer instead?[1]

R.R.E.'s review moved me very much, what he says about my animal love for this life is true, but it hadn't occurred to me. What he says about soundness, realism and the <u>heightened sense of commitment</u> hits the nail on the head too. (How will it go now with me how shall I get total control over myself, I'll go under if I can't find more power in my world.[2]

My Finnish is only so-so. I think it's started getting worse, when the translation comes out send me that rather than the original. Do you think it'd be all right to send my last copy of The Rose Altar to Sillanpää. I thought the bit you quoted very good. Do you know Sillanpää personally?

But Else Lasker-Sch.[3] is heavenly and wonderful, I only knew her earlier poems. I hope you really will flood the columns of Pressen, and this stupid country, with new lyric poetry.

I'm not up to translation work, we'll survive March all right and a mob of soldiers will be coming here for the summer, so I'll be able to photograph soldiers with their sweethearts, that'll be more fun and bring in more money. But some work for the spring period would be no bad thing.

I had Spanish flu very badly, to be honest I thought I was about to make what Muralt and his assistants used to call a crossing over into more respectable world regions. D'you know, I've read 'Woman' again and the bit about 'the rising song from the copper horn of space'[4] was really delightful and so was much else. It's so precious to me that you've been born to be an initiate. Don't forget me.

What's your present address? I need it.

OLSSON: R. R. Eklund's article (*Dagens Press,* 2 February) had been written in connection with the publication of *Motley Observations* but took the form of an evaluation of Edith's poetry as a whole. Here for once she could enjoy being rated at a higher level than usual. Those of Eklund's views which most cheered Edith are worth emphasising even today, at a time when the 'cult of the word' is in the process of stifling the living spirit of lyric poetry:

> The secret of this lightness and freshness is that, despite the originality of her choice of words and images, Edith Södergran is very little involved in the cult of the word. She keeps her distance from æstheticism. Nor is her uniquely intense sensitivity and sensibility the central point of her poetry, as it could easily seem to be. Perhaps it is precisely despite this sick person's sensitivity that the resources of strong life and sound thought, which her best poems disclose to those who know how to read them, have been driven forward and have become the most deeply valuable aspect of her poetry. This is a rare quality, as are her sometimes frankly animal love for life and the realism - I make so bold as to use this word - of her poetry.
>
> He goes on to maintain that what is important to her is her subject matter and the proclaiming of it, and that this 'carries the words on its back': 'With a heightened sense of commitment towards what she has powerfully experienced and found essential, she wants to speak out so that all will hear.'

Edith preferred to wait for my translation of Sillanpää's *Hurskas kurjuus* rather than read the Finnish original as I had suggested to her. My review of Else Lasker-Schüler did in fact mostly consist of quotations from her poems, and my idea was indeed to familiarise the reading public in 'this stupid country' with new lyric poetry.

Edith's next letter gives some idea of what she went through during the harsh last days of that winter, and how she reacted to this experience.

36/132 [Raivola, 16 April 1920]

Dear Hagar! I haven't written because the green mauve ribbon on the bonbonnière I'm now sending you with the ring isn't really right and I want a black one for it. This is an Easter egg for you, with two mountain valleys. Dischma valley was Muralt's favourite, Sertig mine.

Has Anna Lenah already arrived. If she has say hello from me.

It really scared me that you'd talked to Schildt and the Society of Authors. I don't want to become a burden on anyone if it can be helped. At the moment I can't stop you doing this, things are desperate, but as soon as there's a turn for the better I shall burden neither Schildt nor the Society of Authors any longer. We've negotiated with possible buyers in the hope of selling the great ghost-house but their offers have been unacceptable. If we manage to sell it we shall be able to go on existing. Totti's murderers are in court and it's possible they may lose the sawmill here. If they do it's possible the new 'puuliike'[1] may buy our place.[2] My Steiner training enables me not to distress myself but Mamma grieves and sometimes can't sleep at night. And that's not necessary, I always remember Don Quixote and Sancho Panza who managed to survive every time.

Honestly, no one owes me anything for my poems, they are pure trash and my next hyper-obsolete book will be more of the same trash. I now know what a mature human being is like. And that everything I've known till now has been infinitesimally little. I have to start everything from the beginning again. It scares me you want to talk to the Society of Authors, I think that's an enormous shame and scandal, almost as if one were a beggar.

I'm thinking of joining the Anthroposophical Society,[3] that way one can get books one can't get in any other way. But to have to meet members of the society would be really horrible. To hear his followers talk about Steiner would be like seeing him as a most disgusting caricature. He is able to put up with them because he's cosmic and pure, impurity doesn't exist for him in the way it does for the rest of us. Shall I join the society, wouldn't that be horrible? Ugh! You know, the very word 'society' makes me feel ill. It's tragic to be stuck with everyday people when it comes to one's faith.

Your card with the cat moved me, it was Totti. The little thing was shot in a tree they surrounded in the Russian priest's garden and the revolver belonged to the Galkins, so two families had plotted together.

I'm beginning to want to write, but I'd really like to see you.

The Germans in general are so friendly towards Finland now. A German couple (big industrial people) have offered us several thousand Danish kroner, but we wouldn't really have been able to profit from it because of the exchange rate. One can end up with an enormous burden of debt on one's back. But it was very friendly of them.

It's a terrible thing to have to live on the favours of others, one can't even manage to feel grateful, just humiliated. I understand the tragic atmosphere in Shakespeare, that's life. So much harder than one thinks to find security.

Went yesterday to the administrator's[4] to try to palm off on them a bottle of perfume and some lace combinations. They were interested to begin with, then forgot the matter. Today I'll go to others. They look askance at you and you feel like a beggar.

Now the bottle of perfume has been sold, but I feel shattered. If things go on like this I shall go under. You can save me, but much more through <u>friendship</u> than through material support. If I can really be sure that you and Ragnar[5] belong to me, it will do much more for my spirit than material security. The loss of our property never upset me, but Totti's death has hit me hard. Mamma's spirit can't cope with it all. She's had too much of this kind of thing. It destroys you. To go like a beggar to the most common ordinary people and foist on them things they perhaps don't need to buy. I'd really rather have kept this secret even from you. O how things are for the poor, I've gained just the tiniest bit of insight into that. If we don't know what suffering really is, Hagar, we have no ~~insight into~~ knowledge of life. But it's degradation, humiliation, spiritual anguish without end. One has to suffer so very very much to become mild and understanding like Dostoievsky.

The woman who lends me Steiner's books[6] is a vulgar person. You wouldn't want to have anything to do with her. But I'm forced to for the sake of the books. And every time I've been with her it's taken me several days afterwards to shake off her influence. (And it is ungrateful of me to talk like this, alas how ungrateful.)

You and I are bound together by destiny. But I don't know your real life. I bow down before it, I look up with the greatest reverence to what you and Else Lasker-Schüler have in you. That's the one thing I really value now in you and Else L.S. I've seen Sallinen.[7] For what is not mystic is <u>small</u>. I shall never go back again into the narrow, crowded pen. You have known the nearness of God deep inside you, that is the inaccessible high point I look up to in you. You don't know me either, just as I don't know you. I'm a sword, you don't know what my nature is. I'm nothing but a sword. That's another story. But this will eventually unite itself with mysticism. I will never commit any acts for reasons other than religious ones.

I have only one thing of value to leave you both - my great teacher's name. And I want us one day to go even further than he has gone. We bear responsibility for the whole of mankind and all its anguish and for the animals, the poor animals. I refuse to die until I've achieved something which is more than a mere drop in the sea. Tell me he's a charlatan, rip him apart with critic's claws, but to ignore the living Rudolf Steiner, that's impossible! So long as one has both feet on the ground and has ever set eyes on even a single green leaf. That's my kind of heroism. It fails me when I'm faced with such trivial challenges as the need to sell off a few trifles. But it must not fail me. I will grow into a fully mature person. I will conquer myself. One isn't worth a bean if one pulls a face when things get rough. For shame! There can be no place for weak warriors. Sallinen has such a grave face, d'you know him personally? He and

Ludendorff[8] have pretty impressive physiognomies. Farewell, write, say hello to your friends.

An obsolete poem. (I think I've finished my career as a poet).[9]

3 2 1

All are we homeless wanderers
and we are all brothers and sisters.
Naked we go in rags with our knapsacks
but what do princes possess in comparison with us
Treasures stream to us through the air
that cannot be measured in weight of gold
The older we grow
the more surely we know we are brothers and sisters
We have nothing to do with the rest of creation
but to bring it our souls.
If I had a great garden
I'd invite all my brothers and sisters in
each would take away a great treasure
Since we have no land of our own
we could become a nation.
We'd build a trellis round our garden
so no sound from the world could reach us
From our silent garden we'd give the world a new life.

I believe that you my sister, that we are karmically[10] connected to each other and that much is yet to happen between us. So I'm sending you the ring. I believe R.R.E. also belongs to our destiny-group, and that important things will happen through us.

Steiner has given me air so I can breathe!

Out of conscientiousness I've also read a few things by Annie Besant and the cat-loving old bishop Leadbeater.[11] He's an uncommonly nice old Englishman, but not to be taken seriously by anyone who has discovered Steiner. In any case it's possible the theosophists ramble somewhat (perhaps considerably more than somewhat), since Steiner says there's a lot of 'Irrlichtereien'[12] that he deliberately doesn't disclose.

I've thought of a way of making some money. I'd happily translate 'Woman and Grace' and 'The Earth Altar' into German if a German publisher could be found. What d'you think? I've already translated parts in my mind, it's very easy, German's my best language and these are books I'd be happy to translate. In any case I want to translate your next book into German, I think it'll be even finer. I guarantee a faultless translation. D'you think we'd find a publisher?

The absolutely most important thing you and R.R.E. could possibly do for me would be to find out about Steiner. 3 pairs of eyes see more than one. And if you will be my friend to the extent of taking 'The Portal of Initiation'[13] a play in your hand and leafing through it you will be doing me a greater service than any other you could do for me. It's miserable to be alone with these things. You can give me courage and save me. I have a lot of confidence in Ragnar in this respect, he's so calm and sensible. I'm not certain whether these things are the truth but I'm sacrificing everything for their sake since everything that is most powerful in me tells me they are. So you can see what a fateful path this is for me. How much strength I've devoted to it and everything I might have written during the last six months. Save me, sister, don't abandon me morally, inwardly. Come into me, I'm sick and bleeding. If I can be sure we're bound together I'll be able to bear everything with a light heart. I've always been afraid you may abandon me at any moment.

OLSSON: I don't think anyone who has read this letter could ever forget it. It's a piece of concrete reality of such originality and simple greatness that all attempts to express in words what one feels before it must be superfluous. The most overwhelming thing about it is its tone: so free from bitterness and complaint, so unselfish and pure, so full of compassion for those who are suffering in the world. A tone of natural modesty and spiritual emancipation that breaks through the oppressive darkness of the road to Calvary, an intense feeling for what is universal in the condition of all living things.

There are no illusions here, no falseness, just reality as it is. It's a heavy letter that sinks to the bottom like a lead-and-line enabling us to measure the depth of such universal words as poverty, suffering, degradation. The humiliation and tragic helplessness of the exhausted is almost unbearable to watch even in such a tiny incident as the attempt to sell the lace, described so unaffectedly. Yet there is no sign of powerlessness or defeat in the letter; it radiates courage to live and courage to fight, extraordinary willpower and a permanently wakeful critical sense. To read it is to be inspired by the indomitable nature of life, and by one's own good fortune in having the opportunity as a human being to share in human destiny.

At the same time as she sent this letter Edith also sent me the afore-mentioned 'sister-ring', which I have since worn all my life.[1] She had beautiful rings; the skill of the St Petersburg goldsmiths was rightly world-famous and the one she gave me was the one that had fascinated me most. To me it was 'mystically beautiful', a solitaire diamond set in black enamel at the centre of a stylised rose with two small brilliant-cut diamond dewdrops on its petals. The carefully chosen packaging that contained it was a Swiss bonbonnière which must have been very dear to Edith: on it were pictures of two extremely beautiful mountain valleys, one her own favourite and the other the favourite of her unforgettable doctor. What a delightful combination! It was as though, in the form of this old bonbonnière associated with a thousand happy memories, Edith wanted to send me a greeting from nature, the ever-fresh source of strength in her own life. But she herself had already entered other worlds, and I felt this lie like a shadow over the ring when I put it on my finger. Though the realisation distressed me, I knew I could never follow her down the road of Steinerian occultism; indeed I could feel resistance to it growing inside me.

There was also strong resistance inside Edith herself though she'd made a firm decision to overcome it. She pined for life-fulfilment, a mystic coronation from which power would stream towards something that would be more than a mere 'drop in the sea', and when she thought she'd found the path to this she set herself with inflexible determination to follow it. The result was a spiritual crisis whose harrowing and painful development is reflected in her letters from now on. A characteristic and ingenious saying of Paul Claudel[2] comes to mind: 'Connaître, c'est co-naître', to gain knowledge is to be born again with that knowledge. It was in this way, this difficult way, that Edith dedicated herself to this new knowledge. She strove to be born with it and to become a new person with it, to build it up within herself from its foundations. To be born in this way is to die. She already writes 'I am sick and bleeding' in this letter, which was the first to make clear to me how powerfully Steiner's personality had come into her life. To me it seemed occult forces were already in action like shadowy hands groping for Edith's heart so they could squeeze the red juice out of it.

Edith loved extravagant words, and expressions like 'vulgar person' and 'most disgusting caricature' must not be taken literally. She simply couldn't accept the fact that people could commit themselves to Steiner and at the same time go on being just as commonplace and boring as they'd always been; hence the violence of her reaction to them. She herself devoted all her strength to changing herself and growing towards the truth she had embraced, but people of such high ethical quality are as rare within the anthroposophical movement as they are everywhere else. One should also remember that Edith often gives words a meaning of her own, so that for example 'vulgar' for her merely means ordinary, commonplace.

The German couple who offered her Danish kroner were a Herr and Frau Bogs who had been family friends ever since Edith and her mother had come to know Frau Elise Bogs at the Hotel Meierhof in Davos.[3]

37/134   [Raivola, 4 May 1920]

It hurts me terribly, it breaks my heart, to hear that la tristesse has come over you again. You can't believe how much it hurts me, right in my heart. I wrote at once to Barbara Ring[1] with heartfelt joy, certainly in a style that would please her, and now following your advice also to Schildt. Now I'm saved, we can live handsomely for two months on this. And if Totti's murderers lose their case a clothes and tapestry factory will come here, and we may be able to get a good price and then we won't need help any more. Everything depends on this. You've been a great help to me. Mamma's started a new life, it's as if she's become a new person. I think Vilhelm Ekelund should be very happy to get a copy of 'Woman and Grace'. He's so friendly and appreciative, really special. I think it would warm his heart. I feel my life's beginning to rush forward like an express courier. If I had lots of 'Rose Altars' I'd send them to lots of people, it pays off abroad. Today's such a lovely day, wonderful things are beginning to happen in the garden. God is strong, one day you will achieve grace. Heart-felt greetings from Mamma, she thanks you as much as I do. I'm very worried about you. Write.

OLSSON: When Holger Schildt acquired the right to translate the works of Barbara Ring, the Norwegian writer - kind and generous as always - made available a thousand Finnish marks to be awarded at the publisher's discretion to a Finnish writer. It was Edith who got the money. For me it was a great relief to see the money accepted so contentedly. It strengthened me in my intention to continue on the same path without taking the bitter objections Edith had raised earlier too seriously.

38/136   [Raivola, 14 May 1920]

It cuts me to the heart that you're in pain. I've constantly felt a great need to write to you. I think it'd be a good thing for you to come here, perhaps on the spur of the moment. My days of destiny have begun, now I'm joining the Society, the books will become accessible to me and I look on the other followers from a cosmic perspective. 'There exists neither abnormality nor marvel' according to Nietzsche's bird-wisdom. Reading Steiner's second play 'The Soul's Probation'.[1] All my doubts have melted away. I feel like a simple wayside flower before this play. His plays must be read in <u>German</u>, they are about the same people. Compared to this, absolutely everything is thin and flat. But Nietzsche has gone up in my estimation even though he is so thin compared to this. He has a mature <u>brain</u> like no one else's and ~~this~~ therefore can <u>fly</u>. Zarathustra and Steiner, there are my two destinies. Your suffering upsets me. Sallinen is of course much greater than Nietzsche, but the light is a thing in itself. And Steiner's willpower is a thing in itself. And my strength a thing in itself. Steiner's coming to Stockholm in May,[2] he has a system for the threefold organisation of the state.[3] This is certain to be the system introduced in Europe. He is naïf and strong: one single man planning to solve the social problem and organise the whole of Europe. I understand that. It's what has to happen. I'm sure Anna Lenah agrees with his idea, doesn't she. The social democrats certainly like it.

Then it's possible he may come to H:fors[4] in June. My old spinster[5] will see him and question him concerning me. She won't be able to convey everything I need to discuss with him, but some meditation may be possible. Your suffering must surely soon be over. I once tried to imagine eternity and was filled with such terror that I broke into a sweat and my teeth rattled. You must be wearing such a crown of thorns. You poor, poor blessèd child. No tristesse affects me now. A fragment of my destiny has been revealed to me.

Oh how I long for the eternal homeland of mankind.

I'm so anxious about you deep inside myself. This tristesse business cannot go on long. A change will come. It can't go on like this. I have so very much to tell you. Oh if only I could talk to you, because there are ways of getting rid of horror.

A person suffering from horror can't do the least thing to overcome it herself. But there are conquering expanses to envelop one. There are messengers with words of power on their lips. There are eyes that do not fear. All glory can be found in a secret cup. There are messengers who know the Messenger who said: Where two or three are gathered together in my name I am among you. And it is with you that I shall see the eternal Messenger. All our scintillating genius is nothing, it calls forth <u>the storm</u> from the eternal depths. We must sacrifice our genius on the altar of the other world.[6] Our teacher loves us, he knows us, he watches us from afar. He shall deliver those who suffer, he shall liberate the greater being in them. They shall become beautiful and strong. This is God's kingdom, where everyone flowers in purity. I go to my father, to the father of my destiny, he speaks to me words which open the door to my destiny. I shall hold the chalice of purity in my hands. I shall kneel and guard it day and night. But I shall know my teacher by his own language, by his poetry. I have spoken these words to my sister so she may divine where destiny lies. My sister must not scoff at my words when I sing, my sister must know I sing of truth.

- - -

Come, it's lovely and green. Mamma says hello to you. General Tunzelmann,[7] Second Division, Viipuri castle, can help you get here. You must apply for a permit ten days in advance.

Mamma bids you a warm welcome.

Most likely Steiner knows me already, and if you are part of my karma he will be aware of you too. All I need do is say a word about you and he will hear the sad moving song rising from the depths of your being and will know more about you than you can ever know yourself.

Oh how I long for the eternal homeland of mankind.

I shall find the eternal homeland of mankind.

OLSSON: The threefold social system that Dr Steiner set out in his work 'The Threefold Commonwealth' is here touched on for the first time in Edith's letters. She takes for granted that it will be introduced in Europe. This was not so naive as it might seem now. In those days Rudolf Steiner was a figure of European stature who had substantial influence far beyond anthroposophical circles. His social ideas had developed under pressure from the terrible mass unemployment and confusion in Germany after the First World War and they were widely seen as a possible solution to the problem. What he wanted was to break the universal power of the state and hand over control of the economy and the spiritual side of life to leaders independent of, and uninfluenced by, the state. As things are we have neither a free economy that can function in harmony with its own internal laws nor free research and education, since the state administers the whole. Steiner suggested a thorough reorganisation of society, a division into three parts, so that political, economic and spiritual life would be administered and represented by independent bodies which would maintain essential contact with one another via delegates. It was an attempt to create something which would be neither capitalism nor socialism but would include the best of both systems, and above all would ensure living-space in society to the talented individual regardless of economic and political factors. This did not remain a mere theory on paper, but a real movement grew up round the idea and the question was discussed at a large number of conferences and congresses while major political and economic leaders sought Steiner out and maintained active contact with him. One of these was Hjalmar Branting.[1] It was noticeable that social democrats in general were extremely interested. Then many things happened to alter the direction of developments, and Steiner himself died in 1925.

In education Steiner's contribution was ground-breaking and anticipated much that only became apparent to youth psychology later. He took the opportunity to found a school for the children of workers and other employees at the large Waldorf concern[2] in Germany, and this was the beginning of a type of school which has since gained a footing in many countries and spread the concept of a freer and psychologically more realistic kind of education than that which unfortunately still remains the dominating system today.

39/137   [Raivola, 26 May 1920]

How are things? Wos ischt?[1] When are you coming?

Have you already written to the Second Division staff officer?

I've had such a delightful dream about you, that you had the ring on your finger and were so pleased about it in the dream. Last night I dreamed we were dancing together. We'd be able now to lie on the grass, I'll hold you in my arms and comfort you. It's so lovely, come. I've been sunbathing for ages already and soon we'll be able to go in the water. I want you in some way to transfer your sadness to me, I shall go to the fairy lands to seek a cure for it. The couple in Berlin are incredibly kind, they've insisted against our will in sending us 200 Danish kroner. I know it costs them a lot to buy Danish kroner.[2] Mamma says hello.

40/138   [Raivola, 22 June 1920]

I'm frightfully, frightfully happy you've found Steiner. It's a huge relief to me. Mamma and I are both so grateful for what occurred between you and the Society of Authors. Now we can live in style for the rest of the year, after which I hope we'll be able to arrange our affairs in such a way that we won't need any help. Really, I can't find words to say how grateful we are. Come and stay for a reasonably long period, at least a week. You won't be wasting your time, it won't hurt you to be an animal and lie on the grass. Rest is something you can't do without. I'm rather tired too. Shall I write to the Society of Authors or what? I'm not sure what to do. Really, all this has been guidance from the spirit. I've got so much to talk about, don't want to bore you with letters. Look forward to seeing you, Mamma says hello. Say hello to your family.

OLSSON: That I had 'found Steiner' is one of those misleading expressions typical of Edith. It simply means I had taken an interest in the matter and written to her about this. Until now I had not been able to bring myself to read Steiner despite Edith's persuasive attempts to get me to do so, because it would have required careful study and I hadn't the time. But his social ideas had woken my interest, added to which I'd found a very pleasant Steinerian contact in my dentist, Dr Axel Aspelund, a charming and eccentric elderly gentleman whose heart was in the right place. He was a pillar of the anthroposophical movement, very much a dreamer but at the same time manly, robust and full of humour, and this combination enchanted me. I had by now made a firm decision to find out in one way or another what anthroposophy was really all about.

It had been with no light heart that I'd turned to the Society of Authors and tried to get it to loosen its purse-strings a little. Much earlier, when I first clearly understood how critical Edith's economic position was, I'd drawn the Society's attention to the matter and asked one of its committee members whether they could consider making Edith a grant. The response had been 'The Society of Authors is not a charitable institution'. This time things went better.

41/140   [Raivola, 1 July 1920]

Looking forward to seeing you. Longing for it most frightfully. I'm very happy that you have doubts too, I thought you'd think me old-fashioned and faint-hearted. Wrote you a letter yesterday, but I'm glad I needn't post it now, I've so much to tell you. Write and let me know which train you're coming by. I have a confidence deep inside me, a sense of trust, that quietens my doubts and in no way disturbs my delight in Steiner. I believe everything, everything in the world will be cleared up one fine day. Mamma's so much looking forward to seeing you. Here's Filisur, one of the most enchanting villages, a heavenly village.[1] We must try and make sure you won't find it too uncomfortable here in our simple home. O come, come, let nothing get in the way of your coming. Lots and lots of love. Say hello to your family.

OLSSON: Of course I fell ill when just about to start out, a fate which has afflicted me all my life. As I lay sick and in a most miserable state many letters full of reproach reached me from Edith.[1]

42/141   [Raivola, 13 July 1920]

My dear child
Why didn't you come? On top of everything else I know it's terribly hot for

travelling. I'm lying in bed and have been spitting blood. 'The Spiritual Guidance of Mankind'[1] was the first thing I got hold of by Steiner. At the time it seemed to me sheer madness. Now I've got rid of about 70 per cent of what I used to think mad. I haven't much confidence in the theories about Buddhas and Boddhisatvas. I've read 'Occult Science',[2] 'The Way of Initiation',[3] 'Theosophy',[4] (which is excellent, fundamental, a little book, probably best to read it first, I value it very highly) 'The Akasha Chronicle'[5] (very interesting, it made an immediate impression on me.) These four books are essential, when you know them you understand the plays of which I have read the two first 'The Portal of Initiation' and 'The Soul's Probation'.[6] The plays show his genius very clearly, after them you understand the great genius of the other books. Since I first got to know Steiner I've done nothing but study him. I've pushed everything else aside as a waste of time.

Forgive me for not expressing myself more clearly, it doesn't take much to affect me. I don't know 'The Threefold Commonwealth'[7] but judging by all the others I would assume it has to be the right thing. Certain parts of 'The Spiritual Guidance of Mankind' still seem to me suspect at the moment, but I don't remember the book very well. Don't let anyone foist Annie Besant on you it puts me in a bad mood every time I read her. I'm also very much afraid you may come to have too much contact with the blessed society.[8] That's looking at Steiner in a distorted mirror, the worst sort of caricature, horribly embarrassing. I've read two thick books by Leadbeater, 'The Hidden Side of Things',[9] he bears no comparison with Steiner. I've read the 'Bhagavad Gita', it's very fine but to anyone unfamilar with this kind of thing it may seem just an ancient Indian mish-mash of disjointed trifles. I know from my own experience that it's not logic that makes one rebel against these teachings, it's simply that the fantastic and unfamiliar elements make it all seem so suspect, a kind of old-fashioned quality in oneself. Can reincarnation still seem fantastic now hundreds of our countrymen have actually flown at the fair?[10] Today one is thought mad if one believes in reincarnation,[11] but in another three years even the sparrows on the rooftops will know about it. Everything that is destined to happen in the human world will come about of its own accord; all we can do is hurry it on a bit or delay it a bit.

The plays are glorious. In them one can find something of the personality of this impersonal man. One can never be too suspicious or cautious, it would be very feeble to fall into such a trap. But what is purest in me has no doubt, there's something moral inside me that simply believes. The person who lends me the books[12] is a clairvoyant, as are her maid and her 86-year-old mother. This is the lower perception, astrology. The old lady sits at the window all day and gets an extraordinary amount of enjoyment from looking out at the garden. She sees something lovely and her eyes change in harmony with nature. They're ordinary folk in themselves, but something very noble has been grafted on to them. I haven't allowed myself to take lessons from them, but I'd willingly listen to something from you. There's yet another oracle here, Dr Sonck,[13] head of the Theosophical Association. I don't go to him. Also, in Kellomäki there's a Frenchwoman who according to him is 'very psychic'. She's said to know her incarnations, but she's no Steinerian and with the theosophists everything's so disconnected and jumbled up. What I hope for you is that you have a chance to come into personal contact with Steiner, but not so long as you keep on thinking he's a charlatan. I've turned over a few pages, no more, of a book called 'The Inner Realities of Evolution'[14] which seemed to ring very true. A little booklet called 'Three Poems'[15] shocked me frightfully, the satire seemed to me devilish and inappropriate, but after a bit I calmed down.

My dearest, how did you get the money together. Tell me that. Whom shall I thank and how shall I write the receipt? Have you perhaps gone to see Anna-Lenah now?

I'm so terribly worried you may have had difficulties over the money?

It's now the fourth day since I started this letter. A Registered letter has arrived for you. That's why I was expecting you to come. The postman's holding the letter. If you do come we'll have to leave a blessing there. Don't forget this place.

I don't want to torment you if it's too hot, but it would be good if you could.

I'm not going to summon you, you must feel yourself that it's right for you to come.

Lots and lots of love.

43/142   [Raivola, 15 July 1920]

Just got your card. It's destiny getting in the way. Is it Spanish flu? I'm so worried. The postman has your letter at his place, just send him a billet-doux and he'll send it on to Räisälä. It came from Siuntio.[1] You must have overdone things. Look after yourself. Lots of love from mamma. Get well. I'll be thinking of you. I'm glad Axel Lille's all for the threefold state, was very surprised by his article. Lots of love.

Come for a long stay. It's such a lot of trouble for just a few days, more worthwhile to stay longer.

OLSSON: On 27 and 28 August Dr Lille published two articles on Steiner's social ideas in *Dagens Press* under the title 'Towards a New Society'. I've been unable to discover which article Edith had already read in July.[1]

44/143[1]   [Raivola, 29 July 1920]

You haven't come. But you still will come. We've thousands and thousands of things to talk about. I've now read 'The Threefold Commonwealth' and 'Adult Education'.[2] A rather duller picture of the future than how I think it'll be. In this country the threefold state would have come about by itself. But it's of incalculable value that he has been able to see the lines beforehand.

It's not possible for a sober, practical and exceptionally intelligent human being[3] to produce nothing but rant and verbiage. I've languished and longed for you. Want to hear something about your condition and ecstasies. Come for a week or better two, come for ever. I want to 'get on with the job'. We absolutely have to build a little group of people around the world who can totally understand one another and the position, and who will unite together like a single flame. I so much want to talk with you. I don't know what there is to be found in the world of our people and the young. Is there much 'Irren~~haus~~farsorge'?[4]

And it'll be exciting to see the will of the world being broken. We shall insert for the first time into this seething struggle a stranger from outside, the spiritual will of the world. We'll need a great deal of capital (which we should be able to get easily from ~~the Bolsheviks~~ or from ~~Stinnes~~.[5] I don't mean we should necessarily make use of these particular sources. I merely use them as examples to show how dependent we are). But it's important to stick to the workforce, that's the strongest element. A propos, Branting[6] has definitely spent two weeks with Steiner, he's very interested.

We should have a home base somewhere in Europe, a large hotel for instance, and we should attract to this home people important to us like Steiner, Barbusse,[7] Branting, etc. But the home must be <u>ours</u>, because only <u>we</u> (how many are we in the world?) have that spirit of superhuman boldness which speaks in its own pure language and pulls strongly at the past. We must remember that Steiner is old and he is not as we are. We'll give fragrance and direction to the whole even though we ourselves as yet have no fragrance. We are <u>decadent</u>... 'Adult Education'[8] is an important book.

In this house all the 'highest' will go in and out. Socialist leaders and all those who can influence the times. We would bring together the various groups already formed, Clarté and the Movement for a Threefold Commonwealth and the German-Austrian spiritual-workers. We should gain insight into everything one has not been able to have insight into before. Steiner got some of them with him as early as Whitsun 1919 Hermann Bahr, Hans Thoma, Habermann, Eugenie delle Grazie[9] and perhaps other names that one does not know. Now he's having much greater success. Don't you agree? This is why I want to translate your books, incorporate you into German-language literature and make the presentation of your work easier. I shudder at this letter of mine it's so red and worldly, when I write to you I'm filled with the most sinful spirit and now I'm tired and sleepy. Come here, I want to lie with my head in your arms. You're such a delicate and individual being, you'll be roughly handled everywhere till you find an environment which shares your perceptions and will take care of a wonderful flower which earthly hands don't understand. He's said to have an intimate circle of disciples with a very strong aura. I feel myself more and more sinful every day and I'm far too tired, I can never cope with purity except when I've had a good rest. On such days I try to control every thought; when I do I live in purer air. Being pure is damn hard work. In Björnson's 'The King'[10] I've found a splendid partial confirmation of Steiner. Once the wonderful bit on death in Goethe's 'Prometheus'[11] was also a confirmation for me. Pygmies may confirm the Titan's word.

I dreamed last night I drank milk from a great black mare and a great bear sniffed at my lap. Soyez la bienvenue, three times over.

I think in 'Threefold Commonwealth' and 'Adult Education' Steiner has stepped down from his height. The earthly does not suit him. And I see he's ~~somewhat~~ very maniacally stubborn and self-willed, traits that need watching sharply. I'd so much like to know what you'll decide about him, I mean when you've studied him as long as I have.

Who exactly shall I thank for the 2,000 marks. I've written a provisional receipt on a visiting-card.[12] I want to know. Tell me, who procured us this undisturbed summer. Where are you? What are you doing? If I were now as I was before I'd say I was bloody insulted that you don't want to see me. But I won't say that, I've become a different person.

OLSSON: In this and the next letter Edith is still full of the sense of power her intoxication with the future was bringing her and which had supported her so long; what follows is of an entirely different nature. She looks out over the world and weighs against one another the currents, problems and names of the moment in the full conviction that the situation at the time if assessed correctly can be exploited to create an opposition movement concerned with what for her was the one great goal, the goal poet and artist never lose sight of: *the spiritual conquest of the world.*

Naturally I do not remember exactly what I wrote in answer to this particular letter, but I do know that as far as 'getting on with the job' was concerned Edith and I were one heart and one soul, and the concept of a 'little group' which could become a spiritual centre in the world is something that has been with me as long as I can remember. In those days many had similar ideas and elite groups of various kinds were actually established though they seldom achieved any influence beyond particular limited circles. There's no knowing what Edith might not have achieved if she had been granted health and strength, had lived at the centre of Europe and had written in her best language, German. She was richly endowed with what she herself calls the 'spirit of supernatural audacity', that total lack of fear which is essential when something new is to be created, and she also had what spiritual workers so often lack: a sure eye for the realities of life.

Of course to many the ideas of this sick girl confined to her distant village of Raivola belong to the realms of sheer fantasy, believing as she did that she would be able to juggle with such powerful elements as the industrial and economic giant Stinnes, the Bolsheviks and the Socialist leaders as if it would have required no more than a wave of her hand to get them to serve the cause of the 'superman'. I think it was magnificent and moving, and that in such an attitude there is more of the true spirit of poetry than can be found in those specialised writers of our own day who seem to feel they have reached their goal when they have succeeded in 'establishing their position in literature', as the saying goes. It may be that a literary specialist can produce fine literature - mostly distilled from other literature, of course - but he is bound to seem tame, not to say domesticated, compared to a poet who knew her responsibility and importance as an instrument of the spirit in this world.

45/144   [Helsinki, 7 September 1920][1]

I waited yesterday and today. It should be easy to get the permit. Want to ask you about a thousand wonderful things. I've read the third play,[2] love him much more than before. Dreamed one night I kissed your neck, we travelled an adventurous path together. Love.

OLSSON: When this card was posted I was already on my way to Raivola. It was addressed to Räisälä but was sent on from there to Helsinki, and it is only on the Helsinki postmark that one can make out a date. I must have come on my third visit to Edith a few days before 7 September. On the next letter the Raivola postmark is clear; it may have been written the very day I left.[1] Edith had come with me to the station and called on Fröken von Schantz on the way home. There was smoke in the air, a sign that forest fires were burning, perhaps in Russia.

46/145   [Raivola, 10 September 1920]

Enfant adoré. Thought I should suffocate on the way home, realised it wasn't my lungs but the smoke. Fröken S...z[1] received me with <u>respect</u>, the reason being that Aspelund[2] had expressed his joy at my incarceration in the Society[3] in front of one of her acquaintances. I'm fully conscious of the comic aspect of the situation, imagine to yourself a large well-fed lion purring in a narrow cage. I will stand up for Steiner no matter what he may be, so long as he's mine. And besides he's the real thing. <u>A deeply respectful observation was also made</u> on the subject of Hagar Olsson. The Aspelund snowball could grow into an avalanche. Lille and Ruin[4] are not merely a sign that the threefold division is growing old but also that the dead are waking up ~~everything that is sleeping~~, and all this is beautiful, beautiful. I call <u>our</u> group with Nietzsche Superman. A <u>Superman</u> will never concern himself with little social odds and ends, cutting out patterns for chairs, researching the causes of the world war, building temples and ~~the directing of~~ directing plays. Humanity has organised a great war and must certainly learn to organise itself. We need only reach out with full hands. Action is my repose. I shall never worry about poverty, I shall never be afraid to accept money. I am the one the world shall obey. I shall never pick up a crumb. I shall never doubt that anything I undertake will succeed. I am 'mere flesh and my whisper shall be heard throughout the world'. ~~Yea~~ My urges are no wilder in this respect than before, for ~~my~~ I have the lord inside me, my flesh has become lord. I have delivered myself up to my almighty flesh. I have the confidence of a drunk and am not human but mad. Now there's going to be the grand triple-division meeting in Jena.[5] Are you going?

Wonderful. I bathe in blue electricity. The words 'Adult Education' are proof that Steiner's a nice old man. The gods do nothing they merely continue to exist. But what he says is worth gold to me for whom there is no other way to the spirit. Action is a shell out of which I shall creep. My action can take the form of bringing together Steiner and Barbusse and leaving them to discuss which is the better, threefold division or communism. None of that concerns me a scrap any more. The second part of the action, the part that still has some attraction for me, is the celebration of the meeting with the Superman. It should take place high up in the chaste mountains.

I should travel to Copenhagen and from there to Dornach and then to Paris. Pierre Drieu de la Rochelle is an honest person I'd very much like to meet.

Send me Sillanpää, Overland and Hasenclever.[6] I'll send them back as soon as I can.

I wonder if Schildt means to bring out my book in the autumn.[7] The poems I sent in the spring were just an addition, some of the weaker poems can be left out to make room for them. Could you sniff out what Holger's[8] intention is. If it takes any longer it'll become completely useless and out of date. I'd rather not have Lagorio's apes on the cover this time. If Schildt doesn't mean to publish it yet I shall certainly get after him to do it.

Kanerva[9] has got her parcel. Lots of love from Mamma. I hope with all my heart you'll find company for the journey. Write, write what impression Steiner makes on you. Tell me about him, be as venomous as you like, but tell. Aino and Martti ask to be remembered. Thank Rautell[10] for the serial, from an unknown reader.

OLSSON: I now made my way to Switzerland where my main purpose was to be present at the formal opening of the anthroposophists' 'temple' at Dornach, the Goetheanum, and to stay long enough to hear the lectures on various subjects which were to be given there on this solemn occasion. I hoped in this way to gain some concentrated insight into the sort of contribution anthroposophy might make to world culture. I can only say that I was impressed and felt strongly that something new was in the air, not least in the mathematical sciences which to my surprise were represented by a large number of extremely talented researchers. It seemed to me that in medicine and psychology particularly, people were coming up with new and ingenious ideas, a result of their lively understanding of the close connection between the physical and spiritual aspects of the human organism, but such disciplines as physics, chemistry and mathematics also appeared unbelievably fascinating in the light of esoteric interpretation. Since then I've been able to follow only sporadically what anthroposophically orientated researchers have achieved, but it certainly seems to me that 'official' science had every reason to take their findings seriously, at that time particularly in medicine.

I got no real impression of Dr Steiner himself, the soul of the whole thing; naturally it wasn't possible to get much impression of him simply by listening to a number of lectures. His transparent white face, burning dark eyes and great black silk bow-tie gave him the appearance of a sorcerer, and I, who had not read his works, became perhaps a trifle wary.

Spellbound, I put my impressions in an article dated Basel, 2 October.[1]

Dr Aspelund was my companion on the journey and my fatherly protector on the spot. Naturally I also made a number of excursions on my own and got involved in adventures which still make me shudder when I think of them.

'Lagorio's apes' refers to the designs by the Baltic-Russian artist Maria Lagorio with which the publishers arbitrarily and, in Edith's opinion, maliciously adorned the covers of her books.[2]

47/146   [Raivola, 29 October 1920][1]

We've been speculating here that you must have caught cold but Frk Schantz says Aspelund's the sort of daddy who would be sure to take good care of you.

Did you talk to Steiner? What did he say to you?

Do you think the threefold state and Steiner will succeed now? Did the public seem influential? Were there many people there? Does Steiner really understand your character? You're in love with Steiner, to use a profane expression, I here swear on my honour and by Totti's memory that I shall thrill with pleasure for him, though I understand you infernally well. We've rented out the big house to the defence corps for 1,000 marks a year, but with the condition 'kauppa rikkoo kontrahti'.[2]

You've now seen our delightful property. We've been offered 48,000 for the big house plus garden, should we grab the chance? They only want to buy on spec. A respectable gentleman said yesterday we ought not to sell under 50,000 and we might get upwards of 100,000 for half of it. Others say if Galkin loses his court case we could ask any price we like. The defence corps moved in almost violently, we aren't happy with them as tenants.

Is Maria equal to him, is their marriage inwardly motivated? Is Steiner the one who shall come? I don't believe he has the boundlessly rich and warm heart needed for healing the wounds of war.

Could Steiner be the one who shall come while we are as blind as the rest of our contemporaries? But I think even Steiner's decadent, he grates on the Gospels like rusty iron. Christ is sweet, chaste, majestic, a child. 'Blessed are the poor in spirit'.[3] St. has no knowledge of grace, the secret of the kingdom of heaven; his great subject of research has been the last and most cunning of the veils Ahriman[4] casts over him. I've moved from Steiner to Christ, but I can't do without Steiner for a single day.

It was strange about young Lille, I've thought such a lot about that. Is that the way it'll go with me? Did you see Lille there? Oh I wish I knew what to do with my life? If I was physically up to it I'd go at once to Steiner.

Mamma sends love. Tell me all!!! Can one decently settle down for long stays at Dornach? Get well, bless you.

OLSSON: 'You're in love with Steiner' - another of those delightful fantasies Edith was always ready to think up to make life more exciting. As usual it was my job to serve as her double and take on feelings that were secretly her own but which she dismissed in the same breath. I would never have tried to talk to Steiner. I wasn't bold enough. I wasn't even an anthroposophist and I'd gone there merely to form an impression of what the movement had to offer. I only once saw Steiner close up, happening to be with Dr Aspelund when he exchanged a few words with Steiner out on the hillside. It strikes me now for the first time that Edith may have hoped I would talk to Steiner about her.

'Maria' was Frau Marie Steiner,[1] a Baltic lady who was one of Steiner's most devoted disciples and whom he had married at the beginning of the war. What one must admire about Edith here as always is her critical eye which remains vigilant and implacable even towards those she responds to with her deepest feelings. She revered Steiner as a spiritual teacher and was wholly dependent on him but nonetheless saw him clearly as a human being.

'Young Lille' was Dr Axel Lille's son[2] who was seriously ill with tuberculosis. I saw him a couple of times at the lectures sitting in his wheelchair. He died at Dornach.

48/150   [Raivola, 9 November 1920]

Thanks for the Sillanpää![1] Wonderful that he doesn't wear the uniform of culture, lebend, packend.[2] I'm suffering horribly from the contrast between Christ and Steiner. Perhaps it only exists in my own mind. Tell me what you think, solve this agonizing riddle. Compared to Christ all is night, the New Testament kills everything, all thought, all culture. 'Every plant, which my heavenly Father hath not planted, shall be rooted up.'[3] Steiner's interpretations of the Gospels are inspiring and correct.[4] But grace can only be found in the Gospels. I cannot express in words how much I love Christ. Write to me about Steiner. Write about the difference in detail. O what an agonizing struggle I am torn between two worlds. What did you think of the country, of Switzerland. Tell me. Nothing is stronger than grace, 'at the sight of it all things die'.

OLSSON: It's clear from what Edith writes here - on an open postcard - that she was coming near a decisive turning-point in her religious life. One can already sense the first intimations of whatever it was, perhaps heavenly love, that was to silence her muse.

The spiritual help she constantly begged of me was something I couldn't give her. I was shocked by the painful conflict which was torturing her and didn't know what to do. Superficially my attitude to anthroposophy was much the same as hers. It offered visions and incentives one couldn't find elsewhere, above all a view of humanity as a cosmic phenomenon and of the whole universe as a living, pulsating spiritual unity shot through with creative life; but on the other hand it set out a complicated spiritual thought-structure which in Steiner's presentation seemed far too artificial for one to be able to accept it as objective truth. And faced with Steiner himself in the flesh I felt as Edith did that there could be no doubt that here was a great spiritual leader and even from a prosaic point of view an uncommonly rich and deep intelligence, but that despite everything there was something about him which gave rise to doubts, perhaps above all a certain rather chilling self-sufficiency.

What I couldn't understand was why the 'contrast between Christ and Steiner' Edith had discovered could so convulse her, and this shows better than anything else how deeply her relationship with Steiner differed from my own. Mine had to do with my intellectual quest and was something I could equally well accept, reject totally or reject in part. But for Edith it was a matter of life and death. She had literally gambled all on Steiner, devoted all her time and all her strength to him and assimilated what he had written not only intellectually but through a constant inner working, a subtle training of all her powers such as I could never dream of achieving or even attempting. Much was at stake for her. She didn't allow herself to silence her own critical faculties but for her to criticize Steiner was to cut her own flesh ('I am sick and bleeding'). Yet the more deeply she immersed herself in him the more she felt she was getting lost among his minutely and pedantically mapped-out invisible worlds with their exactly defined hierarchies, and she could no longer suppress her irresistible longing 'for the simplest things, for the natural sources of the heart', a state of affairs which finds expression in a most touching way in her next letter.

The one who now brought into Edith's life a power of illumination compared to which all else was dark was Christ. And he also brought her the Gospels' central message about 'the kingdom of God' only being open to those who come 'like a child'. In a purely intellectual sense it isn't easy to understand what the kingdom of God might be but the child image gives a hint. A child is a creature that can achieve nothing if it relies on its own strength; it is in a position of dependence, a symbol of humble submission, but at the same time it possesses a freedom and independence those who rely entirely on their own strength can never attain: the child is the prince among us since it lives protected by love and gets everything 'for nothing'. This is the secret of 'grace': sweet dependence and boundless freedom.

I've gone into this matter in such detail because I believe we should not allow ourselves to dismiss Edith's long, relentless and painful inner battle as superficially as has often been the case in literary studies. I hope people in time to come will feel able to bypass all the philosophical and literary verbiage and take the trouble to get to grips with a spiritual development which led her from grandiose dreams of the assumption of power by Superman and a spiritual elite to the simple concept of the 'child'.

This hard year at the end of which Edith's muse deserted her reached a bitter climax in December with the reviews that greeted her greatest collection of poems, the infinitely rich *Framtidens skugga* [The Shadow of the Future].

Arvid Mörne (17 December) was icy in *Dagens Press*. He had much admired Edith's first collection but could now only lament that *The Shadow of the Future* lacked the romantic charm that had made her first book so captivating. He grudgingly acknowledged 'many poetically strong lines and excellent manifestations of a brilliant skill with words' but went on: 'there is no fundamental mood, so that often everything dissolves into empty words and fine but artistically weak phrases'. Finally he summarised his impressions: 'whatever the cause, we are forced to admit that the overwhelming majority of these poems leave us unmoved'.

In *Hufvudstadsbladet* (22 December) Henning Söderhjelm devoted a few negative lines to the book, stating that the poet 'showed no new aspects to her strange art' and ending with a frank and rather revealing declaration: 'For his part the undersigned can only state that *The Shadow of the Future* seems to him weaker than Edith Södergran's earlier poems; quite simply, the new book says absolutely nothing to him.'

I will refrain from quoting the insensitive and utterly unintelligent comments of the provincial press.

1921

49/154   [Raivola, 30 January 1921]

Thanks for the letter!
I've had hellish neuralgia and toothache for a month, went to Sonck to have the tooth out but fled at the sight of the forceps. Frk Schantz has been so kind as to give me a portrait of Steiner, such strange magnetism radiates from it, I have a share in him as if he were here. I suspect one can share in him just as one can in Christ. I take him so seriously now it's almost sacrilege for me to talk of him. I've read his secret[1] books on St John's Gospel etc. I've put so much work into studying him, no one could be more diligent. But for me it's a burden that he's a philosopher, my heart, my heart cries out for the sources of feeling and faith, for the simplest things, for the natural springs of the heart. Such overflowing springs must exist. I'd love to see an ardent catholic. Between you and me, in the long run philosophers are bearable only to themselves, everything else can be found in every heart. But all this seems nonsense when I'm face to face with the splendour of Steiner, I'm irresistibly and uncontrollably drawn to him. Come to us now, we've got fine wheat flour, we've had aid from the American Red Cross.[2] Till now we've been living on your money, that's how much you've done for us. Now we can expect rent from the defence corps, they haven't paid the insurance for the house though they faithfully promised to pay three months ago. Last autumn our bath-house was burnt down uninsured, Aino, the miserable creature, dropped a match there while her mind was far away dreaming about boys. Now we have an old hag called Miina instead. I hope with all my heart Steiner will pull it off with the threefold state, it's good facing up to evil, for the sake of all the suffering in the world I want that. I wish him all the success he would wish for himself. No Superman would ever play about with ideas like the threefold state, but perhaps it's the great Christian labour of love, a thing so great one can hardly expect it to come about so soon. Steiner is so genuine he could stand slap in front of you and you wouldn't recognise him. I'm dying to know what you really honestly think of him deep down??? Was he surrounded by lots of scientific superficiality (I mean in his environment). R.R.E. was clever and brave today in 'The Crown, the Sceptre and the Apple'.[3] Last autumn I had a raging attack of Nietzsche, difficult to break free of him. Sometimes I weep with longing for the Superman, purely physical longing, like the whim of a pregnant woman. But I try to seal all this away hermetically for the sake of the vine.

Deep inside me I feel we'll yet get the house sold. Frk Schantz has shown me my caricature in V. Krönika.[4] What idiot drew it?

Have you given up Steiner? How can you? How can you? But tell me honestly: is there something warped about him?

I wrote expressly to Schildt to leave certain poems out but he hasn't removed even one. No proofs, no payment, not even an agreement on royalties. Who are the members of the 'lunatics' club'. Which of them want to come here? Tell me that to compensate me for your visit that never was.

It's virtually impossible for me to write. I just get all entangled in what I want to say. The words have no power. This letter's contemptible if it isn't full of what I'm feeling.

[Warmest regards from H.S.][5]

50/156   [Raivola, 16 March 1921]

Thanks for your letter. One seems to go about on a permanent high, such exciting things are happening, I hope the poor sailors will manage all right![1]

Runar's[2] been so magnificent I'm overwhelmed - 700.[3] Up to now I've been a blunt knife, but now Steiner's writings are beginning to live for me, I can perceive what is natural, healthy, simple, innocently childlike in the cosmic. Now I'm beginning to love Steiner, to be grateful to him. He's as innocent and wise as the trees and Råttikus.

You've done so much for me, I owe this business with Runar to you

In my own way I understand so well what you say about concentration. Inessentials simply become invisible, our future is our guide.

Dagens Press is a really Bolshevik paper these days and yesterday it didn't come at all. What d'you think about Steiner's incarnations? I'm not sure Frk Schantz hasn't got it all mixed up. Has he gone down or up in architecture or sculpture? I've compared the head-shapes of the various incarnations, and there's no doubt the master has kept his bone-structure. Strange how fate pushes your nose into anthroposophy. A delightful day today. We had a great Finnish-Russian anthroposophical evening in the big house arranged by Sonck. Mysticism has been spreading rapidly in these parts.[4] I've given up the Superman, believe it's my doppelganger. If you know Steiner's incarnations, then tell me them. Frk Schantz can be fantastic about anything to do with the 'respected teacher'. I suspected him earlier of the Jewish incarnation.[5] But don't tell anyone at the society I'm talking about his incarnations. It's wonderful this constitutes evidence to support the doctrine of incarnation, because you can't make any mistake about whether you were or were not this or that unless you're a downright fraud. I've always had. That would be quite unnecessary folly I must say. This letter's getting positively antique.[6] You can have no idea how difficult it is for me to write. I can only think of one thing, of the sun. O it's such hard work to write. I saw the sun for the first time yesterday, you may have seen it earlier. The way is so straight-forward and so steep. What do Lucifer and Ahriman and all the obstacles in the world matter compared to the sun. Everything I've said up to now about Steiner has been absolute rubbish. Total and absolute rubbish. He who possesses the sun is high above all my silly judgments. Everything would now fall into my arms if I had the physical strength. According to Nostradamus[7] the holy spirit will come in 1921. Will it be Steiner or someone else? Who is the holy spirit? This entity can be found in Steiner. Jesus brought the Father down to Earth, and Steiner will bring the Son out into the world.

Don't give away anything about the incarnations. It would be terrible if such things were broadcast around the world.

Write. What's R.R.E.'s attitude to Steiner. When are you coming here? The gunfire from the sailors is making the windows rattle. There's smoke like last time you were here, it must be from fires in Russia.

Lots of love. I'm expecting you this spring. Love from Mamma.

OLSSON: Naturally I knew nothing whatever about Steiner's incarnations and hadn't the faintest interest in the subject since I'd never been able to take incarnation theories seriously. It sounds here as if Edith was doing her best to believe everything Frk von Schantz with her great powers of persuasion was telling her, but I would think the effect was transitory.

The shooting that was rattling Edith's windows came from the sailors at Kronstadt.

51/157   [Raivola, 27 March 1921]

Very best wishes for Easter. I'm lying in bed, have spat a little blood. Today's crucifixion day,[1] everything else just rushes by. My whole being is concentrated on a single point: God. Steiner's his true servant, they speak truth. Though I do think he's hurrying things a bit, but perhaps I'm seeing things from the angle of my own imperfection. You write very well on Spengler,[2] I read it in passing, I can't take in philosophical stuff any more. You and R.R.E. have been writing some exceptionally fine articles lately. Spring's wonderful at the moment in this little village. Come here and tell me about Steiner, the Raivola spring sends you best wishes. So does Mamma. I'd so much like to do something for Steiner but sacrebleu, je suis paresseuse.[3]

OLSSON: 'This little village' where spring was wonderful in March was the Swiss village pictured on the postcard.

52/158   [Raivola, 17 May 1921]

Steiner is sweet as sweet and kind as kind. When I imagine the shape of his head in life, I feel such compassion for him constantly having to put up with my sniping and mistrust. I've sniped so nastily at him in my thoughts, I really can't swallow that stuff about 'Master Jesus' in his interpretation of St Luke,[1] it's really too much. Every time I get out his portrait I feel strong antipathy and begin to have doubts. And then I feel so sorry for him because I've doubted him. I always feel this antipathy and I can't explain it. Did you feel anything like that when you saw him in the flesh? Do come, the spring is so lovely.

It's a sorry business about the Kronstadt refugees. They get 400 grams of white bread a day and thin soup with dripping and groats. I've talked to people who've been to see them and handed out gifts. 4,500 people in the deepest misery. It makes you ashamed to eat, ashamed to lie on your bed. When anyone brings them food their eyes glisten they're so happy to get something in their stomachs. Once when eggs were being distributed among the children the mothers said lucky children to get eggs. But they're happy to be able to stay here where no one will kill them. Most of them are neither Bolsheviks nor anti-Bolsheviks but just ordinary people who've been caught up in events by accident. We need a woman like Anna-Lenah in this district to do something for them. These refugees lie heavy on my conscience, never allow me a single moment's peace. All this nameless misery should be seen and described so compassionate hearts can take pity on them.[2] The Russian priest[3] here often goes over to see them and often talks about them.

53/159   [Raivola, 24 May 1921]

I see daily proof of your existence in the newspapers, but you've forgotten I exist too and that I'm accessible here on earth. I had such a vivid dream about you the other night: you were here and I held you close against me while you told me about the Goetheanum. When are you coming?

I've been working at Steiner constantly and I've come to the conclusion he isn't saintly enough, I think he and Goethe are two great sinners and that no one alive today can attain the kingdom of heaven.

Now I'm going to trouble you over something again, I'm afraid, but come what may I must find some work. I <u>can</u> and <u>will</u> not live on <u>charity for ever</u> and I ought to be able to get some translation work or something of the kind. Can you give me some advice or should I turn to the Schildts? I'm absolutely ready to do that because when necessity grabs one by the throat one can certainly cope even with work one isn't used to. If it's my destiny that something will come of me, my life must go forward in such a way that I again get a chance to take up my own inner work. Please don't see my wanting to earn some money now as a crime against my inner vocation. Ne te fâche pas, chère enfant,[1] you've always been my protector and adviser. And there's no way out but work. If I'm so widely notorious that translations in my own name won't do, I can always find myself some pseudonym, in fact I'd prefer that. I've just been reading II Corinthians on God's boundless clarity.[2] The truth can be found only in the New Testament and nowhere else in the world. I need Steiner all the time, he's my greatest saviour and my most dangerous enemy. I believe every everlasting word he says (even his interpretation of St Luke's Gospel) but I distrust his spirit, the sophistry of Ahriman in him. But how can spirits that orbit with the planets be mistaken? At this point my understanding reaches its limit and I don't know which way to turn. Come here and tell all. Things have become strongly theosophical in Raivola through Sonck.

Give me some advice about work, but no more charity or I shall never be able to turn to you again. I enclose a letter for Anna Lenah, do with it what you like and think best. I have to do this, they are in such a pitiable state. If I didn't try at all I'd be acting contrary to Christ, the poor Kronstadt refugees weigh on my conscience. Come, it's nicer here now. Such a wonderful radiant day, but have you completely forgotten me? Is your address still the same.

OLSSON: For once Edith's bitter reproaches for not writing to her found me innocent. I'd been struck down with acute appendicitis just after reaching Räisälä[1] and rushed to Viipuri by night on a goods train. Like it or not, I was forced to spend much of that summer lying in the district hospital.

Edith knew through me that Anna Lenah Elgström was one of the directors of Save the Children in Stockholm, and she hoped that something might be done there for the starving Kronstadt refugees.

54/161   [Raivola, 12 June 1921]

You poor, poor child that's had an operation. One knows so little, I thought you were at Räisälä. If it wasn't so damned expensive I'd so happily come and see you. My decision to do some translating has become firmer. If I get a chance to translate Steiner I'll translate nothing else. If I can't get Steiner I'll apply to the right people and take anything. Mamma sends you her warmest best wishes and really hopes you'll get well soon. Martti says hello too.

OLSSON: I hope it hasn't been forgotten that Martti was Edith's dog. Now in all modesty he had to take full responsibility on his own for the greetings that had previously come mainly from the incomparable Totti/Råttikus.

55/163   [Raivola, 9 July 1921]

I'm writing in a hurry to send you my love. I'd already suspected something was wrong, it's tedious to be so far from your parents' place. Forcing myself to be a Christian is breaking me apart, I'm hungry as a wolf for Dionysus. If you write to A.L.[1] tell her the story of the refugees can be dropped from the agenda, they've already been taken away. I'd so much like to sit with you and talk, but what can't be can't be. Mamma sends her love and so does Martti who remembers the person who was gracious and gentle with him and tout Raivola sends regards and the forest trees wish you a swift recovery.

56/164   [Raivola, 23 August 1921]

It's a very long time since I last heard from you. The reason I haven't written is I've nothing to tell. Anyone who can find Christ is fortunate. I've never stopped looking for him.

Yesterday I saw the latest portrait of Steiner by Wolfhügel,[1] the aura-like yellow. I think it makes him look more interesting, infinitely deep and mature, if embittered that the threefold-division idea hasn't been accepted. He's supposed to have said: Zu spät![2] Europe's culture won't survive.[3] Write sometime, you haven't written a letter for more than six months, I think. And tell me about Steiner's piece of sculpture, I mean the ideal human being.[4]

When Mannerheim[5] drove over that sheep in Räisälä why didn't you climb into his car and get him to drive you here. Is your appendix behaving itself now? Do you live <u>much in the spirit</u>? What did your dad say about your illness?

Dreamed about you last night. Very often dream about you.

Aino paid us a visit yesterday, that was a little ray of light for us. She's at the sotilassairaala[6] in Viipuri, in a paradise of bliss.

I've read six of Steiner's 43 secret cycles[7] and I'm in the middle of the seventh. 'Von Jesus zu Christus'[8] had the strongest effect on me.

I can't doubt Steiner but it bothers me that he isn't saintly. I believe he's a seducer. This for me is the central question, the one I put to myself a thousand times a day. Do you know the answer to this question? If I was a saint myself I'd see clearly, I wouldn't doubt for a moment, I'd know Steiner was a sinner. I'm writing to you so you won't feel hurt, while I shudder inwardly myself, it hurts me so deeply to write to you. I really bleed inwardly at this humiliation.

I believe I shall never see you again, something serious is happening to me, 'the bucket is leaking at the well', the whole organism of my soul is being destroyed.

How was the operation? Aren't the doctors rather simple and stupid? How dreadful to give oneself into the hands of coarse fumblers. Sonck believes in all the incarnations both past and future that a Frenchwoman from Pborg[9] serves up to him, like the badly constructed romantic novels of a dressmaker. Write or not, as you please: I'm bloody hurt. Mamma sends you regards.

OLSSON: This time Edith's hurt feelings weren't justified. I'd been ill and miserable all summer, bedridden for several months partly in the hospital at Viipuri (twice) and partly at home. Complications had developed because the operation[1] had been left so late. 'The firs are already sighing over your grave!' was how an angry and hardly tactful surgeon greeted me as I was carried into the hospital in the middle of the night after a horrible journey. And this was how I felt all through, and I didn't at all feel like writing letters.

When at last I was well enough to travel to Helsinki and start dealing with all the work that had been piling up for me there, I decided to go via Raivola so as at least to set eyes on Edith. I didn't feel like spending the night there, I think partly because I was uneasy and depressed and always found staying with her a strain, but mainly because of the nervous tension which has been my lifelong cross and has spoiled most things for me. So it was a short visit, and Edith didn't like that either. One can understand her bitterness if one remembers the dreadful spiritual isolation she suffered in the environment in which she lived. It would have been ideal if I'd had the sort of home at Räisälä where I could have invited her to stay with me. But Edith was far too oversensitive and eccentric and my father too unpredictable for me to dare to risk such an experiment.[2]

One gains a very moving moment of insight into the loneliness of Edith's life from her comment on Aino's visit: 'a little ray of light for us'. And this was the irresponsible girl who had once lived in the kitchen and been so obsessed with daydreams about boys that she had accidentally burnt down the bath-house. Now she had found her ideal workplace: the military hospital!

What Edith says in this letter about the 'organism' of her soul being 'destroyed' can easily lead to those speculations about being on the edge of madness etc that a self-satisfied world so readily reaches for when faced with the phenomenon of genius. Edith could be as fanciful as you like but she never lost her balance and her sharp critical faculty and sense of humour were always at hand to keep things in proportion. Her sense of humour is a subject in itself; there are glimpses of it everywhere in her letters, often half-hidden and so subtle that those who have not come to know her well may have difficulty in detecting it at all.

It is hardly surprising that Edith herself could sometimes feel she was losing her foothold, so intensely concentrated on a single point was her inner life. Only those who have experienced the pressure of loneliness themselves can understand the inhuman stress of having no companion or friend for conversation and emotional contact, of having to carry their thoughts and sense-impressions shut up inside themselves as if in a closed container year after year, with no opportunity for diversion or relaxation. And if on top of this, like Edith one has concentrated one's whole being on God with heightened emphasis on everything a passionate temperament and energetic nature can demand, then one lives under such continuous psychic high pressure that occasional backsliding or lapse of concentration can hardly be avoided. This does not imply any kind of going to pieces but is quite simply evidence of a healthy reaction.

One need only read the two last poems Edith's mother found after her death - 'Landet som icke är' (The Land That Is Not) and 'Ankomst till Hades' (Arrival in Hades) - to know the radiant clarity and extraordinary fineness of perception her soul was capable of even when her body was totally exhausted.

57/165   [Raivola, 28 August 1921]

So terrifically happy I'm going to have a chance to see you. Write and tell me what train you're coming by. I'll meet you with the horse at the station. Don't forget the stupid pass. I didn't know you'd been in hospital a second time. Wasn't upset by what you said about Steiner. I don't understand the spirit, but I don't think you're floundering in the nets Steiner wants the whole world to flounder in together with himself. I also have a feeling you know something about Christ no one else knows, that perhaps not all the apostles quite grasped. With you it's instinctive spiritual freedom, with everyone else it's just commonplace platitude. But I'd better not talk about things I don't understand. I am myself hopelessly commonplace, superficial and helpless. Well-meaning helplessness is the common lot of all Christians. The flesh is too superficial to be capable of understanding the spirit. If only I could inhale a whiff of the fresh air of your spirit. You could bear the arms of the spirit better than anyone.

Steiner's previous incarnations are entirely sunless (I'm talking about the sun in art as I understand it). He's a child of shadow. But R.R.E. is certainly also a child of shadow. I'd find it easier to believe that R.R.E. is descended from Steiner's Italian incarnation than that Steiner himself is. But a piece of sculpture is Steinerian to my mind.

Steiner maps out the hierarchies of angels using all the material world's geometrical common-sense. But this is what the founder of the new culture must do. And it's precisely this culture that I don't trust. One must become a child to comprehend the kingdom of God, the most a philosopher can do is found a human kingdom. This will be a false paradise, an artefact, something that looks alive but is in fact dead.

You have permission to hack away at my poor dear Steiner as much as you like. Are you on a special diet? What are you allowed to eat? It's really terribly sad you've been ill for so long. I'm sure Fröken Schantz thinks your illness is the result of a blasphemous attitude to Steiner, she once told me that anyone who blasphemes against him can expect to be totally crushed: when a young woman fell from a balcony and broke her leg Frk Schantz was convinced it was because she'd blasphemed against Steiner.

Don't overdo things and take care on your journey. If for some reason you can't let me know in advance about the train leave all your stuff with the postmistress,[1] Miina's[2] efficient, she'll be able to look after everything. But try to arrange things so I can meet you with the horse.

Mamma's really looking forward to seeing you. Martti too is most humbly expecting you. Every one of us that lives and breathes is waiting.

58/167   [Raivola, 7 October 1921]

It's a wonder you're still alive after that dreadful villainous cart, which I'm sure you chose on purpose to destroy the work of an elderly surgeon. What was the point of spending a few hours honouring Kanerva and me? A wandering tour, an Odyssey! I see from my period that exactly a month has passed since Hagar Olsson graciously condescended to visit our humble border lands.[1] Did you know A.L. has done something for the Kronstadt refugees, 'Save the Children' has sent Fru Nobel-Olennikov[2] to them with some money. A splendid woman, Anna Lenah!

I'm so thoroughly cross with you for the brevity of your visit that I feel anger alone could take me all the way to Helsinki; fortunately this can't happen. I've been having severe Dionysiac attacks and need to throw myself physically into the air and dance and dance. If I were well I'd run in the woods and dance tens of kilometres and the Superman is physically a thousand times stronger than man and I'm a wreck. Can one dance with Christ or is dancing only for the devil? You're the specialist on Christianity, tell me!

I've now joined the Society of Authors, which is pleasant and peaceful. As a result I don't need financial support, I feel more capable of work than before, I'll get myself some work, do you think it's a good idea for me to write to Proco,[3] perhaps he'll be able to recommend something for me. I'll be happy to translate any kind of report, absolutely anything. Do nothing for me, excellent child, I want work and I shall have it. Here I've begun to make prints from fine negatives of views of Raivola in the hope of selling them but it won't pay, the locals can't tell quality photographs from common picture postcards. I'll make the most of any opportunity that comes my way to photograph faces though in this there's a good deal of competition.

Do you think I've been written off as a wastrel or outsider or too dim to be given work?

I wonder what human beings are incarnated for, whether it's to darn stockings or the like. Tell me if anywhere in the world there's a man bewitching enough to distract one from religion. I'd like to meet the man who could make me forget everything.

We're united with the churchyard now, the fence collapsed in a storm.

OLSSON: I don't think I did meet Elsa Kataja (consistently called 'Kanerva' by Edith) during my visit. She lived, I think, in Terijoki though admittedly this was not far from Raivola. She is here ironically pressed into service as one of those who should feel honoured by my visit to the district. Absolutely anyone who had even the slightest acquaintance with me became a useful figure to Edith in her isolation. It was the same with Anna Lenah Elgström. I really have no idea who took the initiative at 'Save the Children' in providing help for the Kronstadt refugees, and Edith must have known even less about it than I did. But since Anna Lenah was one of my friends Edith assumed it must have been her.

59/170   [Raivola, 31 December 1921]

Heartfelt thanks for wanting to see me but it can't be, it would be a crime against our little household budget and I refuse to travel as a beggar, it makes me uncomfortable and turns everything into humiliation.

As far as 'Woman and Grace' is concerned I think if there's any chance for it at all it's best you return the manuscript to me, I do think if there's any solution to be found I have one, i.e. through our acquaintance in Berlin, I think if Herr B.[1] can't instantly find a publisher for it, it won't find one at all. I'll copy it out very neatly, and I'd be very glad if you can pay for an exercise book (or whatever paper I ought to use).

Read through the munuscript, if there's any word you don't like just mark it. Would you prefer 'Magd' or 'Dienerin'. 'Magd' is of course the Biblical expression but 'Dienerin des Herrn' is also used in the modern language. Will any written formalities be needed for the German publisher such as the author's permission and the like?

Now I've done the greater part of the job I think it's worth doing the lesser by approaching Herr Bogs so my work won't have been wasted. Herr Bogs is enormously enterprising and rich, enormously kind and enormously reliable, and he'll be enormously childishly pleased to be able to have a finger in a literary pie, so far as we know him.

I translate very fast and enjoy it, I almost missed Elkanah's woman when I'd finished with her. I'm thinking very seriously about making an anthology of contemporary Finland-Swedish poetry. There's no doubt at all it would be accepted in Germany. You could be represented in it by a long extract from Elkanah's woman. As for R.R.E., I've already translated his best poems in my mind. There's only one poem by Grotenfelt, 'Det vita och det röda vinet' [White and Red Wine][2] and I've already translated that in my head. Mörne has really beautiful things in 'Skärgårdens vår' [Spring in the Archipelago][3] and I believe he has written some really beautiful prose-poems which being freer in form would be easier to translate. All I've got of Hemmer's is 'Pelaren'[The Pillar].[4] Can the best narrative in his latest book be treated as poetic prose to the extent that with a little elevation of style it could be included in this collection? I can certainly translate anything Hemmer has written in fairly free form but strict verse-forms cramp me too much. Schildt can write whatever he likes and I'll put it in.[5] If you have any of Hemmer's and Mörne's latest books (in your capacity as reviewer) give them to me.

I don't plan to take on Gripenberg, Proco, R. Ekelund, Tegengren, or Lybeck[6] (I haven't even read anything by the last two), but if there are easily translatable and representative things by them I will of course happily translate them. Shall I write to Hasselblatt[7] and ask him to ask the writers for permission? But if it's going to lead to nothing but trouble and irritation and discontent from those who've been left out and discontent from those who've been put in then I won't do it!

Happy New Year! Tell me something about yourself to make up for our failed meeting.

Both Mamma and I wish you a really first-class and successful year.
Give my regards to your Mamma too.

OLSSON: I'd spent Christmas at Räisälä and planned to stop for a couple of days at Viipuri with my mother on the way back to Helsinki. This gave me the idea that perhaps Edith could come to Viipuri at the same time so we could meet, it wasn't very far and it seemed to me it might do her good to get away for a breath of fresh air now and then. She gives a negative answer in this letter, but when I insisted and made clear that I would of course finance her trip since the whole thing had been my idea, she agreed.

In this letter the unhappy idea of the anthology emerges as a serious project. Edith had taken it upon herself to translate *Woman and Grace* (sometimes known as 'Elkanah's Woman' or 'The Elkanah Family') into German. I thought this was stupid and meaningless and didn't in the least share her naïve belief that one would be able to place a book of this kind by an unknown writer in Germany, but she was so eager and seemed so reinvigorated at the prospect of having such a project on her hands that I hadn't the heart to say what I thought.[1] While she was working on the book the idea occurred to her that she could also translate other Finland-Swedish writers and put together a whole anthology that could introduce us to German readers. I thought this idea made more sense, especially since she had an excellent contact in Germany in Herr Bogs. I knew how she suffered from being imprisoned in the Finland-Swedish rat-hole and was particularly pleased her voice might now have a chance to be heard in the outside world. Even if this meant only a few of her poems appearing with lots by other people, at least they would be interpreted in a way no other translator could approach. But unfortunately the work of translating taxed her strength, especially since she felt a duty to include so much material that was alien to her and in consequence difficult for her to translate.

All the trouble the project brought her and the fact that it all came to nothing in the end eventually dealt her a blow from which she was never to recover.

Edith Södergran

1922

Bon, then I'll come on Wednesday 11 January. I'll take an earlier train which gets to Viborg about 11am. Can look up a few acquaintances. I even think it might be possible for me to spend the night with people I know, but I'll have to look into that beforehand. If it's convenient for you I'll wait for you in the second class buffet at the station or shall I go to the Hospiz?[2]

So tell me where we should meet. If you've got that new German anthology[3] you once talked about with you at Räisälä I'd very much like to give it a passing glance. I really wonder what the Elkanah family's fate will be? The decision to translate it came to me from nowhere and I sat down to do it instantly. I'm extremely curious to see what becomes of it. Love from Mamma, here's hoping we meet up all right.

OLSSON: It didn't turn out all right at all, and even now I can't understand why Edith behaved as she did. I'd written to her plainly and clearly that my mother and I would be staying at the Hospiz and she herself had said she might be able to stay with people she knew. But when we met Edith demanded that I share her room - I can't remember if it was at her acquaintances' or in a hotel - and when I refused she took offence. It has always been difficult for me to share a room with another person, and I'd slept alone since earliest childhood. In any case I had my mother to think about; she and I were already installed at the Hospiz and as always she was sad that I was just about to leave her for a long period.

I found it very tiresome that things turned out like this since I'd planned the whole thing as a pleasure trip for Edith, a little bit of change in her monotonous existence. Perhaps she lacked self-confidence because she wasn't on home territory. She was used to being waited on day and night by a mother who lived for no one but her, and she must have felt rather lost on her own. Also, this was the first time she'd met me away from her own world and seen me in a context that bore no relation to herself. When you've lived as long in introspective isolation as Edith had such a situation can seem strange. In this context the anthology project was a blessing in that it gave her thoughts a new direction and served as a counterweight to her intense and relentless concentration on inner things. Once the idea had come to her she wouldn't let go of it, for it aroused in her long-suppressed hopes of life. Her dream of conquering the world seems to have burst into flame one last time and destroyed the bonds of religious celibacy she'd imposed on herself. The anthology took over her imagination as a 'sweet madness', a last promise that she would be allowed to breathe freely in a world wider than the one in which she was slowly suffocating. And she threw herself into the struggle to make reality of it with the passionate determination of someone who risks all on a single throw of the dice.

In the new year I too was drawn into a vortex of new tasks and experiences. Up to this point I had stood alone in the struggle for a new sensibility and for the poetry that would give it expression; now Elmer Diktonius appeared on the scene and we entered into a long-lasting blood-brotherhood which was essential if we were to have the slightest chance of holding our own against the pressure of conventional opinion. The battle in the world of the arts intensified, and little by little plans for a new review took shape. This was to be bilingual in Finnish and Swedish and would be called *Ultra*, the first modernist review to be published in the Nordic countries. *Ultra* was to make its first appearance in the autumn of that year, 1922, but before that happened I had to help launch Diktonius. His first book had been published by a small house in Sweden[1] but he was still totally unknown. For this I made use of the highly respectable periodical *Nya Argus* which I managed to persuade - with the help of the well-disposed Hans Ruin,[2] if I remember rightly - to accept my dangerous article.[3] But all the time I was thinking of Edith sitting alone in her wilderness, and I could find no peace until I'd packed off Diktonius to Raivola to see her. He only stayed two days, but he and Edith became good friends and corresponded with one another. Diktonius was a fine letter-writer and consciously developed his style for this purpose. It was a great relief to me to know that Edith had at least one literary figure apart from myself to scold and admire and share her thoughts with.

Thus Edith and I were both deeply engaged in practical literary work, each in her own sphere, and her letters give evidence of this. They now begin to have very much the character of a journal of work in progress. All these sober discussions of suggested translations and tiresome negotiations may not seem very exciting, but as the final chapter in Edith's life they have a pathos of their own. She sacrificed the rest of her strength to this major project, and when it finally came to nothing there was nothing left for her but to die.

61/172 [Raivola, 4 February 1922]

I think many <u>changes in the plans for the anthology could be made</u> still in connection with Bonnier's Finland-Swedish anthology.[1] I'm quite ready to agree with Ruin's suggestion, but I think such an important (let's face it) work as this anthology <u>will be able to choose</u> its own publisher. I don't accept the idea that one must rush wildly to the nearest top publisher, and there may well be others with a better appreciation of artistic values. I think we should ask Mörne's advice, he's the oracle on the subject of <u>anthologies</u>. <u>I'm certainly willing to translate</u> prose, in fact I like translating prose best.

If I can translate Lybeck, Zilliacus[2] etc. I'll do it, but if they're very difficult I certainly can't. I'll have to see their work first, I've never seen it. I'm not sure about Finnish, but anything that's been translated into Swedish will probably be all right. Though I won't be able to go on translating indefinitely at a low rate of exchange.

But to Ruin <u>yes, yes, yes.</u>

Won't you go to Mörne and ask his advice?

Das 'Weib und die Gnade' isn't a suitable title.[3] The Biblical word for 'hälleberg' [bedrock] is 'Felsen'. In Swedish we are used to the stately word 'hälleberg' but it isn't something the Germans feel any need for, Felsen is good enough for them. There is no word in German for 'skär' [pure (as of a virgin)]. One could use 'zart', 'hell', 'rein', or 'klar'.[4]

'<u>Feurigkeit</u>' isn't really quite right, but mightn't one say '<u>Glut und Flammen</u>'?

I don't understand what you say about 'Bote' and 'Botschafter', can't find the place in the text. By all means change it, I don't think that'll do any harm. 'Wort des Menschen' is better than 'des Kommenden', it isn't used in German the way it is in Swedish. 'Mensch' is a large concept of something. If one is to be linguistically conservative it's best to avoid as much as possible expressions like 'Geburtswege' [birth passages]. They would make a <u>strongly unfavourable impression on all bourgeois natures</u>. I tell you, if you want to <u>avoid stumbling</u> blocks leave out anything that would attract attention for its sexual content. You're a thousand times better off with phrases like 'pious madonna' or 'chaste and womanly'.

I shall also select the tamer stuff from among my own poems.

My main aim shall now be to make 'Woman and Grace' as irreproachable as possible. I really <u>want to check her over before she's sent off</u>.

Instead of <u>Kindbetterin</u> one could say <u>Wöchnerin</u>.

(Though I think the former is probably better.)

Instead of 'barst an den Bergen aus Blei in diesem Lustgarten der Wüsten' one could put <u>brach an den bleiernen bergen in diesem Lustgarten der Wüsten</u>. (note that I've added n at the end of <u>Wüste</u>)

It was good that you took out 'aus Schuld und Angst' and left 'der du so licht und träumend dem Bette ~~Blut~~ meines Blutes ~~Better~~ entsteigst'.

Best to leave 'zu einem schwachen und mächtigen Zeichen der Gnade' as it is; 'gebrechlich' inclines too much towards fragility or decrepitude.

The long section about 'det enda ordet, människans ordet' [the only word, the word of Mankind] cannot be replaced by something newly made up; anything not part of the organic context of the act of creation will kill the living nerve in it. Modern art is much more sensitive in this respect.

Instead of 'als der Geist der Ernte einfiel' one might put 'es war zur Zeit der Ernte' or 'im Monat der Ernte'. Where it says 'süsser, zarter Freund' you could have 'holder z. Fr.' In 'Rösten' [The Voice] you could replace 'die in uns war' with 'die in uns wohnte'. The whole would then read: 'Noch weilt in uns der Erinnerung jener Tiefen Milde die in uns wohnte'.

For 'kvävande ring' [stifling ring] I've put 'beengenden ring', 'erstickenden ring' is impossible, there's no way round it.

It must be: 'Weil wir ihm nicht einmal so viel vertrauen wie einem unserer schwachen Brüder'.

'Beklädda med Guds sköld' [clad with God's shield] is well enough translated, 'decken' is precisely the expression one uses of shields. Or, if you like, one could put 'gewappnet', but 'bewaffnet' would be scandalous in this context.

That acrobatic trick of putting the ear to the womb's horn is certainly a stumbling-block, but to take it out would be to spoil the passage. 'The Voice' should now be ready. Don't have it typed out till the whole lot's ready. I can't remember what's still missing. If you could get this poem[5] into Finsk Tidskrift I'd certainly send it to them, only I don't know the address.

Argus won't take anything of mine, Gunnar Castrén is my enemy.[6] Lots of love!

52/173   [Raivola, 18 February 1922]

I leave it to your judgment whether a fair copy should be made or not, you know more than I do about how tidy the handwriting of a manuscript must be. In no circumstances may the relatively tidy pages be written out again. If you want to improve the overall look of the thing you can have at most about five pages copied out but only with the greatest care and attention. This would already be a major improvement. But if a lot is copied out it'll be that much harder to control it. You've done a good job, you've worked through the manuscript very carefully - and even so Mamma and I have spent four days looking for small errors and finding them. So copying it out would be dangerous. Though a few pages, well done, could improve the total impression. But you must do as you think best.

If I could get a firm foothold as a translator with a good publisher it would be a lifeline for me, even though the Germans pay so little that at present it doesn't make sense financially to do much work for Germany. I won't take on translation from Finnish but I'll happily translate Swedish prose. The anthology is such an excellent thing I'm extremely unwilling to let it out of my hands. But I'm not sure how I'm going to cope with strict verse forms.

I have no difficulty translating R.R.E., yourself, Grotenfelt (in his case we need so few poems apart from the white and red wine), myself and Hemmer (though his work will cause a considerable degree of fuss and bother). The rest are very difficult to translate. A translator of verse must be inspired if the result is to be any good; work done with nothing better than good intentions is bound to turn out unsatisfactory. And the anthology must at all costs be high-class, anything less would be pointless. What would you advise in this connection? I found 'Skärgårdens vår' [Spring in the Archipelago][1] and some other books in the attic and was mightily disappointed - no free verse at all. But I'm afraid an anthology containing only younger poets would cause bitter feelings. To say I'm deliberately adopting a careless approach is the most unjust accusation that has ever been made! Good luck with the woman![2]

63/174 To Elmer Diktonius[1]   [Raivola, 25 March 1922]

Your letter was unreadable. Assumptions and poison. What a miserable loss that I didn't get a chance to hear more of your music, the little you hummed woke my longing.

Sorry I have so little understanding of the finer points of punctuation: I put it in with despair merely because it has to be put in - in the hope that Holger Schildts Publishers will improve it for me. Strange that you were here.[2] What is destined to come to one comes in through the door, while one can so to speak search the whole world for a buttonhole and find nothing.

The act of writing is heavy as lead. Every word that doesn't go through God is wasted. All in vain.

Your coming was like a liberation from ancient chains.

I am no woman, I'm holy in no Christian way because I'm dedicated to my purpose.

One thing I will say to you: you can do nothing smarter than find out a little about old Steiner (whether he happens to be a charlatan or not). If you ignore this man then you're absolutely nothing more than one of the crowd no matter who you are. If the humblest and most ordinary person acknowledges Steiner he will have a star over him and a crown on his head.

If you're planning never to come back here again you're nothing but a 'reisu sälli'.[3]

Say hello to Hagar and tell her I know nothing of the new plans she's talking about. Do you know Pierre Drieu de la Rochelle? If not, I'll send you a cutting with some of his poems. If you have his book, send it to me.

Send me lots and lots of your own poems. I think the true faithful among the anthroposophists worship Steiner rather than Christ, which of course is like trying to milk a billy-goat.

Do you know who I am? Do you know my music?

Write so I can read what you've written, or I'll certainly come to the conclusion evil cunning lurks behind your words. I mean exactly what Bismarck means: someone capable of creating a new world-order is just what we need at the moment.[4] But one factor is constant - and I've already mentioned it. It's why humanity can never achieve anything through its own willpower alone. Only God's will can prevail, and if we hold close to that we can win. Everything else just thunders furiously into the abyss.

You can write to me as freely and unconventionally as you like. Give Hagar my love.

Mamma and Martti send regards.

64/175 To Elmer Diktonius   [Raivola, 4 April 1922][1]

Please send about 10 poems for translation. I've translated the six.[2] Will you be staying long enough in the country to get them when I send you a fair copy of the whole to check, or shall I write them out ~~and check them~~ for you immediately now? There are two things I particularly like in your book: what you say about the artist who lives so long before his time that he doesn't hear the shrieks from this inferno we live in and the bit about laying about oneself with an axe. (Of course it isn't the axe that appeals to me but the spiritual meaning.)[3]

But tell me, what will you do to help people out of the mire they're in?

I'm 30 today, an old hydra. I've determined to start a new life from today. Mother's been laid low by a sudden back spasm. Here are the young Frenchmen.[4] But send them back, I don't want to forget their names or a single poem.

You write to me stiffly like a real fox.

Pity you're a man, with Hagar things are so free. Did you and she have fun? But Hagar deserves to be drowned like an unwanted puppy or kitten for running off to look at Steiner like an English tourist in a picture gallery. (But for heaven's sake don't tell her this).[5]

I'd rather use 'du' than 'Er' with you so as to be less conventional, but never mind.[6] Boldness or, to be more accurate, the audacity of immaturity has so far been my special characteristic. And for this very reason I shall go for prudence since it comes naturally to me to prefer indiscretion. I behave like a teacher towards myself.

Miina has just said of Herr Peck, the hermit who used to live in this room, 'he lived like a man and died like a man'.[7] A genuine epitaph from Miina's mouth. Write a lot to me, whenever a thought occurs to you write it down and let the letter compose itself. One often thinks of saying something to one's friends and then it never gets written down. And it can often be more important than what one actually does put in letters.

There's no one I feel so inwardly similar to as Almkvist.[8] I've only read 'Drottningens juvelsmycke' [The Queen's Jewel] but I've never found anything I've related to more closely.

It's a really horrible, disagreeable, inner likeness. I love Almkvist but I'd never want to be him. If you want to know me read Almkvist. Ugh, the dust that swirls from this letter. Ugh, how horrible it is to write intellectual letters. But give me your solemn promise that my letters will never fall into the hands of the worms that infest dead bodies and write biographies.

65/176 To Elmer Diktonius   [Raivola, 6 April 1922]

I've read your book[1] very, very closely so as to understand it properly. It's very, very fine. Pity you're under a curse and don't even know it, like a dumb animal. I do know about my own curse but I've nothing to set against it but my abstract will. Up to now I've believed I can sow the seed of myself anew from the ashes, but now I don't believe that any more. The road's too long for me. I think religion broke me. I'm not the least bit pessimistic, but tired, tired, tired. It kills me to be aware that at 30 I don't even know my A.B.C.

How can you help others out of drifting sand when you yourself are the one sitting deepest in it? We who believe ourselves creative poison the general spiritual atmosphere of the world more than London's chimneys poison its physical atmosphere. Although we don't realise it we create substances that prolong the agony of creation. In producing a poem we give the strongest possible support to those powers that make human beings burn and torture one another or put out each other's eyes or, like Lloyd George, observe famine with unfeeling detachment.[2] Creation sighs as it waits for the child of God to appear. Just as our physical breath mixes with material air, so in the same way our feelings and thoughts mix with the general spiritual atmosphere and alas, what an effect they have!

I'm so childish I've always wanted to see my siblings. I've wished we could

1.ES with 'Totti', 1917

2. ES contemplates the world from her sickbed

3. Hagar Olsson at her parents' home, Räisälä, c1920

4. The Södergran's 'ramshackle' villa at Raivola, which Edith and her mother had abandoned in favour of a small cottage in the grounds by the time Hagar Olsson came into their lives. Troops were later billeted there.
Photo by ES

5. The 'little cottage' by the Orthodox church in Raivola, where Edith lived with her mother during the years of her correspondence with Hagar

7. *View of Lake Onkamo and Raivola. Helen Södergran and her dog Martii out walking. The Södergrans' house can be glimpsed on the right.*

6. *R. R. Eklund*

8. *Elmer Diktonius*

have a party and meet. But I can't wish for that any more. I know the thunder, the atmosphere, we'd produce would be a curse. Even if we were to go and cut off the heads of innocent children we wouldn't cause as much damage.

Don't react to anything I say about religious matters, it's painful for one who knows to hear one who knows nothing speak. You may be where you like and stay in whatever camp you like, but I want this to bite into your heart with iron hooks: I torture people with my art, crucify them, my poems make them kill their horses, I have legitimized every atrocity that happens for it happens in my camp.

My outward destiny has three pronounced lines: loneliness, illness and lack of fulfilment of earthly desires. When I was 16½ years old I became ill. Abraham's daughter was in agony for 13 years.[3] He who loosened the bonds of her who had been in agony for 13 years may perhaps loosen my bonds, who knows?

Forgive this long tedious letter. I write as I can. Give Hagar my love when you see her.

We are exceptionally strong characters, you and I, which is why we look more mad than others who are as mad as we are.

Can you introduce me to Barbusse?

66/177 To Elmer Diktonius   [Raivola, undated][1]

I waited till I'd done the remaining poems so as to send off the whole lot in one go. The van Gogh poem becomes somewhat unwieldy in translation, I'd be grateful if it could be replaced by another.[2] Send all these back, and the remaining ones - at least 6. Barbusse was a misunderstanding, I was talking about the man not the book.[3] I haven't taken any particular care with the punctuation here. The piece with the three flowers is very beautiful.[4] What's Hagar doing? What's her address at the moment?[5] Give her my very warmest regards and tell her to answer the questions on my card. How much longer are you staying in Finland?

If Hagar's too lazy to answer the questions herself get her to do it through you. Best wishes from Mamma, Martti and the old lady, who does have other things to do besides writing letters to young lads. Now I shall go the way I have to go - which is in all respects the way of self-denial. That's why I'm no great letter-writer.

67/178 To Elmer Diktonius   [Raivola, 19 April 1922][1]

68/179 To Elmer Diktonius   [Raivola, 29 April, 1922]

Let me see Barbusse's letter if there's anything very big or important in it.[1] Meanwhile I'm sending you these.[2] Please send them back soon and the others with them. I want to start making a fair copy at once. Send also sequences of poems if convenient, and I'll choose as beautifully (I mean from a literary point of view) as possible. Now be very nice to me and tell Hagar that a letter has come from Bogs in Berlin and that I want to send off the anthology in a few weeks. Ask her to send the original my manuscript[3] at once (never mind if it was only scribbled out in Viipuri) or the typewritten version and at the same time ask her which passage I should take from it for the anthology? I should most prefer the beginning up to Elkanah's death or that plus another chapter as well. Do this, be a real angel.

Hagar's the kind of person (between you and me) who may not write unless she's in the mood for writing and by doing this she could disrupt the whole anthology for me. Make sure I get these papers absolutely at once, send them yourself or (if she doesn't do it) do what's necessary to get them to me. When you've gone there'll be no way out for me. Say nothing to Barbusse about me, my former self is dead and my new self hasn't yet come into the world. I also represent the poor if anyone does.

What route will you take to England?[4]

Tell me, must I ask Grotenfelt's widow for permission to use the two poems by him for the anthology?

I've already translated some of the Hemmer, but I haven't asked him. What are you and Barbusse going to do together?

69/181 To Hagar Olsson[1]   [Raivola, 12 May 1922]

I'm pleased with your selection.[2] You're right. (Though I'm very fond of the woman's conversation with the messenger!!) But do as you like. It's very lyrical, the bit you chose.

I don't intend to steal the manuscript, you'll certainly get it back. But I want to work through it so every word is right, so there will be no errors in it when it's copied out.

The anthology contains Diktonius, Ekelund,[3] R.R.E., Grotenfelt, Hemmer, Hgr O., and E.S. Since Diktonius comes first alphabetically, 'Jaguaren' [The Jaguar] will be the first poem in the book. Shall we add a greeting to young Germany or shall I write a poem of greeting in German from all of us to them (if I can manage it)?

I'd be very grateful if you can get permission from Hemmer, Ekelund and R.R.E. Give the enclosed letter and poems to Hemmer when you see him (the letter only if you think it's all right).

I want to make as neat a fair copy as possible of the whole anthology. So there would be no point in typing out particular bits. Hr B.[4] will accept neat handwriting but he doesn't like bad writing (whether handwritten or typed). If need be it can be typed out in Berlin, there can't be any shortage of typists there.

Naturally it's best to keep as quiet as possible about the whole project.

Shall I write a similar letter to Ekelund? The reason is I want them to give me books, they're so expensive to buy. I haven't yet translated a single one of Ekelund's poems because I haven't got any of them. Make arrangements for them to let me have their books, I'll give them back immediately as soon as the translations are done. Send me a list of the poems Pastor Israel has translated.[5] Might he claim later that I've plagiarised him? Should I ask Grotenfelt's widow for permission?

I've still got some of your money left over from the Viipuri trip. I've thought of using it to pay for a typescript of 'Woman and Grace'. But more of that later. Say hello to Diktonius. Martti's very ill, he's licked poison or been beaten up. What I have at present has already been translated, very little still to be done.

I'm very, very tired and have a bit of a temperature too. All this fuss about getting permission is too much for me on my own. I hope you and Diktonius will help me.

70/183 To Elmer Diktonius   [Raivola, 16 May 1922]

Thanks for the package. I'll follow your instructions. As soon as I'd posted the letter I realised that 'wieder geh ich dir entgegen'[1] weakened the original. I'd be happy if you could immediately send a really fine set of poems, it needn't be long, 3 poems will do, so you will be adequately represented in the anthology (but more would do no harm). No, nothing old-fashioned, they'd be impossible to translate. Hemmer has caused me more trouble than the 4 of us put together. The strain of the anthology is nearly making me ill - Hemmer, I mean. I've only got the one poem by Grotenfelt, 'Det vita och det röda vinet' [White and Red Wine]. I'm a very bad translator, I can't cope with strict verse forms.

I think I rate Jaguar III and IV higher than anything else in all lyric poetry without exception. I was so carried away by the Jaguar that I wrote you a proper letter but I've burnt it. Now I've made an iron-hard decision I shall keep to for ever. I have renounced all power - my self - and everything personal. But I do have an Achilles heel - I can't bear Mamma suffering poverty and in agonies because of our economic situation. That's why I'm not a Christian. 'He that loveth father or mother more than me is not worthy of me'.[2] That's why I'm doing the anthology, to help improve our economic situation. I'm selling myself to Satan but I have no choice. I am of no significance. Tell me, <u>which of my poems would you have wanted to choose for the anthology</u>? Naturally I've taken nothing from my first book. Only answer if it amuses you, I'd be curious to see what you choose.

Send me the set of poems at once so I'll have time to send you a translation of them. The poem with the cars[3] is of high artistic quality but both it and 'Sei Wirbelsturm'[4] seem a bit too unpolished for the anthology. You and I are such outsiders, we're only satisfied with our own books. I love the anthology, I want it to be like a miracle. I'm <u>enthusiastic</u> about it (the Jaguar kisses a flower).

An unmarried German lady was moved by the Jaguar kissing the flower: wie lieb, wie reizend.[5] She took the Jaguar for a jaguar. She was herself moving and lieb.

Hagar - has sent the manuscript, bonne enfant. Martti's terribly ill, it's beginning to look like rabies. Your poems are so deep I'd like to include them all, but I want to choose in the context of the whole anthology and at the same time with the deepest seriousness.

Do something for me! I want to ask a big favour of you. I've asked Hagar three times so far without result to do the same thing. When you see Eklund, tell him I've translated 'Kniven' [The Knife], 'Tystnadens Hed' [The Heath of Silence], 'Det Ensamma Trädet' [The Solitary Tree], 'Vad är slätten' [What is the Plain], 'Se drömmaren' [See the Dreamer] and 'Skapare vederkvickare' [Creator, Restorer].[6] Ask him if he approves of my choice and whether he'd like to add or subtract anything? I'm too lazy to write him such a long letter, and if he's absolutely determined to see the translations he can have my not entirely legible rough copy or the fair copy of the whole anthology, which I'm not very willing to let out of my hands.

Hagar has volunteered to get all the younger writers' consent, I hope she'll be as good as her word.

71/184 To Elmer Diktonius   [Raivola, 1 June 1922]

So tiresome to have to pester you again before you go away,[1] but you are under-represented in our anthology. I must have another set of poems. Send one now or while you're on your travels, but at all events before the end of June. So far I've only got twelve of your poems in the anthology, counting 'The Jaguar' as four. I put in the one with cars, it's got style. I'd very much like to have more so as to be able to judge properly which are the most suitable. Hagar's done everything, I've got everything I need from outside for the anthology. All I need is enlightenment for my understanding, so that I'm equal to the task. Martti's still alive but no better, cruelty to animals to let him live, brutality to kill him. Greet the wide world from me! Don't take it as treachery on my part that I'm not sending you the 'wild poem' which would be blasphemy in my eyes.[2] Say hello to Hagar and thank her for me for arranging everything so brilliantly. Have a good journey!

E.S.

72/185 To Elmer Diktonius   [Raivola, no date][1]

Now Hagar's written again. She wants to look after everything. Which is good, I'm dead tired. Martti's worse, certainly dying. He's been so sensible during his illness. Say this to Hagar: I'm happy with her very latest decision about 'Budbäraren' [The Messenger].[2] My annual subscription to the Society of Authors has been paid. We'll only use the best of Ekelund, whatever isn't dull, little but good is the best policy. From 'Pelaren' [The Pillar, by Jarl Hemmer] I want to take 'Pelaren' and 'Offer' [Sacrifice] (some of those already translated could well be added). -

It really moves me deeply that you have put yourself to the trouble of transcribing, - one shouldn't preserve illegible scrawls, it's childish. I expect you've even copied out my mistakes, 'Wille' should have a capital letter and it should be 'des Jaguars', not 'des Jaguaren'. I only point this out in case you want to use the translation in some other connection. I always write carelessly when important things like the anthology are not concerned. But I shall be devilishly fussy about that.

When does your book come out?[3]

Martti has got so terribly thin. He can't eat, but never gets tired of being spoken to affectionately.

Give Hagar my love

You can keep these.[4]

73/186[1] To Hagar Olsson   [Raivola, 14 June 1922]

I was about to send the Siegberg books[2] to you in Helsinki when Kataja[3] turned up and told me you're at Rälsälä. It'll feel like having an electric battery nearby when you're staying at Terijoki. Welcome to our frontier lands.

Thanks for the books and for arranging everything so brilliantly. I've been tired and overstressed by the anthology, such never-ending work is difficult for me. When it comes to rhymed stuff I'm an idiot, can't do anything with it. Rhyme's really for negroes.⁴ You'll take the books away with you when you come here, won't you? I haven't got nearly enough Diktonius poems in the anthology, only sixteen. I think he's sent me his worst, what he chooses is always all wrong. And it's a question of us 4 making a breakthrough, or we could be left sitting in the shadows in this benighted little corner of the world till doomsday.

OLSSON: By 'us 4' Edith means herself, Diktonius, R. R. Eklund and me.

74/187¹ To Hagar Olsson   [Raivola, 17 June 1922]

Frk Kataja's address is: c/o Commander Schröder, Terijoki. The idea was that you should stay either there or with a Fru Tchaikovsky. Fru T. was considered first and then later Commander Schröder, it sounds lovely, a fine place, the latter. But to be quite honest I find it hard to decide between the two. Lots of love!

75/188 To Hagar Olsson   [Raivola, 9 July 1922]¹

Welcome to our neck of the woods! I thought you'd slipped past out of pure treachery and were sitting there with Kataja in perfect glory without letting a sound be heard from you.

Come with the train [- - -] arrives [- - -] Raivola so we'll have [- - -] the day time to talk, if you don't want to stay overnight with us. Sonck has left and we gave him a great send-off.

Love from Mamma. Looking forward to seeing you.

High summer this year is so mellow and mild!

OLSSON: I had travelled to Terijoki for a few weeks, naturally not to 'sit' there with Kataja¹ who was presumably in Räisälä at the time, but to bathe in the sea and replenish my energies for the campaigns that lay ahead. I planned a detour to Raivola on my way back to Helsinki and the card gives instructions about the most convenient arrival time. Someone has cut off the corner of the card with the stamp so that part of the text has been lost.

76/189 To Hagar Olsson   [Raivola, 29 July 1922]

I'm afraid this card's going to arrive too late! Damn! Your matchbox and cigarettes are still waiting for you. Come, I've been talking to Fru Laubmann, twenty-five a day.[1] We could talk more about the anthology. I've just had a card from Fru Bogs, nothing in the way of letters could have been more welcome to me at this moment on this green earth. I dream about the anthology, such sweet madness.

D'you think having it typed is <u>unavoidable</u>? The anthology gleams before me like a golden bird, whew, I'm so silly. So: twenty-five a day, five meals - two large and three small of which the first with roll and butter - electric light, south-facing room, situated in the pine-forest, landlady Baltic-German, fifteen minutes' walk from our place. We could lie in the woods and sunbathe. No elegance, tasteless pictures and knick-knacks on the walls, perhaps a little unsophisticated for your taste, but I think the food won't be bad and you can be peaceful and totally undisturbed there. Do as you like. If you write to Diktonius, tell him I absolutely and instantly must have all his best poems. Do as you like. Love from Mamma and Martti.

OLSSON: I don't remember anything about these plans for a stay at Raivola. But I'm certain it never happened. I made Edith a short visit as planned, arriving in the morning and going on the same evening to Helsinki. It was August, and I was with Raoul af Hällström[1] whom I'd come across in Terijoki and who was to join me on the editorial board of *Ultra*.

I had no presentiment that this was to be the last time I would see Edith. We talked about the anthology and *Ultra* and I made it clear to her that she would be the genius of the new review - those of us who launched it considered this self-evident, even the Finnish-language editor Lauri Haarla.[2] The practical work Edith and I had before us filled our thoughts and seemed to bear promise of a brighter future. Even so there was something about our parting I found particularly moving. Perhaps it was a foreboding, one of those shadows which suddenly glide over our souls and would tell us something if we didn't so easily let them evaporate amid the urgent business of the day. When I said goodbye Edith was lying on her daybed on the veranda, and I was on the point of leaving when she gripped my hand and gave me a wonderful look I shall never forget as long as I live. With the warmest of smiles she said: 'One day you will find Christ.'

Those were the last words she spoke to me.

77/190 To Hagar Olsson   [Raivola, 31 August 1922]

Sorry to bring bad news, but my contribution will have to wait till the next number. I absolutely have to see a copy of the journal first. If it has too strong a political bias it will be absolutely impossible for me to take part. You will understand that - taking into account the superficial physical reality which surrounds us most closely and the spiritual atmosphere that goes with it - it would be idiocy of the highest order for me to get myself mixed up with irrelevant political tendencies. We shall probably stay here for the rest of our lives, why should one become a martyr for political beliefs one does not share? I'm sorry if I'm causing you disappointment. I must have Diktonius' poems, if I get them soon there'll still be time to fit them in. You seem to have forgotten your own promises about Diktonius!

OLSSON: It was like a shower of cold water for me to get this reply to my earnest entreaties for a contribution to the first number of *Ultra*. Now with hindsight Edith's initial caution - she was perfectly happy about the journal later - seems quite remarkable. It was probably Diktonius' pronounced inclination to the left and his tendency to use coarse words of abuse in debate that made her fear that similar elements would also appear in the new journal. I felt the very fact that I was responsible for editing it should have reassured her that extreme material of this kind would not be tolerated. The aim of the journal as I saw it was simply to let the poetry of younger writers have its say and bring a breath of fresh air into our stagnant cultural life. In fact the whole project did have political backing, but that's another matter. I hadn't the faintest idea of this when I placed myself at *Ultra*'s disposal, and I was very angry when I accidentally discovered I'd been thoroughly duped by Diktonius and his crony Herr Salava who did duty as business manager.[1] On the other hand it's to the credit of the Left in that period that it believed it could profit from a purely literary and cultural campaign. No political tendency in our own time would rate artistic values so highly as a potential tool for political action.

78/222 To Hagar Olsson   [Raivola, no date][1]

I'm so tired physically I don't know how I'll find the strength to do any more translating. The anthology has taken so much out of me.
    I'm so weak I can't do very much.
I can write down thoughts about the moon and death in nature.
I want to see the journal!

I'm glad you've understood me to some extent. When I saw you were faithful to Diktonius' poems I didn't want to fail you and thought I'd send at once, but then our tenants demanded 4000 from us because they'd patched the roof and in these circumstances I don't want to take any unwise steps that might compromise me with these creditors who are difficult to deal with.

79/191   To Hagar Olsson   [Raivola, 12 September 1922]

Mamma's had an idea, this is her suggestion. Wouldn't it be a good thing if Daimon could undertake to sell a number of copies of the anthology with some more foisted on Schildt. It's possible German publishers might absolutely refuse to take it without a guarantee that a certain number of copies can be sold in Finland. Put your clever heads together and give me a quick and businesslike answer. I don't mean the publishers should serve as bookshops - the public would buy individual copies through the bookshops as usual - but in this way the Germans could be given a certain degree of security. <u>We need to finish the job at once, so that the book can be out in time for Christmas</u>. I want a concrete agreement with a German publisher immediately. Bogs certainly knows all about negotiating. Perhaps we could also interest Söderström[1] with some copies going to Sweden as well. Or could the Society of Authors support the project? From a moral point of view it will make all the difference in the world if a publisher or two or a group of writers stands behind it rather than just me alone.

I haven't received Ultra yet!

Then we must also organise the advertising, we ought to send the German publishers a list of people they should send copies to, and Daimon should send copies out and each one of us should send copies to individuals. We mustn't forget those friends of Finland Franz Fromme and von der Golz and Rudolf Eucken etc.[2] Kind regards to Diktonius and little Raoul.[3]

OLSSON: Daimon was a publishing house founded specially to publish Ultra and new literature that might be hard to place with the more established publishers. Among other things it published Diktonius' *Harsh Songs* and on my initiative Gunnar Björling's first small collection of poems.[1] It also published translations into Finnish, among them Barbusse's *Le feu*.

80/192   To Hagar Olsson   [Raivola, 16 September 1922]

Thanks for your letter! There are fine things in the French journal, the 4 Paris poems of Edmond Fleg,[1] they would do Ultra honour. But impossible to translate, at least for me. If you have anyone who could do the translating I'd recommend precisely these. Poème synoptique sur trois plans[2] sounds impressive, if there is really anything in it it would be important to get hold of it. 'Suicide-assuransen' [Suicide Insurance] is rubbish, obviously by one of Diktonius' friends. I'm not surprised if my poems were not accepted in France, since it was Diktonius who made the selection. Give him my best wishes and thank him for his letter! I've sent off the letter and the anthology to Bogs, what instructions should I give to Bogs post festum?[3] Should he turn to Stinnes or have it sold in small quantities through journals. I said that Bogs should have a fair copy made by a typist specialising in literature and that we would pay for this. I've written the introductory poem but haven't risked letting it go. It's about what the murmur of the German oak means to other people. Under the surface it's an act of homage to Steiner but on the outside you can't see this, it seems a piece of pro-German patriotic sentiment. Dry and dull like an official introductory speech with even rhyme thrown in.

The poem about the moon was written in blood - up to ändlös längtan [endless longing] - and from that point on in ink.[4] That's always the way when I speak of higher things. Take it or leave it, please yourself. Choose what you like. I've got masses of rubbish like 'Fångenskap' [Captivity], I know Diktonius likes that kind of thing. The last poems he sent were perfect, who chose them? You know the poem called 'Kyrkogårdsfantasi' [Churchyard Fantasy].[5] It should be 'vita bruddräkt' [white bridal dress] and the 3 first lines should be repeated at the end. It would be a good idea to use some other word than 'jägare' [huntsman], perhaps krigare [warrior], since the huntsman's wife is still alive and the word might make an unpleasant impression on her, if she gets to see the poem. A woman's voice I heard in the churchyard here by moonlight caused my imagination to make a connection between her and a dead woman buried with her child. Put krigare.[6]

I don't want pictures of me published - absolutely not. And I want no contact with all the interesting things in Ultra. I want to distance myself now from earthly things. I want to avoid all worldly contact.

'Månen' [The Moon] Sept 1922.
Do what you like about Fleg, it's good there's a piece by him still to come.

OLSSON: The bit about Edith's poems not being accepted in France is a reference to a French anthology edited by Ivan Goll and published the same year under the title *The Five Continents: World Anthology of Contemporary Poetry*.[1] Diktonius managed to get his 'Jaguar' included through the agency of Lidia

Stahl, a charming and rather adventurous Russian lady who had at one time lived in Finland but had now settled in Paris and had connections with the radical intelligentsia.[2] Diktonius maintained that it was his intention to get a few of Edith's poems in too. I have no idea what the truth of the matter was, but the fact is that Edith was left out, and also that this had not the slightest significance.

Among other things Edith had sent 'Månen' [The Moon] to *Ultra* and I very much wanted to cut the last lines in the manuscript which seemed to me more thought out than inspired so that they weakened this wonderful poem. She herself admitted that the last lines had been written 'in ink', and with her permission I left them out when the poem was published.[3]

81/193   To Hagar Olsson   [Raivola, 22 September 1922]

Thanks for Ultra! As soon as a poem of mine has been published so that I can extract the cost of the subscription from my fee, I'll subscribe.

The bit to be repeated at the end is:[1]

What is it echoes in the churchyard; my own, my beloved!
Who is it calls in the mist?
it's the warrior's wife hurrying to her man; my own, my beloved.

Here are two more things for you (to use if you want to), give the third poem to Diktonius.

If the Severyanin translation's suitable, use it.[2]

Stylish, that French journal. All of it stylish including the rubbish. Will you take 'Poésie sur trois plans'[3] if I do it, or shall I send it back immediately?

Thanks, it's very kind of you to want to have a portrait bust done of me, but I refuse to have anything to do with anything as expensive as sculpture. The pride of the poor is exceptionally sensitive. It's absolutely out of the question.

Check the Severyanin: should it be aeroplane or aeroplanes? The tragedy of life? or the tragic things of life?[4]

OLSSON: I'd worried for a long time about the difficulty of getting a good portrait of Edith, so I was delighted to take up the art dealer Gösta Stenman's idea of having Edith's head sculpted. He was ready to send a sculptor to Raivola to do the job if I could only get Edith to agree. She flatly refused. It may seem hard to believe that her real reason for refusing was the cost: Stenman knew exactly what he was doing with his money. But to Edith it may have seemed like an insult to suggest she should be the subject of a work of sculpture at a time when she was living in a state of utter destitution. In any case, I'm sure this wasn't the only reason. We can only weep to think that a head like Edith's, so boldly chiselled and full of character, was entirely lost to mortality.

82/195   To Hagar Olsson   [Raivola, 29 September 1922]

Dear Hagar

Something wonderful has happened, a real act of providence. Bogs' answer has come ten days after I sent off the anthology: the production cost of the anthology would be 600 reichsmarks, i.e.18 Finnish marks, per copy. No German publisher today would pay out of his own pocket. The book can only come out if one covers the cost oneself.

So I decided to ask the Society of Authors for 5000 marks to print a limited number of copies of the anthology. And now the 5000 marks has arrived of itself.[1] It must be you who was responsible. Thanks to you and to everyone who has helped me. I hope you and the others fully approve of my plans for using the money. It's the only chance for the four of us to emerge from the shadows. I really must have even more of Diktonius' best poems. And immediately, in a hurry! I believe now the anthology will become reality.

Should I write specially to thank the Society of Authors? Answer! I'll send thanks via Hasselblatt at once.[2] If you haven't published the Severyanin yet, so much the better, I've a mind to do a short series. I've translated one piece by Fleg. I don't know whether that will lead to a series, it's difficult.

I'm sending you the only existing picture of me that can be considered for public use.[3] I do this to please you but you must know it's difficult for me. I want to whisper in your ear: 'Jesus doesn't like his children to show off their faces.' D'you understand me, don't be hurt. But this sort of thing is too crude to put into words, the only way one can say it is by keeping silent.

I want to thank you again for what you've done for me.

Mamma wants the picture back later, she made a bit of a fuss about it.

Shall I send you the German introductory poem? I won't risk sending it off till I know what you think of it.

OLSSON: The anthology was driving me to despair. It had become more and more like a hydra which had Edith in its grasp and was devouring the last of her vitality. I'd moved heaven and earth to get her adequate financial support; no one knew better than I did how desperately necessary this was. And when I did succeed in ensuring her a decent sum of money which would have made it possible for her at least to eat properly, she refused to use the money for herself and determined to pour it down the anthology's throat. Naturally I understood her feelings, and I wrote to tell her so. I knew that the anthology meant more to her than life itself: it meant freedom, an open door, the liberating breath of air she needed so badly after her oppressive spiritual imprisonment. No human being can live entirely without hope of any kind, and for this reason I couldn't scold her. I felt I had no alternative but to 'nag' the Society of Authors yet again and try to extract a grant for the printing of the anthology, even though, to be honest, I knew I had little hope of succeeding.

And I also believed that once the trouble with the anthology was over Edith should have the chance to get a proper rest in a sanatorium where she could at least have appetizing and nourishing food and recover from her exhausting work to an extent that would not have been possible at home.[1] I did a little research and became certain that enough money could be raised by subscription to cover a spell in a sanatorium for her. I was only too aware how much she loathed Finnish sanatoria, but I hoped to be able to win over her mother to be my ally and thought the two of us together could manage to persuade Edith to make an effort at least for a short time. I also wrote to her mother about the matter but without success, as we shall see. I should have realised that she was so totally bound up in Edith that she was simply incapable of seeing things from any other viewpoint than Edith's own. I was overcome by a paralysing sense that there was nothing I could do.

83/196   To Hagar Olsson   [Raivola, 4 October 1922]

Dear Hagar, you can talk to Pauli,[1] but without the anthology. If he wants it in his hands he can leave his German address and Bogs can send him the original or the typed copy.

The book's 160 pages long, I've written a good deal of it straight into the exercise book and I have the rest on loose sheets and in two miserable little notebooks all mixed up with my own poems and poems I've translated but left out. In any number of places there are 4 variants on top of each other, all in bits.If I myself should ever in future need to put the anthology together in a hurry the result would be a meaningless muddle which would put us to <u>shame</u>. Every word has to be worked over and crystallised months in advance. No substandard version of the anthology must ever fall into anyone's hands. I can certainly ask Bogs whether Wolff and Rohwolt[2] might put themselves to the trouble of taking an interest. Ultra's beginning to get lively! I'm really pleased!

[... Edith's lying in bed at present, she's been spitting blood. The second half of the poem 'Månen' [The Moon] can certainly be left out. Similarly the second page of 'Tankar om Naturen' [Thoughts about Nature]³ can also be removed. ... With my very best wishes, also for 'Ultra''s future.

and thanks for everything! H.S.]⁴

84/198 To Elmer Diktonius   [Raivola, 6 October 1922]

Send <u>instantly</u> poems as fine as 'Hunger i London' [Hunger in London].¹ At last something first-class, otherwise your choices have been all wrong. Could you also write an introductory poem for the anthology? Though I can't absolutely guarantee to use it. I've written one myself, but mine would necessitate the book being dedicated to Steiner. Can one dedicate translations to people, or only original poems? Tell me! I shan't do it, though I long with all my heart to. Did you get the poem about the old woman and the cat?² I'm lying in bed and have been spitting blood. Martti's still alive, he's made a wonderful recovery after being poisoned! Once we are gathered together in Ultra, I think we should take control of the world, we young stallions who've been too much for Barbusse's Nobel hacks.³ Destroy Verseilles[sic], etc.⁴ And a little of Stinnes' money for the lyric poets of the world. I liked your latest poems - d'you understand? Things are very bad in Germany the 5000 from the Society of Authors can go to the anthology, a limited edition. Each copy about 18 Finnish marks.

Goodbye, regards from Mamma and Martti. Give me the best poems you've got. Which are the new ones you were talking of? People, I mean.

85/199 To Hagar Olsson   [Raivola, 12 October 1922]

You can use the Fleg whenever you like. There won't be any more of him. I'm busy now with Severyanin. There'll be a series of poems, a picture, there should be an article about the picture too if <u>you editors want an article</u>. Tell me, <u>shall I write an article</u>?¹ Here's the picture, presumably done by a detractor, no chance in hell of a proper likeness. Then to follow this series I've got other ideas.

Here are two more of my poems. Use them if they're suitable. But no payment need be made for them, they're hallowed. If from an artistic point of view they don't suit, don't use them.²

As far as payment for the other poems goes, you can put the short ones together. Two or three short ones can be counted as one.

Keep an eye on Diktonius, make sure he sends the poems. So far still nothing.[3] And make sure he doesn't write anything nasty in his article about me, it comes so easily to him.[4]

Tell me whether you'd like me to follow the Severyanin series with an article about Steiner's plays? I need to know whether you'll take it. I want to concentrate on mystic things, I suffer horrible torments over Severyanin and his like.

OLSSON: The portrait of Severyanin was a cutting from a Russian paper, its original according to Edith drawn by Denisov and exhibited at the non-aligned exhibition of 1916. It's a savage piece of work; the poet is presented as a woman in a corset with coquettish bows on his bare shoulders. I had no use for this faded sketch and was pretty surprised that Edith could have wanted to illustrate her article on a poet whose work she loved with such an unfortunate caricature.[1] She was capable of the most heartfelt admiration but her admiration was utterly free of sentimental idealisation.

86/200 To Hagar Olsson   [Raivola, 17 October 1922]

Here are two Severyanin pieces for you. Soon you'll get a third, so you can use them whenever you like. But I implore you: if the picture makes him a figure of fun don't publish it, we mustn't hurt Russia in the person of her leading poet.

Tell me, what did you think of the picture?

I'm happy that you understand me.

Will Ultra take what I write about Steiner's plays? Thanks, I've just got your card.

Ultra's full of life now, brilliant.

I was happy you put in one of my poems, it's nice to be involved even to one side - to live.

Here's a cutting from 'Hamburger Fremdenblatt' which Bogs sent me, you understand.

Lots of love from Mamma and Martti and me.

You can do Kyrkogårdsfantasi [Churchyard Fantasy] just as it is, that's the simplest.

I'm so ashamed you're still pestering the Society of Authors, but I'm overwhelmed by the size of the grant.

I'd be interested to know why Hemmer's a nonentity.[1]

My life, my death and my destiny June 1922.

Instead of 'To the charnel-house, Marat' it should be 'To the charnel-house with you, Marat'.[2]

OLSSON: It was the poem 'Min barndoms träd' [The Trees of My Childhood] that was published in the October 15 number of *Ultra*. It was very badly placed, literally 'to one side' - one of the typesetters made up our pages for us![1] - but even so it gave Edith pleasure, a first breath of air. In the next number we presented her more effectively with a portrait, the poems 'Zigenerskan' [The Gypsy Woman], 'Hemkomst' [Homecoming] and 'Månen' [The Moon], a piece of 'critical homage' from Diktonius and a little poem about her contributed by Björling.

The newspaper cutting she enclosed which Bogs had sent her was about how expensive it was to produce books in Germany and how writers needed to find another way to earn a living if they were to survive.[2]

87/201 To Hagar Olsson   [Raivola, 20 October 1922]

Here's the article on Severyanin. It's a bit on the tame side, since la Rochelle has put paid to Severyanin as far as I'm concerned.[1] Use it if you think it suitable. I couldn't finish the poems, I've lost the mood. You know, I'm really ashamed you talked to the Society of Authors, I'm so overwhelmed by the 5,000, it seems to me utterly shameless to ask for yet more. I've just had such a warm letter from Hemmer (but I like to be discreet and not talk about it if anyone writes to me). He says he'll do everything in his power to get help for the printing, but that I should send in my application before 1 November together with the publisher's terms. Bogs has written again but he hadn't yet had my letter about the 5,000. So far I know nothing about publisher's terms etc.

You've heaped so much kindness on me I really don't know what to do. Diktonius and Hemmer are so well disposed towards me too. I'm completely overwhelmed by it all. Have you perhaps already talked to Hemmer about the matter? You called him a nonentity, what did you mean by that? He's so terribly friendly and wants to help. Don't be cross with him if he hasn't come up to the mark in some other respect.

Perhaps it's best to say '*ilade* jag till estraden' [I dashed to the stage], it's stronger.[2] Of course I'll translate some La Rochelle but it would be 'theft', there's the copyright. Don't you have to ask permission, so they don't sue Ultra for stealing? My head's in a whirl, I will not put pressure on the Society of Authors, I want to find some other way.

I'll be profoundly hurt if you and Diktonius think I'm leaving you in the lurch. Of course I'll write for Ultra, if Ultra uses what I write. But I'm seriously turning away from material things now. Only use the Severyanin article if it suits you. It may be no good. Don't send me any new books after La Rochelle. I'd really like to work full-time for Ultra, but I can't. I must go to God. If I don't I'll die of grief. Now I really am leaving the old things behind me.

OLSSON: Of course I was the one who had spoken to Hemmer; who else would have done so? I think he was moved when he heard Edith was ready to sacrifice money she needed to survive for the sake of an anthology in which he himself was represented. He was certainly ready to do what he could, but when the anthology couldn't be published his help came to nothing. Later he showed he hadn't forgotten Edith's plight. There was a reason why I'd written in some connection that Hemmer was a 'nonentity', and since the matter had come up once again and embarrassed me it's probably best if I explain how it came about. I heard some very disagreeable stories frivolously spread about by Hemmer concerning the time Edith came to Helsinki and had an evening out with him and Grotenfelt which she described as one of the 'most beautiful memories of my life'. To distort such a thing and add colour to the reactions of a spontaneous young woman seeking contact with more sophisticated people is typical of some men, particularly those who pride themselves on their so-called 'high ideals': the repressed side of their imagination looks for an outlet in this way. It upset me more than all the lies about myself ever could, and I could never forgive Hemmer for this exhibition of vulgarity.[1] Obviously I couldn't give Edith an explanation when she asked me repeatedly why I thought Hemmer a 'nonentity'.

88/202 To Hagar Olsson   [Raivola, 23 October 1922]

A bloody mess. Bogs has approached Rohwolt (Rohwolt has been fined).[1] Here's Rohwolt's answer. And Bogs makes no mention of the 5000. He considers the matter now closed and proposes to send the manuscript back to me immediately. That they write 'mit grossem Interesse' gelesen [(we have) read with great interest] must mean that they might take it if it was paid for. What the devil shall I do? Perhaps Bogs can't stand Rohwolt for political reasons, I don't know what the hell to do. I can hardly apply to the Society of Authors for a publication grant when the position's so unclear.

Don't use the Severyanin yet, I may have another poem for you, I'm not sure, but it's possible.[2]

OLSSON: Rowohlt had written briefly and firmly that conditions in Germany made it impossible to publish the work of German poets, let alone that of young Swedish-language lyricists in Finland.

89/203 To Elmer Diktonius   [Raivola, 27 October 1922]

Thanks for the poems! Excellent from an artistic point of view but one mustn't talk about children like that.[1] And those who want to draw attention to certain poems from my first book - they're making a fundamental error. Those are early poems, written 'when the dew of ignorance still lay on life'. As for the anthology, things are going wrong. Bogs tried Rohwolt, who answered that he'd read the anthology with great interest, but that at a time when young German 'Versbücher'[2] couldn't come out, geschweige då 'Junge schwedische Lyrik in Finnland!'[3] And Bogs disobeyed my instructions about the 5000 and sent the manuscript back to me. He believed from his German standpoint that this is not a suitable time for an anthology. He thought he was doing me a service by saving the 5000. Now all that was left for me was to apply to Rohwolt on the basis of the 5000. Who knows whether he will answer. I have great doubts. My agent failed me. A great grief. I've been up again a long time now and I'm feeling fine again. This kind of thing isn't serious, you just have to rest quietly. I think Nicolas Beaudouon and Rèné Ghil sound fine, there's no example of their poetry, but one can feel a breath of air from their direction - top quality goods. Claire Goll is fine, but I don't understand the exotic, have too little experience of it.[4] You know from 'The Shadow of the Future' that I am a very strongly concentrated person - my whole being draws together to a single point. This has an effect on my brain, I can't split myself up into all the pieces I need to be able to leaf through a collection of poems. My destiny is moving towards its fulfilment - I can't make promises about translations. Martti thanks you for all your kindness.

90/204 To Hagar Olsson   [Raivola, 7 November 1922]

Dear Hagar

In the end I didn't manage to write. The portrait was hilarious, a raw coarse soldier's face, an indigenous highwayman in woman's clothing.[1] You can see how things are now from Rowohlt's card.[2] It'll be best for us now to keep quiet about the whole thing and leave the Society of Authors in peace. If Rowohlt takes the anthology I'll hand over the 5000, it was because I'd offered this that he asked Bogs to send the manuscript back to him. But Bogs had it sent to me.

He <u>will</u> not help bring about something he considers madness. You mustn't blame me and reproach me if I let Rowohlt print it. I - am the life force of the anthology and can't do things any differently. None of you must blame me. I feel tired and weak, all this fuss is a bit much for me. How long will Ultra survive. Use as much of me as (!) you can in Ultra, so I can live this winter. 'Kyrkogårdsfantasien' [Churchyard Fantasy] must wait till I've made a new fair copy. But use Severyanin and Fleg. I've still got more of my own poems, but to avoid swamping Ultra I ought to try Argus or Finsk Tidsskrift or 'Allas Journal'. I have some left from the old days. <u>What are the addresses of these journals</u>? What do they pay? I have a long poem, epic-dramatic, from 1915, a Catholic girl tells her story to a nun. It's got plenty of life in it and perhaps some artistic value, 13-15 pages, perhaps suitable for Finsk Tidskrift.[3]

If I can put together a little over a thousand marks, I'll be able to have a rest. I'm now totally exhausted, there's a lot of work and trouble with the anthology still to come. I don't think I want to fleece Ultra, I have a feeling its economic position isn't brilliant and it hurts me to be forced to extract fees from it at all. Say hello to Diktonius, I'm not up to writing just now, thank him for including <u>Martti</u>.[4] Thank Björling too if you conveniently can, who is he?[5]

I got another letter from Rowohlt today. (A matter for discretion). He wants the manuscript and first estimate. If the estimate adds up he'll take it. I've a firm feeling <u>the most important thing</u> is a <u>German-friendly</u> introduction.

With this in mind I've written a new poem, 'Zueignung' [Dedication]. But Diktonius was of the opinion that you or someone <u>not involved in</u> the anthology should write a <u>short introduction in prose</u>. Simple and full of warm fellow-feeling for Germany. Get one, write it yourself or get someone else to do it. Send it to me within a week. Make sure it's first-class.

I offer the following two versions of the first line of Severyanin's 'Trettonde' [Thirteenth].

<u>Ett palats uti tolv våningar jag äger</u>

or

<u>Ett palazzo i tolv våningar jag äger</u> [6]

<u>I suggest also</u>.

<u>Jag skall stämma harpan, harpans gyllne stränger</u>[7]
(which is better, <u>luta</u> [lute] or <u>harpa</u> [harp]? Severyanin has Harp.[8]

Isn't it absolutely vital for Ultra to print something on the German Expressionists.[9]

OLSSON: For our special Södergran number we'd got an artist to draw a portrait of Edith based on a photograph, and she couldn't find words strong enough to condemn it. No one can honestly say the portrait was a success, but one has to admit she exaggerates wildly. She is much more impressed and touched that Martti is mentioned in Diktonius' article about her. The relevant passage is: 'With a little red-cheeked old lady who is her mother, and a black dog who is her friend.'

In his card to Bogs, Rowohlt asks to have the manuscript of *Junge Schwedische Lyrik in Finnland* back so as to be able to give further thought to the possibility of publishing it. If Herr Bogs had realised how much publication of the book could have meant to Edith in the form of new hope and belief in life perhaps he would not have set himself against her 'madness'.

91/205   To Elmer Diktonius   [Raivola, 14 November 1922]

I'm sure you're angry with me. You're thinking: I've gone and written a fine article there[1] and she's so ill-mannered and inconsiderate that she hasn't sent me a single line about it. Yes, it was splendid that Martti was mentioned. That rascal has a way of getting in everywhere. But <u>tell me</u>, can you show me a single shrew in the first book, a single woman worthy of that name??!!²

Now things are looking more promising again for the anthology. I've no idea what's essential in your poems and what isn't, what carries spiritual content for you. When you talk about 'the longing of the ashes for life' I don't understand you. The spirit of Dostoevsky and Fröding[3] is not in me, I lack the necessary organ for detecting the divine in Dosteoevsky. To me 'Animalisk hymn' [Animal Hymn][4] is an unimportant poem, you yourself have read greatness into it. The nerve of my life is entirely other, don't you know me? Or were you too tactful to mention it? How can I know. We are all incognito to each other. But if you don't know me, who in the world can know me? I don't know whether 'Evigt lever jag' [I shall live forever][5] is a deep fundamental feeling in you, or just a fleeting impression. For me the whole of Animal Hymn is a fleeting impression. The central thing, the centre of gravity of my soul, lies in entirely different poems. I have never had mysticism in me, though nature-mysticism has begun to appear this autumn. I've lived in the atmosphere of death and the moon. It's been wonderful and delightful, I've become a child of nature. You're very kind and you have a good heart I think. Why don't you like Severyanin? Don't stop Hagar using my Severyanin translations, they cost me a lot of work.[6] Greetings from Martti, who has an abscess on his chest, caused by the bite of a rival. Say hello to Hagar, Mamma sends her regards.

92/206   To Hagar Olsson   [Raivola, 16 November 1922]

Thanks for your letter. It'd be good if you could produce the article instantly, or at least as quickly as possible (if you can manage it). I shall not send off the manuscript till I have the article to go with it. It's the most important thing of all. It can be quite short. Write about Young Germany and greetings and sympathy etc. You can do this best yourself. I don't think the introductory poems I've written will do. I'll send them so you can have a look, but they're not worth using as a model. Absolutely not.

Tell me, what do you think of these two poems?

Send the poems back again.

The article is utterly vital.

93/207   To Elmer Diktonius   [Raivola, 28 November 1922]

Thanks for the book.[1] I'm really, really happy with it. I've never before been so happy with any book I've been given. I must not tread such paths or let my thoughts even once begin to move in that direction, but I have to say it has been like sunshine to me, I love the quality of truth in it. I'm glad you're such a winner and belong in our country and in our anthology. Mamma liked the Cornwall poems,[2] she sends you her regards.

You need to be seen as a whole, the ragged peaks of all your Alps at the same time. 'Jag slunga vill' [I shall hurl out][3] is very hard to translate, I haven't managed it. I've had flu, 4 days in bed. Better now. It was awful.[4]

What sort of a bird is Ivan Goll,[5] I thought the pyjama-drama a fussy piece, though a certain sense of style can't be denied. I have no understanding whatever of the exotic. I know nothing of van Gogh,[6] have never seen any of his pictures. D'you think the spirit's domination of the world should only be valid for art, or what? Isn't it art that's contemptible and should be destroyed? Art - the most expensive luxury - and aristocratic. Anyone who wants to feel with the masses should renounce all spiritual superiority - all virtues, including the moral ones, and be spiritually poor - this is the heavenly mean. I've just had a letter from Hagar.

94/208   To Hagar Olsson   [Raivola, 7 December 1922]

Here's the rubbish for you. It's more important to me that you don't leave out the last nature poem, no 3 in the Ultra series. If you use 'Mitt liv, min död och mitt öde' [My Life, My Death and My Destiny],[1] don't put it on the same page as the spiritually-tinted poems, they'll clash.

Love

Mörne was less cold and hostile to Dikt. than to R.R.E.[2] Did Kihlman include you, R.R.E. and Diktonius?[3]
I'd like to include Severyanin most of all. Here are some changes in Severy. Trettonde [Thirteenth].
1. Skönt det vore att engång i detta rummet [Wonderful would it be once in this room to]
  (altered word order)
2. I suggest three variants (you choose the best)
var av dem de andra i sig själv fullkomnar [each of them perfects the others in himself]
var av dem de andra genom sig fullkomnar [each of them perfects the others through himself]
var av dem de andra uti sig fullkomnar   [each of them perfects the others within himself.]

> Don't believe, don't believe dryasdust science.
> Don't believe, don't believe powerless doubters.
> Don't believe, don't believe what the whole world says and echo repeats.
> Don't believe, don't believe your own surface nature
> Don't believe your prejudices
> Don't for a moment believe in your doubts
> All is nonsense and madness
> Believe, believe that there is only one truth

> You must live him and
> he will compel you
> with the force of his spirit.

The poor wayside flower cannot help, though she would so much like to. But she can tell about him who lives in the truth, he is her teacher. He can do it.

You have beheld the Messenger, for you have been called to a great task which is not of this world. Only them does he approach. And you will become angry every time you see him. The dark powers within you will become angry. And my dark powers defy my teacher, I will go with defiance and laughter to him who will be my father.

95/209 To Hagar Olsson   [Raivola, 12 December 1922]

Do the best you can with the punctuation. Call the poem 'Novembermorgon' [November Morning] or 'Senhöstvandring' [A Walk in Late Autumn] or whatever. It has no title of its own.¹

Love

96/210 To Hagar Olsson   [Raivola, 16 December 1922]¹

Here's a piece from 1915, I'd be grateful if you could place it for me. Since Argus is hostile to me² and it's too long for A.,³ I thought perhaps 'Finsk tidskrift'. It should be long enough and tough enough for them. I've got another double the length, parallel, girl and nun but not religious.⁴ These two should be added to 'Dikter' [Poems] some day. I'm not feeling too well, staying in bed for the time being. I'm not going to be able to do any work all winter, it'll be something if I can manage to make fair copies of old stuff, translating out of the question. That's why Larochelle never got done, even though I'd already translated some bits in the autumn.⁵ I'm very curious about the Kihlman anthology, but it's bound to be so stuffy one'll go mouldy just from setting eyes on it.⁶ Was Diktonius dissatisfied with Mörne's review, or did he think it was simply well-disposed, relatively speaking.
Love.

97/211 To Hagar Olsson   [Raivola, 30 December 1922]

A Happy New Year from Mamma, Martti and me. I assume you're at Räisälä. A pity Ultra went under.¹ I sent the manuscript off to Rowohlt on 28 November precisely, so far no response, - a bad omen. In the autumn letters took about seven days to get here, maybe the ships are slower now,² or perhaps it's the Christmas rush, or perhaps times in Germany are getting even worse.

I've decided not to touch the 5000 for about another month, and after that if there's still no answer or a negative answer - I shall begin to eat into the 5000. It upsets me not to be able to do something for you after you've done so much for me but no one could have taken more trouble over the anthology than I have done, it was Bogs' fault for sending the manuscript here just when Rowohlt wanted it, after which the whole thing went cold. If he had kept it the matter would surely have been sorted out by about the 10th of November.

How pleased were you with Ultra's career? Did it work? It would amuse me to know why you all made such an attack on Hemmer?[3] As thrilling as bullfighting.

We were so very young once, when we first knew each other four years ago. Everything shone so for us. Now it's all become so sober. Nothing shines, nothing gleams any more for me. Now that Stenman has rejected Austrian art[4] - now there can be nothing but a chorus of whistles for the anthology. No doubt about it. I hope Rowohlt says no.

If you can manage it without difficulty it'd be a great help if you can place some of my work for me so I can survive till this matter is cleared up. And if Rowohlt accepts - in which case extra income will be essential - I'm really weak now and can't think of doing any work.

However I hope from a full heart you haven't yet placed the unhappy 'Undret' [The Miracle]. It should say 'nunnedräkten' [nun's habit] rather than 'nunnedoket' [nun's headdress, wimple], change it, don't let the poem out of your hands till you've changed it. I had a temperature and managed as best I could. Maybe have a look through all the rubbish, to make sure there are no language errors.

It would be fun to meet but of course it's impossible. What are you going to busy yourself with and are you going back to H:frs[5] again?

Love

1923

98/212 To Elmer Diktonius   [Raivola, 5 January 1923]

Here's Father Christmas, a bit late, with greetings from Raivola to the Jaguar's alcove,[1] - but of course he'll be around till Twelfth Night.

Oh yes - one of us lives in an alcove, and the other's walled in and cooped up in her own weakness. I've been constantly ill, weak and very anæmic. I haven't been able to work at all during this time and shan't be able to work for a while yet.

I've given up all hope for the future now, all I can manage is to vegetate for a while.

On the 20th November[2] the manuscript was sent off. to Rowohlt. Silence. Bad sign.

Was it you who stopped Ultra accepting the two long Severyanin poems or was Ultra timid? Do you loathe Severyanin from a social point of view? Tell me, I'd be interested to know. Or are they so feeble in H:fors that not even Ultra has the nerve to print a few harmless love-poems.

I very much enjoyed the extracts from van Gogh's letters.[3]

What should one do about anæmia? Give me an answer, Jaguar! I still have my prescription for iron, but the damn doctors have to have everything signed and paid for.

Are you living with your mother? And she's let your old room so you have to live in the kitchen? Is that so?

I really ought to be writing to Rowohlt rather than to you and asking him for an answer. But that sort of letter must be written with such wisdom and I'm tired. I'll never be clever enough to write to Rowohlt. We've got a little Christmas tree (in the hermit's room).[4] I feel so cold all the time from lack of blood. Why were you so stuck up last time you came here that you stayed at the hotel.[5] I've often felt bad about it since, knowing there's not much in your purse.

Kind regards from Mamma. Are you going to join the Authors' Association now?[6] You are hardly a favourite there. Why did you attack Hemmer so fiercely? I'd be fascinated to know. Something did happen between Ultra and Hemmer! But what?

Adieu

99/213 To Hagar Olsson   [Raivola, 15 January 1923]

Why didn't you come? Depriving me of my winter happiness. I'm really as if buried alive here. By 'it's impossible to meet' I meant of course that you shouldn't travel in winter weather and without a permit. What d'you think about Steiner's temple being burnt down?[1] R-w-lt has written: economic conditions at present catastrophic. German lyric poetry must come before all else, so he can't publish foreigners. He thought the terms favourable. He said the book would have strengthened 'die kulturellen Beziehungen'[2] between Germany and Finland but that his firm had to give up many fine plans.[3] - So that was fate. I hope you won't be disappointed. I'm a bit better now, I've taken some iron and really forced myself to eat. One victory to announce: the dog Jeppe has left the district.[4] I've now started to use the 5000, 1500 will go to the milk bill etc, and we'll live through this year on the rest. Enormous relief now that I'm not arbeitsfähig.[5] If without too much trouble you could place a poem or two for me it would be brilliant I'd splash out and get myself a patent medicine from Switzerland. But if you do don't forget to change 'nunnedoken' to 'nunnedräkten' (it's right at the beginning) of course there's a grammatical error anyway ('doken' should be 'doket').[6] D'you know of any preparation that has a powerful effect on horribly severe anæmia? I wonder if there'll be a new journal again? Martti asks me to thank you for remembering him and gives you a little bark of delight because you managed to give him a couple of lines.

Love from Mamma.

A Happy New Year for your plans![7]

100/214 To Hagar Olsson   [Raivola, 17 February 1923]

Lovely that you're coming, knowing this has as it were given me new life, living here is like living on an uninhabited island. It'll be nice to meet your friend Fru R.K.[1] Mamma says about your trip to Uusikirkko that you should dress for a long journey of 18 or 19 kilometres and take good care of yourself. Everyone's longing to see you: Mamma, Martti and the undersigned. Write and say when you're coming or phone Galkin, Raivola and leave a message. Would you like a horse at the station?

101/215 To Hagar Olsson   [Raivola, 8 March 1923]

Dear Hagar,

I feel really overwhelmed and embarrassed deep inside. This spoils me. I had enough to live on to the end of the year, this is too much - to take away any shadow of worry for the future.

I wonder whether it was Fru Rakel Kansanen who did this. Thank her most sincerely from me. I would so much like to do something nice for her.

It was your great good fortune you didn't come the first two weeks, the weather was quite exceptionally harsh and cold, but this week we've had delightful sunny days bringing new life. We were so looking forward to seeing you - you Old Testament women! I've been curling my hair and brushing and combing Martti nearly every day and Mamma's been baking gingerbread and we've listened for every sound at the train times. And the famous Helsinginvieraat[1] never came.

The first days of sunshine have as it were given me new life. I've certainly been too anæmic to be able to cope with extreme cold. The fierce frost has ended with the fine weather. You and Diktonius have no doubt been mewing to my generous benefactor that I'm extremely ill. One can't be sure how ill one is - one can't tell whether the illness is getting worse or not or whether it was extreme anæmia. Now good times are back!

Thank the <u>unknown person</u> and thanks to you as well and also to Diktonius if he's been thinking of me too. Love from Mamma, I must hurry to the post.

102/216[1]

I enclose a piece of embroidery, a book-cover I made in Davos. It has lain ten years in a table drawer awaiting its destiny. Give it to the <u>Unknown</u>. I want her to have it as a small reminder of me. It can't make a public appearance as handicraft and isn't 'salonfähig'[2] but the little marchioness is alive and wants us to share her walk in the autumn crocus-meadow and her conversation with the goose. - I'm so fortunate to have met with so much generosity, it makes sense of everything that has happened to one.

I know all about what you wrote to Mamma last autumn about sanatorium plans (it happened quite naturally that I read the letter before Mamma did).[3] And recently a few days after you had announced you were coming here and also going to Halila[4] it occurred to me that something similar must be brewing. I see now that I was wrong, though I wasn't entirely unjustified in having suspicions even if I was suspecting the wrong thing. But now I simply hope and pray that there will be no new surprises any more. I already have too much to bear and I'll oppose any such plans with all my strength. I have everything I shall need for a long time to come.

I wish so much I could talk to you. Has Fru Kansanen some relative at Halila? I wish so much I could see her.

There's so much to say and ask, but we can put that off to another time.

Where will you be living this summer. Love from us all (including Martti).

OLSSON: I had got to know Fru Rakel Kansanen, a well-known personality in the art world at that time, a collector and connoisseur very enthusiastic about the work of young artists; among other things she was one of the first to fully perceive Sallinen's[1] brilliance. I particularly wanted Edith to meet her, so when for some reason we planned a trip to Halila, a tuberculosis sanatorium in eastern Finland, we decided to make a detour to Raivola to see her. But in accordance with a law which has ruled my whole life and decrees that all plans shall go wrong, the journey was cancelled and Fru Kansanen instead had the idea that very spring of asking me to her home in Geneva - her husband was secretary to the delegation[2] at the League of Nations. This presented me with what in my situation was the dizzy prospect of being able to spend a reasonable amount of time in the heart of Europe and even of making a trip to the Riviera. I've seldom been so happy as I was at the beginning of that journey and no ghostly voices whispered to warn me of what lay in store.

It was while the aborted trip to Halila and Raivola was being planned that Edith got 3,000 [Finnish] marks from someone who wished to remain anonymous. She thought it was Fru Kansanen, but it wasn't. It was Jarl Hemmer. No one had 'mewed' to him about her illness, least of all Diktonius who didn't even know him and in any case had no inclination to raise money for others. I had earlier described Edith's economic plight to Hemmer, and now when he received a large grant from Sweden his conscience pricked him - he did have a conscience - and he came to me of his own accord and told me with considerable embarrassment that this three thousand was 'more than he needed' and that he wanted Edith to have it, but on condition she didn't know who had given it. I was very happy and thanked him for his kindness. But I wasn't quite so happy when Edith asked me to give the embroidered book-cover to her unknown benefactor. Aware of her deep feeling for the spiritual content of gifts I felt unable to pass the little marchioness on to someone who had made her the butt of coarse male jokes and in no way shared our artistic aims (I'll never forget my embarrassment when at some meeting Hemmer poured scorn on Diktonius' poem 'The Jaguar' on the grounds that in the places where jaguars live there are no fir-trees for them to hurl themselves over!).[3] I allowed myself to clutch at diplomatic evasions, and when Edith in her next letter characterized Hemmer from a purely theoretical standpoint as 'quite unsuitable' I considered the problem solved. In this way the little marchioness came to stay with me.

103/217 To Hagar Olsson   [Raivola, 16 March 1923]

That it's a man does change things a bit. It could be suitable or unsuitable depending on who it is. Uncle Proco[1] (to take him as an abstract example) would be eminently suitable. Hemmer (as an abstract example) ~~absolutely~~ very unsuitable. In a word, it might cause gossip and discussion that could sully the purity of the soul. From the most profound point of view it would be suitable in every case, but superficially embarrassments should be avoided. Judge for yourself and do as you think fit. If the person in question won't care a fig for the marchioness it would be pointless to give her to him. If it was Diktonius (abstract example) I absolutely would give her, he is far above all gossip and calculating. Decide for yourself what to do, since it is not for me to know a secret which would make it easier for me to deal with the matter. But of course he might be totally unknown to me in any case. If he is unsuitable I want you to keep her, that would be a happy solution to the problem.

The spring is glorious, utterly wonderful. When are you coming? They're cutting down the forest here.[2] It would be good to be able to talk sometime. What's Diktonius doing and where is he, give him my best wishes. Love from Mamma and 'Rackeli'[3] who has the best possible memory of you even if when you threw a stick for him he found it instantly.

104/218 To Hagar Olsson   [Raivola, 31 March 1923]

Happy Easter!
What you wrote was a great relief to me. I was afraid the marchioness might jump into the wrong box. But no, not in this case. So long as you don't despise the poor creature I'd be happy for you to give her sanctuary. I'll be very happy if she stays with you. This is Max Linder, if you're wondering.[1] Mamma sends her love. Are you still thinking of a trip to Halila with Fru R.K.?

105/219 To Elmer Diktonius   [Raivola, 7 April 1923]

I was very happy to get your letter. Yes, I'm sure it's lovely just now in the country near Jyväskylä.

You wrote an awfully fine article.[1] Mamma was very happy with it, she's always very happy and grateful when you write nice things about me.

You want a merciless critique. Well, what can I say, there's nothing incorrect except what you say in connection with 'Animalisk hymn' [Animal Hymn]. You review <u>music of your own</u> that you read into the poem and not my poem itself. The fact is, the poem is a feeble piece compared with what <u>you</u> read into it. And everything you attribute to me in this connection is false. A critic must write about the object that lies before him, not about himself. He must give <u>facts</u>, not fantasy.

You promised to send some 'things', I'm very excited.

I'm a little dizzy as I write, didn't sleep well last night. The independence monument is to be unveiled here on Monday, Mannerheim, Svinhuvud and others are expected, nothing but spring-cleaning and raking and sweeping and a triumphal arch here - and - making garlands and excitement in the air.[2] It'll be a relief when it's all over.

You're a very nice boy.

What d'you think of Steiner's temple being burnt down?[3]

Send your poems!

Best regards from us all.

106/220 To Hagar Olsson   [Raivola, 26 April 1923]

It's good you're escaping to the wonderful south.[1] This is certainly the best time for Lac Léman.[2]

I shall continue faithfully to write to you, you can depend on that. I was so happy when I saw how well the Society of Authors had dished out its money this time. It was really a sight for sore eyes. Particularly that Diktonius got something - it bodes better times.[3] Very clever to travel now, it's bound to be enchanting. Give my love to my dear, dear Switzerland.

You'd make Mamma very happy if without giving yourself too much trouble you could send her a picture-postcard of Nôtre-Dame. She's always dreamed of being able to see it one day and Diktonius has told her about it.

I wonder if you'll be able to eat cherries soon in Geneva, certainly at the beginning of June.

Martti, who's been ill, is now well again. We all send our love and wish you a happy journey! When are you coming here.

I'm feeling a bit better, but I'm so anæmic I have no periods. Don't forget us completely on your travels. I'm already missing you, I have a gut feeling that something warm and benevolent is moving away, receding.

I'm very curious to know what impression Paris'll make on you! It'll enchant you, I'm sure! Give my regards to Anna-Lenah if you see her in Stockholm.

Give my regards to Fru Kansanen and Harry Blomberg[4] if you see him.

OLSSON: These greetings to people she'd never met who could be presumed to be favourably disposed towards her make an oddly moving impression here: the names represent a wider world, people who had heard of her, and a greeting is after all a form of contact if a very insubstantial one. It is as if Edith were reaching forth her arms one last time from her loneliness, out towards a world she was about to leave without its having even been aware of her existence.

107/221 To Elmer Diktonius   [Raivola, 19 May 1923]

I'm sure you're angry with me. But I shall use this letter to put in an appearance and ease my conscience.

Profiteering sharks and forest speculators are cutting down the forest here, the forest of my childhood. -

Martti is ill again, in the same way as last year.

The younger of his mistresses has revived with the spring, the frost has vanished with the coming of the warm time of year. I'm a bit weak and rather thin - don't be too hard on a sick girl if she sometimes pauses in her writing.

I feel very fortunate, not wishing anything more for us here.

It's such an abstract process writing to you when I don't know whether you even exist. And even if you do exist, I don't know whether you will ever again be ready and willing to write to me.

When does your book come out?[1] What are you busy with? Kind regards from Mamma.

Say hello to Hagar. Martti and I are taking this letter to the post at once.

108/223 To Elmer Diktonius   [Raivola, 20 June 1923][1]

[Here is a last greeting from Edith Södergran - she left me today midsummer day tell Hagar if you know where she is.

And accept my thanks for all the kindness you showed her!

                              H.Södergran]

I've seen in the paper that the author of 'Harsh Songs' has had some tender ones in Argus. Congratulations.[2]

I was happy to get your letter. You unconsciously chose the right moment. I'm very ill now. Short of breath with the slightest movement, almost unable to walk. Cramp and fits of choking at night. No sleep at all. My nerves - 500 raging electric pinpoints in each hand. Strong medicines paralyse the organism. The

155

doctor says: asthma originating in the heart's nervous system.

Don't forget me now, Strong Storm. I've had one card from Hagar, a field of narcissus at Les Avants.[3] This is a really hard time for me. Weak. I can't stand light or noise.

[Hagar Olsson to Elmer Diktonius   Golf Hotel, Bandol, France, 2 July 1923[1]

We're very much alone now. Olsoni[2] has sent me a telegram saying Edith's dead, it hit me in a way I'll never forget. Horribly guilty conscience that I never went to say goodbye to her before I left. It was so extraordinary with Edith, she was so strongly alive it was almost impossible to realise she might die very soon, even though she was so ill [. . .]

I feel terribly empty. It's so strange, as if everything was lost. But God it's awful to have left her so alone, not to have gone to see her more often. Perhaps she felt bitter about it. Latterly I didn't even write, just constantly expected letters from her - and could never understand why she didn't write!

In a few days I'm leaving here for Geneva. Write and tell me everything you know. There's something mystical about this death, it knocked me off my feet, I don't understand myself what it is, but I'm desperate with anguish. Perhaps the best thing would be to follow sister Edith.]

[Helena Södergran to Hagar Olsson   Raivola, 8 July 1923[1]

Well, now our Edith has gone from us, calm and patient, as she lived and suffered. For although her illness had already been wearing down her strength for many years, this last year was especially difficult with her shortness of breath getting worse and worse to which were added in the last weeks insomnia, extreme weakness and neuralgia, while in the very last week she found it difficult to swallow. Medicines only made her condition worse.

If her heart had not been so weak she might perhaps have been able to go on suffering longer, but it gave up its work before her lungs. In her agony she wished God would take her away and she had long understood that the condition she was in could not continue very long - she had of course had the chance to see the same course of events in others during the times she spent in sanatoria. Her anxiety was for me: 'I can't bear the thought of leaving you here alone'.

I don't think Edith felt any bitterness towards you, Hagar, for not coming to see her before you set off on your journey; she knew you were not going alone and that you may have had to take your fellow-traveller into account. But she certainly longed to see you and on the day she died she said, 'I wish I could see Hagar and Diktonius here.' And she was full of gratitude for all the kindness that had been given her, and the day before she died she said: 'We've received so much helpfulness and kindness that I ought to write a book of thanks, if only I could manage it.' And she often remembered all the things you and Diktonius had done for her. - And she forgave or ignored what she had experienced of offence and malice in her so quiet and retiring life, because her heart was too rich, affectionate and understanding ever to suffer the usual marks of extreme poverty: envy and bitterness.

She got your card from Les Avants.

For several years she had been busy destroying all her old papers - 'I'm not leaving anything for the worms,' she used to say. And today I understood how right she was when I saw an account of her origins in *Svenska Pressen* by someone from Närpes. It was accurate enough apart from one error I must correct: I am not Russian, my father came from Perniö and my mother from Nauvo.[2] For if there were any sense in the idea that Edith was of Russian origin on her mother's side the fantasies and speculations about her poetry would never end.

She went from one philosopher to another, from Nietzsche to Steiner, and then turned to the New Testament. She wanted to believe in reincarnation. The last piece she felt up to reading in the paper was about the success of young artists in Gothenburg and she was delighted by this, but sighed: 'When will it be literature's turn?'

Thank you, Hagar, a telegram did come from Eric Olsoni and such a warmly sympathetic letter from your father. The sun shone the last day she was above ground. Now she lies close to her home, just by the fence, and when I'm out in the fields I can see her grave.[3]

Keep well and thanks for everything!

Edith's mother.

Will you be spending long out there? It's so strange, Hagar; it's as if the three thousand[4] had been intended for her last journey.]

[Helena Södergran to Hagar Olsson   Raivola, 8 August 1923[1]

Thank you for your letter and for promising to make me happy by coming to see me and Edith's grave; it will make her happy too. I so long to be able to talk about her with someone she loved.]

OLSSON: Edith's mother gave me a small piece from the cover of a notebook on the inside of which, in lead pencil, in extremely weak and partially illegible writing later inked over by her mother, Edith had written a few words, her last communication with me:

109/224[1]

Has she forgotten me Hagar aren't we bound together in life and death From [deep inside] me rises a spring of devotion, in my purest moment I call on you Lord offer up my heart's blood in the loveliest limpid moments I remember Hagar

The End

Appendix

The essay which follows, 'Diktaren som skapade sig själv' (The Poet Who Created Herself), was written in September 1940 by Hagar Olsson as an introduction to her 1941 edition of ES's poems and reprinted in 1949 as an introduction to Tideström's collected edition. It was written at a depressing time for HO. The 'Winter War' between Finland and the Soviet Union (November 1939 to March 1940) had preserved Finnish independence but had resulted in the loss of the Karelian isthmus, including Viipuri, Räisälä and Raivola. At the end of the First World War ES and HO had been young and full of hope. They had believed in the power of the arts to influence the direction the world would take out of the melting-pot into which the war had thrust it (HO touchingly describes this youthful confidence in her commentary on Letter 6/95). But by 1940 it was clear they had failed in what they had set out to do and that the best years of their lives had been nothing more than a parenthesis between two terrible wars. HO felt she had doubly betrayed ES: she had not been there for her in her time of need, and she had had little success in making reality of the dreams they had shared. She had also let down Helena Södergran, who had looked forward to seeing this first collected edition of her daughter's work. It had been planned in 1939 but HO had put it aside to concentrate on her own writing and Helena, evacuated from the isthmus ahead of the Soviet invasion, died before she could see it. It cannot have helped HO's permanent guilty conscience about the Södergrans that when Helena died (in a communal home at Joroinen in January 1940) she herself was once more abroad - this time in Sweden. The title of the essay is based on a surviving fragment from a lost poem by ES (see HO's 1955 Introduction to the letters, note 13).

The Poet Who Created Herself

Hagar Olsson

Edith Södergran possessed a very individual and seductive charm that cannot easily be captured in words. I have no idea what wood-nymphs are like as with our clever modern eyes we can no longer see such creatures, but to the extent that I can imagine such mysterious females of the forest I would say that she was like one. Be that as it may, I have never come across any other human being who gave such a strong and immediate impression that she had yet to separate herself from that mist-shrouded world which is the source of fairy-tales and mythical nature-concepts, forces which seem all the more inclined to drape you in floating veils the more you try to limit their influence. This is particularly striking since she had an intellect capable of needle-sharp perception and judgment, and a character, an ethical will, which struggled relentlessly for the full moral development of her own personality.

It is this combination of genuine child of nature, questing critical intelligence and morally serious personality that makes Edith Södergran the great poet she is.

From the point of view of biographical research as well as in a purely spiritual sense the disappearance of her notes and half-finished drafts has been an immeasurable loss. The little I was able to see of them before they were destroyed in accordance with her own last wishes gave me the impression of a clear and uncompromising analysis which forced its way to the very foundations of her self-contradictory being and explored the most intimate ramifications of the creative process. These notes would have been priceless not only as an explanatory text for her poems but because they gave a clear picture of her sensitive critical sense. It is so easy to fall into the trap of believing that a poet with a temperament like hers, one who so openly lets herself be carried on a wave of inspiration and cannot bring herself later to complete a poem she did not finish in that first inspired moment, will also lack the ability to assess her own resources critically and pass judgment on them. This was not the case with Edith Södergran who wrote:

> Can I ever be capable of the simplicity my perpetual but unsatisfied longing and my powerful but unsatisfied innermost poetic judgment demand? Is not my joy too violent? Am I not a savage, the sort of child that runs to grab everything that excites her with its glitter? Am I strong enough to sustain my showy and dangerously unbalanced brilliance?

Hardly any poet has ever succeeded in expressing more clearly and objectively what she is trying to achieve and what she needs to master in herself. She had a certain weakness for all that glittered and was gaudy both in words and colours, but she also had fine poetic judgment that enabled her to transform into beauty even what lay perilously close to banality. And more than that, she had that powerful natural inspiration which is a surer divining-rod than even the most fastidious sense of judgment and the most critical understanding. She knew this, and it gave her the divine freedom from care she needed in the midst of the anxiety and labour of creative work. As she wrote:

> The spiritually penitent need not seek ethical perfection in their poems; all they need do is give full rein to their passion, riding roughshod over stock and stone, vanity and banality, and they will reach a height where they will suddenly be transfigured so that all weakness falls away from them like scales.

Even those who doubt the truth of this theory will see this transfiguration fully achieved in her remarkable last poems.

Fortunately one day her letters will be available, and it will then be possible for the first time to understand fully the strength and originality of her character; power and supremacy are in every flourish of her clumsy handwriting. In the collection of her letters that I possess there is not a single line that is not moving, and moving precisely because of her harsh but spontaneous sincerity. These letters are human documents that will remain of value so long as people have any feeling for the great bold lines of the basic struggles inherent in human life. She mixes humour and seriousness just as we all do, and battles resolutely to find the best way to ensure her life is fruitful and useful.

'Alas, I don't know what to do with my life,' she wrote in one of her letters at a time when she was not sure which spiritual lead to follow. This was her urgent mission here on earth. Not just to write poetry, to speak out, or to create shapes with words, but to shape her whole life, investing all her powers to the full in the attempt to create a whole without defect or blemish. Every line she wrote, like every other aspect of her private life, related organically to this shaping of her life and its full genuineness and validity can only be assessed in this context. As she put it: 'I do not make poems but create myself, my poems are for me the way to myself.'

This is why I want to say: Don't read her poems as literature. Take them for what they are: the many-coloured sparks that flew from the anvil on which a life full of suffering and simplicity was hammered into a block of truth.

I am convinced the way to do her poems full justice is to let them speak for themselves.[1] Each one is like a quivering fragment of life in which one is conscious of the rhythm of breathing and a subtle pulse-beat. The right atmosphere for such poems is the solitude of the individual. If you read them without reservations and with the sensitive insight which every true original poem demands of its reader, you will be able to experience without intrusive æsthetic analysis the poet's living personality, and you will come to love the human being who reveals herself in them. Even so it could be useful for the reader to know something of the poet's fate and the circumstances which formed the concrete background to her poetry and gave it its characteristic local and personal colour. The milieu she lived in was so unusual and the circumstances of her life so sad that it is almost impossible to understand the subtler nuances of her lyrical language without some knowledge of the practical material from which she wove her dreams.

Edith Södergran's homeland was the Karelian isthmus, that border-land which Finland has now lost together with the rest of Karelia.[2] She lived most of her life in the Russian-Orthodox village of Raivola, a typical frontier village with a mixed population and a picturesque assortment of more or less dilapidated but highly ornamented wooden houses[3] embedded in luxuriant vegetation. The district had earlier been famous for a great larch-forest planted long before by the Russian Tsar Peter the Great, and in more recent times this sylvan renown had been supplemented by a budding reputation as a place of poetic pilgrimage.[4] Many lovers of poetic secrets would make their way to the modest grey wooden cottage close to the Orthodox church, hidden from the world's gaze by the luxuriant bushes of a garden run wild. Once one has seen this place and its expressively beautiful trees that seem to guard the peace of existence,[5] and has looked across the river with its wide inlets, and seen the precipitous shore where dark-trunked trees grow down to the water's edge, one can no longer have any doubts about the origin of her pantheistic mysticism and the gloomy yearning dreamlike quality of her depictions of nature. She has interpreted the nature and special temper of this Karelian landscape, imprinted with the melancholy of its tragic history, with a living fervour which speaks immediately to anyone familiar with the Finnish countryside. She is the only recent Finland-Swedish poet to have made any impression on Finnish-language readers and she has exerted a decisive influence on young poets writing in Finnish; the fresh and entirely original tone of her poems, springing from the very heart of the time she lived in, has naturally been the main reason for this, but another very important factor has been that readers have recognised the purely Finnish quality of her landscape and the Karelian mood of her lyrical descriptions of it. She was the first poet, and she may also have been the last, to succeed in spreading an undying lustre over this province we have now lost. That she should have done this in the Swedish language is the best possible evidence that all the way to its very easternmost border Finland is spiritually at one with the Scandinavian north.

Edith Södergran was descended on both sides from the Swedish-speaking communities of Finland. Her father, Mattias Södergran, was of Ostrobothnian peasant stock and her mother came from the south-western coastal district near Turku. Mattias Södergran was born in Närpes, studied technology in Vaasa, and worked for various engineering firms in Finland before moving in the 1880s to Russia where he was employed by the Nobel company. His first marriage was childless, and after his first wife died he married in 1890 Helena Holmroos, daughter of a well-to-do iron-founder from Perniö (Swedish Bjärnå) who owned a workshop and foundry in St Petersburg; her mother was from Nauvo (Swedish Nagu). This marriage produced one child, Edith.

She was born in St Petersburg on 4 April 1892, but was only three months old when the family moved back to Finland. Her father bought a property in Raivola where he interested himself in a sawmill and set up various business concerns. After his death in 1907 his widow and daughter continued to live there. From 1902 to 1908 they spent part of each winter in St Petersburg where Edith attended a German church school, the Petrischule,[6] as her mother had done before her. But when a year after her father's death she developed tuberculosis, the disease which had killed him, she was taken away from school and the periods spent in Petersburg in winter also ended. From then on her only home was Raivola.

For a few years more, until the Russian revolution, she was able to travel, particularly to Switzerland for treatment for her illness but also elsewhere abroad, and this gave her an opportunity to take in new impressions of nature and art. During a period of remission she was also able to attend a high school in Helsinki to prepare for matriculation. But economic disaster caused by the Russian Revolution and deteriorating health soon put an end to all such expeditions. Throughout the last ten years of her short life she was restricted to what a quiet life in the idyllic surroundings of her Karelian border village could offer in the way of nature and spiritual stimulation.

There has been talk in some quarters of a 'Russian' element in Edith Södergran, and a tendency to detect something unSwedish in her 'Byzantine' poetic diction with its antitheses and enigmatic quality and use of free verse. 'Romantic' would be a better term for this than 'Byzantine': it is a quality one finds in some of the most talented lyric poets in the literature of Sweden and Edith Södergran was herself conscious of her relationship to, for example, Almqvist.[7] There may indeed be a Slav element in her temperament and imagery, but only to the extent that they belong to the part of Finland which was her poetic homeland and are in many respects typical of its population. A closer examination would certainly reveal that much of what to the uninitiated can seem foreign in her lyrical imagery is recognised by readers whose native language is Finnish as deriving from the soil of her border homeland. For all her cosmopolitan attitudes and world outlook Edith Södergran was sensitively and intimately bound to her own home district and its people.

The great city where she was born and where, during a few dream-filled early years, she absorbed the decadent attitude to life of the boudoir-poets[8] and the mysterious dark secrets of a brooding sea of people was to be for her nothing more than the overture to her creative life. She herself, in her poem 'Fragment', has given a suggestive summing up of the two worlds in her life, and like so many of her words these have now[9] taken on a strangely prophetic tone:[10]

Petersburg, Petersburg,
from your pinnacles flutters my childhood's enchanted banner.
It was the time before the deep wounds, before the mighty scars,
before rejuvenation's bath of oblivion.
Petersburg, Petersburg,
on your pinnacles lies the glow of my youth
like a pink curtain, like a light overture,
like a veil of dreams over the slumber of titans.

Is not our miraculous citadel rising from the sea in Helsinki ?
Do not watchmen stand there with blue and red banners never seen by
    the world?
Are they not leaning on spears, peering out to sea,
-the granite of destiny in their petrified features?

Two demanding yet in their own way generous forces took charge of Edith Södergran's destiny after the light overture as her richly talented spirit prepared to take over her life. These were Poverty and Death, the two powers that had so often intervened in the destiny of her people, strengthening them as they chastised them.

Her father died of tuberculosis when she was fifteen, and it is reasonable to regard this as the decisive turning-point in her life. Carefree times were over, to be replaced by fear and the necessity to test her own resources. She lost interest in school and expressed a wish to be allowed to leave. After this first warning she seems to have wanted to concentrate her strength on what was essential in the mission that her life was to be. A year later what she had secretly feared happened. Following an attack of pleurisy, tuberculosis struck her in the autumn of 1908 and at once took such a severe form that her illness immediately became a decisive factor in her life. After some time at a sanatorium in Finland she travelled with her trusty companion, her mother, in the autumn of 1911 to Switzerland to undergo pneumothorax[11] treatment in the most favourable conditions possible. According to her doctor this was 'fairly successful'. Her severe cough disappeared, she recovered her spirits and the glorious natural surroundings became a source of refreshment and delight. Her Davos doctor, Dr Muralt, also became an important and positive factor in her life. She was passionately attached to him and never forgot him. When she returned home in the spring of 1913 - 'the happy year' - to her beloved Raivola, where her dog and cat which had been boarded out were waiting to welcome her together with the elderly eccentric called Peck who had found refuge in the Södergran's little cottage,[12] she was feeling well and full of intoxicating dreams of the future. She could feel that her wings had grown and she was ready to write.

Her first published collection, *Poems,* grew out of this atmosphere of carefree optimism and the sheer exhilaration of being alive that followed her first brief but profound brush with death. All the brightness and mischievous glitter and the light, graceful, arabesque-like slyness which was so characteristic of her nature flowered in these pages and presented Swedish-language literature with a captivating and intimate nature-lyricism whose ardent yet delicate and spontaneous refinement is reminiscent of the subtlest Chinese nature-lyrics. A morning dew as of paradise lies over the world, and the feeling for life is simple and strong, spiced with the must of a headstrong temperament. It is as if the nature-god himself has for a moment lent his flute for a dreaming human being to play. Nature's pleasure-garden unfolds before the life-hungry soul like a tissue of symbols and promises full of wonder. The cuckoo calls, happiness hovers in the air like a bird far away on the horizon, and the red rose of love falls on a white breast. But at the same time everything is veiled in sadness and to some extent the mood is one of farewell. The miraculous garden of the poems hides a dark secret. Poem after poem is suffused with death, and even the most insignificant flower in this paradise of nature seems to be waving farewell to one who has already lost it.

Perhaps only someone who knew Edith Södergran can understand just how spontaneously she was being herself in these poems which surprised the world with their new language. Her spirit was not afraid to storm the heavens but she also loved the idyllic and had developed a special free and easy way of life full of excursions, name-day parties,[13] cat-stories and an amusing jargon involving fantastic names for things both living and dead, designed with hidden cunning 'not to arouse the springs of darkness'. Boat trips down the river with its romantic tunnels of dark green foliage, expeditions in search of mushrooms, happy hunting with a camera, favourite walks, all these modest delights are the real background to her poetry's 'sunflame-coloured peaks'[14] and show us the friendly powers this child of nature called on during her silent battle to live.

In her next book Edith Södergran was able to say of herself:[15]

I am strong,
for I have risen from the marble bed of death.

All the powers of destruction seem to have conspired to shatter the happiness and courage of this well-equipped soul. As the young poet with her newly-recovered health prepared to come into her own the terrifying figure of Death crossed her threshold, together with Poverty who brought suffering concealed under her grey mantle. She enjoyed barely a year of happiness before the glare from the world conflagration rose above the horizon. World war, the Russian revolution and civil war in Finland washed in a destructive wave over her life's fragile defences and shook the very foundations of her physical existence. The degree of poverty and deprivation that now afflicted the home of these two totally helpless and unworldly women can only be fully understood by someone who has seen such rudderless lives with their own eyes. The harsh demands of destitution also weakened her powers of resistance against the death lurking in her own breast. Her illness grew worse and her life more restricted; it was as if death were encircling his prey. Not only this, but the spectre of poverty took over the whole district and turned what had been a romantic frontier country into a home of decay and mortality, where people stood face to face with the silent annihilation which follows in the footsteps of war.

In these circumstances Edith Södergran showed no sign of breaking down. Rather, she seemed to derive strength from affliction. It was as if the diamond-hard foundation of her character could not show itself when things were easier. The war upset her, tormenting her with compassion for the sufferings of others, but she was not one to complain on her own account. She dismissed her poverty as a joke played on her by fate and accepted it with unfailing humour. Thus her poetry became what it remains today: a voice speaking strongly to us above the misery of total breakdown.

In the collections which followed, *The September Lyre*, *The Rose Altar* and *The Shadow of the Future*, it is as if a young St George, already mortally wounded, is going forth to conquer the dragon that holds the world in its power. The dragon is suffering, corruption and death, those evil powers that control their own destiny and have taken over the whole world as a field large enough for this destiny to come to full fruition. With saint-like self-mastery this dying woman frees herself from the fetters of her own suffering and instead of bewailing the sufferings of humanity celebrates the future, the noble sun and life which conquers all and can never die. Through powerful visions expressed in rhythms which seem loaded with blazing energy from the sun, she builds a picture of the sacred future which is to be the heritage of purified humanity. She is no longer a poet singing for the sheer joy of singing, but an instrument or tool in the hand of a higher power. Her creative power is not for her own benefit, but is a blessed instrument of the future. Within the walls of her sickroom, through days of agonising struggle against weakness, disinclination and physical exhaustion, she dreams of redeeming the world and raising life to a purer plane with the help of those chosen ministering spirits which work silently towards the liberation of humanity.

When in times like those we are experiencing today[16] one reads these poems from the St George period in Edith Södergran's life, constructed on a grand scale and sometimes apocalyptically fragmented but never less than riveting, one is amazed at the primitive prophetic power in them. Her poems have become greater with the passing of time, instead of shrinking in importance like most literature. The more time has shown us its unadorned face and the deeper we have been able to see into what is really happening in the world, the more clearly we have understood the colossal extent of the upheaval which came out into the open in the First World War and whose end is not yet in sight. In parallel with this development Edith Södergran has come ever closer to us and has had ever more to tell us, in a voice that has become ever more penetrating. In a poem like 'Stormen' (The Storm) - to take only one example - it seems that a spirit of genius has grasped the innermost meaning of the appalling and extraordinary drama which at this moment is being played out in our own human world and also, at the same time, above our heads in the world of gods and demons:[17]

Now earth shrouds herself again in black. A storm
comes up from dark ravines of night to dance
alone his ghostly dance above the earth.
Now people fight again - phantom fights phantom.
Wanting what? Knowing what? Driven
like cattle from dark corners
unable to break free, tied to events,
victims of big ideas that drive their prey before them.
Ideas that vainly stretch beseeching arms in the storm
for the dancer knows he alone rules the world.
The world cannot care for itself. Some things will
crash like a burning house, like a rotten tree;
others stand firm preserved by unknown hands.

And all the time the sun looks on, stars shine on ice-cold nights
and man steals off alone toward boundless bliss.

When this and other similar poems were published - during and
immediately after the First World War - no one understood what they were
about. Up here in the Nordic countries, at least, we firmly believed the war had
been a temporary episode and that after it the world would return to the same
normal order as before. But it has become obvious by now to everybody that
our civilisation is being shaken to its foundations and that as we go from one
catastrophe to the next we are searching for a new way to order our lives. Now
perhaps we can understand that an initiate was speaking in those unnoticed slim
volumes of poetry, and that the lonely destitute girl in Raivola no one took
seriously and who was held up to ridicule by a solid mass of stupidity had in
fact seen what no one else could see: the rapacious hand of the future reaching
out for its prey.

One asks oneself where this isolated and physically weak woman found the
power to see so deeply into the demonic and sacrificial character of the age and
at the same time write so freely and lightly and uncomplainingly of a world she
saw as a battlefield for gods. She herself knew the secret:[18]

Where do the gods live? In my heart,
in my torn, painful, blissful heart,
when the song rises.
- - -
O gods, gods!
In all my weakness I find mighty words -
words for you.

This is what we call inspiration. But it doesn't tell us very much. Where does
her eagle vision come from? Who has given this woman who knows no more
than anyone else such immediate, all-revealing, concise and objective
knowledge? Clearly a superior instinct no less than a sharp, penetrating
analytical gaze must lie behind such prophetic certainty. There was also a
moral quality in Edith Södergran that equipped her better than others to speak
for her time. She was fearless. There was nothing timorous or cowardly about
her. Her whole temperament and character blazed with courage. In both her
poetry and her life she met suffering with a gesture of courage: 'Give me a
hammer to strike sparks - from stone image hew out my soul!'[19] She looked
down into the abyss at the dark brooding spirits of war and revolution with the
same inflexible courage:[20]

Demons,
with all that's serious in me I shall stare into your eyes,
with all my being in my gaze.

Unlike weaker characters she felt no need to shelter behind misty images or other kinds of blinkers. She looked cruelty and horror straight in the eye and let them speak in their own voices. This is why even the most seemingly contradictory ideological manifestations of the time can be accommodated in her poetry with its inherent polarity. And we may ask whether the future she foretold will also confirm the accuracy of her claim about the greatness of humanity as stated in her poems and once alluded to rather carelessly in a letter to the daily press: 'The world belongs to those who have the highest music in them'.[21]

If we can hear this highest music anywhere in its full seraphic purity, it is in her own last poems, those marvellous transfigured poems from the autumn of 1922 in which she took leave of life and at the same time opened the door to the 'land that is not'. A poet can achieve nothing higher than the harmony that came to her in the act of creating these poems, a pure harmony of unheard melodies, of spirit and nature and of death and life. And no one can reach higher than the calm, objective perception of the fulfilment and completion of all things that lies behind such poems as 'Hemkomst' [Homecoming], 'O himmelska klarhet' [O Heavenly Clarity] and 'Landet som icke är' [The Land that is Not].[22]

She did not achieve this harmony lightly. First she needed to overcome a great deal of 'Ahrimanic'[23] resistance within herself and master the weaknesses of an over-sensitive disposition before she could attain the humility which releases the deepest power in a strong soul. What makes her life magnificent, quite apart from what she achieved as a poet, is precisely this tenacious sense of purpose with which she struggled day after day to achieve perfection. What she wrote in her letter to the press quoted above was literally true: she lived the life of a saint and sacrificed every atom of her strength to her high purpose. The extraordinary ill-will and lack of understanding that assailed her when she laid her work before the public, to say nothing of the insular and oppressively intolerant character of artistic life in Finland in those days, hit her particularly hard in the distant and poverty-stricken corner of the country in which she lived. It would have driven a weaker and less generous nature than hers to stagnate in a mood of unfruitful bitterness. But she, doomed as she was to geographical isolation, simply persisted in developing her inner life and searching for the purest sources of inspiration. Her restless intellect had always looked to philosophers for guidance but gradually she turned her back on them all, first her early heroes Schopenhauer and Nietzsche and eventually even Rudolf Steiner, the adored prophet of her later years. In the end the only texts she could accept were the Gospels, by whose light she rediscovered nature in the divinely transfigured form it takes in her last poems:[24]

And earth and flowers and stones talk to the child in their own language,
and the child answering prattles the language of Creation.
And God is concealed in the smallest flower
and things inanimate proclaim his name;
even human hearts cast out by the Father
know not how near he lives.

During the last days of her life, while she was pining away and forgotten by a world slowly returning to dust, it was granted her to experience earthly life as fully and richly as only those can experience it who have seen the last veils fall and opened their hearts to the truth of Oneness. 'The mysteries of religion are the mysteries of nature' she noted in 'Tankar om naturen' [Thoughts about Nature][25] and her last poems are simply variations on this theme. Her own garden, which had whispered nature's secrets in her ear even at the beginning of her career, now returned to her transformed, each blade of grass talking to her of God and welcoming her home as if from a foreign country. 'This is paradise,' she said during the last week of her life as she lay on her daybed on the veranda watching the light green of new leaves shimmering on the trees. It is hardly surprising that all human wisdom should have seemed thin and insipid to her once she had been able to experience the grace which comes from understanding simple things.

In this connection it may be worth quoting from a letter she wrote me about Steiner. That he in particular happened to be the object of her criticism was an accidental, and the result of a great deal of soul-searching; the point is the gulf she had become aware of between even what was to her the best of human philosophy and what she absorbed directly from the Gospels, the only thing that could satisfy her soul: 'I don't believe [Steiner] has the boundlessly rich and warm heart necessary for healing the wounds of war. . . I think even Steiner's decadent, he grates on the Gospels like rusty iron. Christ is sweet, chaste, majestic, a child'.[26] And elsewhere: 'Compared to Christ all is night'.[27]

Edith Södergran died on Midsummer Day 1923.

When I look for the most suitable image from her life to bear in mind as I read her poems, I think of the Whitsuntide[28] walk she took every year with the regularity of ritual. Spring was the great wonder, a mystery to be celebrated. In earlier years she had walked as far as Suomenkylä hill, but like everything else her Whitsun walks had necessarily become more restricted year by year until she could go no further than the 'anemone-meadows'. Her last Whitsun walk was the shortest of all, only as far as the 'meadow with the little yellow suns', as she used to call it. There she sat happily on the grass in her own garden, her trusty old dog Maredinierl[29] at her side, and for the last time greeted the coming of spring to our earth.

NOTES

All individuals mentioned in the notes are Finland-Swedish unless otherwise stated. Abbreviations (for full details of books see 'Further Reading'):

ED   Elmer Diktonius

ES   Edith Södergran

FSLH   *Finlands svenska litteraturhistoria*, vol. II (The Swedish Literary History of Finland. vol. II)

HO   Hagar Olsson

SLSF   Svenska litteratursällskapet i Finland (Swedish Literature Association in Finland)

SS1   *Dikter och aforismer* (*Samlade skrifter* 1, redigerade av Holger Lillqvist)

SS2   Södergran, Edith. *Brev* (*Samlade skrifter* 2, utgivna av Agneta Rahikainen)

General Introduction

1   For a more detailed account of ES's family background and early life, see HO's essay 'The Poet Who Created Herself', pp. 160-171 above.

2   Sweden ruled Finland for several centuries up to 1809. Finland then became an autonomous grand duchy within the Russian empire, gaining her independence in 1917. The Karelian isthmus just west of St Petersburg-Leningrad was lost in March 1940 in the peace settlement that concluded the so-called 'Winter War' between Finland and the Soviet Union and it remains a part of Russia to this day. With it were lost what was one of Finland's most important towns, Viipuri (in Swedish 'Viborg' and in Russian 'Vyborg'), and the family homes of ES at Raivola (in Russian 'Roshchino') and HO a little further north at Räisälä.

3   An exercise book survives containing essays ES wrote when studying English with an Australian fellow-patient in Davos in 1912. In the first of these essays she describes the director of the sanatorium, Dr Ludwig Muralt: 'A serious and steady man, surpassing middle stature, with beautiful and noble traits, large shoulders, a little belly (paunch), with something quiet and superior, charming and mild under a morose appearance. He is a charming, clever brown bear. The form of his nose is ideal. His head is noble and round, His hands have an expression of firmness and cleverness, His feet are perhaps a little long, but the sound of his steps is like exquisit [sic] music.

His eyes are grey, with a greenish sparkle, when he is smiling or amused. He speaks german with a swiss accent, powerful and ingenious.' In another English essay she fantasized about him introducing her to a visiting professor: 'Here is my darling between the pneumothoraxes...'

4   In Lönnroth and Delblanc p. 155.

5   Elmer Diktonius, *Opera omnia / Alla verk / Kaikki teokset*, performed by Taru Valjakka (soprano) and Kauko Kuosma (piano), and issued by Love Records (Finland) in 1976 as LRLP 185. In the same year the dissertation *Diktonius: Modernisti ja säveltäjä* (Diktonius: Modernist and Composer) by Matti Vainio was published by Suomen musiikkitietellinen seura (The Finnish Society for the Study of Music) in Helsinki. Schoolfield (1985, p. 221) describes this dissertation as an 'exhaustive study of Diktonius' compositions and their musical and intellectual background'.

6   Aphorisms have been intermittently popular in Finland-Swedish literature since the eighteenth century, and the form enjoyed a notable revival with the modernist poets, perhaps as a natural stage between prose and 'free' verse. See Holger Lillqvist's article 'Aforismer' in FSLH, pp. 112-114.

7   On Salava and his involvement with *Ultra* see Letter 77/190, note 1.

8   *Hufvudstadsbladet*, 8 December 1957.

9   Zilliacus, FSLH, p. 83.

10   John Keats to George and Georgiana Keats, 20 September 1819.

11   Quoted by Zilliacus, FSLH, p. 111.

12   *Hufvudstadsbladet*, 10 November 1946, quoted at length by Holmström, 1995, p. 48.

13   Schoolfield comments that HO's statements on ES are 'often both possessive and hagiographic' (Schoolfield, 1984 p. 13).

14   For more on Kylli Siegberg and her relations with HO see Letter 41/140, note 1 and the Commentary on Letters 55/163 and 56/164, note 2.

15   The essay was 'Jag lever' (I'm Alive, 1948), reprinted in 1987 with a foreword by Stina Ekblad and afterword by Eric Fylkeson. See Zilliacus, 'Avantgardet i öster', in Lönnroth and Delblanc, p. 160.

16   The final section of the Introduction, 'Ett stycke liv' (A Piece of Life), to HO's *Tidig Prosa*.

Introduction by Hagar Olsson (1955)

1   A small resort on the Mediterranean coast of France just west of Toulon.

2   This happened in the summer of 1946. Gunnar Tideström (1906-85) was a Swedish academic with a special interest in Finland-Swedish literature, Professor of Literary History at Uppsala University, Sweden, 1948-71, author of the monograph *Edith Södergran* (1949), and editor of the first standard edition of ES's poems, *Samlade dikter* (Collected Poems, 1949).

3   HO's comments on Tideström in this Introduction may reasonably lead the reader to believe that there must have been a deep and lasting personal antipathy between them. This was far from the case. Tideström first approached HO about ES in 1946, and over the years gave her unstinting moral and even material support while she came to rely on him as an ever-present friend to whom she could pour out her troubles. The main reason for her fiercely negative initial reaction to his attempts to pry into her relationship with ES was probably not so much a dislike of academic literary biography (though her lifelong feelings on this subject were genuine enough) but precisely because Tideström was touching a raw nerve that something had to touch if her own career as a writer were not to stagnate. Holmström argues (1995, p. 191) that Tideström not only helped her come to terms with her deep-seated guilt about ES in *Ediths brev* (1955) but that by compelling her to face up to her past in general he also helped liberate other areas of her memory for creative use, as for instance in one of her most successful books, the reflective novella *Kinesisk utflykt* (A Chinese Excursion, 1949). Writing to Tideström on 7 January 1949 after he had 'bombarded her with Södergraniana', she blamed herself for being unresponsive:

'Dear Friend,
    I have such an odd memory that it only needs something to give it a nudge and such an awful lot of things come to light that I had thought lost, everything is still there alive and intact, it had just buried itself so deep that one thought it had completely gone. [...] You have to understand that all this 'forgetting' of what happened between Edith and me has its roots in the enormous, almost fatal shock I received when the message that she was dead reached me in the hotel at Bandol. That moment is for ever engraved on my soul, with extraordinary clarity, as the most unbearable I have experienced in this life. From that moment I buried everything personal in our relationship as deep down in myself as I could, I shut it out implacably from my

conscious mind: I had to, if I was to go on living. [...]

Alas, dear man, how it hurts me to think of all this, it should be left undisturbed at least for the present. What a strange tapestry our life is. It's only now, in the last few years, that I've understood in my bones the naked truth in Edith's poem 'Livet' ['Life']: 'Life is being careless with one's own happiness and pushing away the unique moment, life is thinking oneself weak and not having the courage to dare.' How could Edith who was so young have understood everything in that poem so clearly - and this too: 'I, my own prisoner'? But that's what she wrote.'

Hagar

('Life' is an early poem, published in ES's first collection *Dikter* (Poems) in 1916 when she was 24. HO here quotes the last three lines and the first.)

4   When *Ediths brev* finally came out Tideström was generous (letter to HO, 18 December 1955): '[...] I'm so deeply happy the letters have now been published and you've made the commentary just as detailed and as strongly personal as it had to be if the letters were to be understood by a wide readership, and not the least reason I'm so happy is that they've had such a warm and enthusiastic reception. Every so often we all need something that can emphatically contradict the impression of insensitivity and apathy we usually get from the everyday world.

As you well know, there are a couple of points in the book where I do feel a bit like arguing with you, but this seems so meaningless set against one's experience of the whole that we can forget it. If I have been even to the smallest extent one of the causes of the letters being taken from your desk drawer during your lifetime and published with precisely your own commentary, then I have something I can feel really happy about, whatever justification there may or may not be for the existence of literary historians and their methods.'

5   Liberal Swedish-language daily evening paper published in Helsinki.

6   Finland had the status of autonomous grand duchy within the Russian Empire from 1809 to December 1917, when the Finnish government unilaterally declared independence from a Russia in the throes of world war and revolution. In the bitter civil war which followed from January to May 1918 between pro-Bolshevik 'Reds' and anti-Bolshevik 'Whites' more than 30,000 people died. The Whites led by General Mannerheim (see Letter 18/111, note 2) were victorious, and the last part of Finland they reclaimed from the Reds was the area where ES was living, the Karelian isthmus adjoining St Petersburg (or Petrograd as it was known in Russia at the time, a name never used by ES and HO). ES's home village of Raivola had a station on the main-line railway

from Viipuri to Petersburg. The Whites wrested control of this station from the Reds on 23 April 1918, and the same day some of them temporarily moved into the Södergrans' 'villa' or larger house. The Södergrans had already vacated this for economic reasons, moving into a smaller cottage in the grounds where they stayed for the rest of ES's life.

7   During ES's visit to Helsinki in 1917 the young conservative poets Jarl Hemmer (1893-1944) and Erik Grotenfelt (1891-1919) spent an evening with her at the Börs restaurant which lived long in her memory as a unique experience of the bohemian side of the capital's literary life.

8   Pseudonym of the conservative columnist Gustaf Johanson (1880-1959). Later he also sneered at HO (see Letter 18/111, note 1).

9   ES was indeed born in St Petersburg when Finland was part of the Russian Empire and later went to school there, but she had moved to Raivola with her parents when only three months old. See note 3 to Letter 2/91.

10   Ragnar Ekelund (1892-1960), painter and writer. Not to be confused with the writer Ragnar Rudolf Eklund, generally known as R. R. Eklund.

11   'Children of the future'.

12   The full context was: 'My confidence derives from the fact that I have discovered my dimensions'.

13   It is unclear which ES 'notes' HO is referring to. The hyacinth figures in a number of ES's poems (sometimes personified as 'Hyacintha'). In *Framtidens skugga* (The Shadow of the Future, 1920, the last collection published during ES's lifetime), it represents in the poem 'Hyacinten' (The Hyacinth) the eternal life-force breaking forth anew each spring through iron-hard ground and snow. In *The September Lyre*, hyacinths are a positive and powerful image in 'Starka hyacinter' (Strong Hyacinths), written in 1916. But the hyacinth image goes deeper, as Ulla Evers has pointed out in her essay 'Vem var princessan Hyacintha? Om en försvunnen Edith Södergran-text och en essä av Hagar Olsson' (Who Was Princess Hyacintha? A Lost Edith Södergran Text and an Essay by Hagar Olsson) in Schoolfield and Thompson, 1995, pp. 145-55. Shortly after ES's death, HO and Elmer Diktonius (ED), planning to collect the best of her unpublished work in a posthumous volume, turned to ES's mother Helena Södergran who at that time held the surviving manuscripts. Among the things Helena sent them was the manuscript of what she called 'Edith's unfinished Hyacintha poem'. ED wanted to publish this but HO was against it, which upset Helena who asked to have the manuscript back. However, the poem continued to prey on HO's mind to such an extent that she wrote an essay about it which she also sent to Helena, who was so impressed that she suggested it be

used as a preface to the forthcoming volume. By 1925 the volume was ready and given the title *Landet som icke är* (The Land That Is Not), but in place of HO's Hyacintha essay it had a short new foreword (also by HO) which quoted some lines from the Hyacintha poem that were described as 'a fragment of a poem about the secret of [ES's] own creative power'. After 1925 no more was heard of either the poem or HO's essay about it for nearly sixty years until in 1984 HO's biographer Roger Holmström, cataloguing her papers after her death, came across a fifteen-page handwritten manuscript entitled 'Prinsessan Hyacintha'. This has now been published as an appendix to Ulla Evers' doctoral thesis *Hettan av en gud. En studie i skapandetemat hos Edith Södergran* (The Passion of a God: A Study of Creative Themes in Edith Södergran, Gothenburg University, 1992). In her essay HO describes ES's work as a prose-poem, a strange, long, dream-like monologue about a poet called Princess Hyacintha who lives happily with divinely gifted people in a fairy castle where terraces of white marble lead down to a beautiful lake. This Hyacinth-figure, HO goes on, is a self-portrait of ES as poet in fairy-tale terms. From the surviving fragments quoted in HO's essay it emerges that the poem, written in 1917, was an enquiry into what it means to be a poet. At times ES freely interrupted the narrative in her own voice to discuss her problems as a writer, sometimes addressing Hyacintha directly. At one point she declared, 'I do not make poems but create myself, my poems are for me the way to myself', which inspired the title HO gave to her 1940 essay on ES 'The Poet Who Created Herself' (see Appendix) and serves as a title for the present volume. Evers comments that it would have been well if HO's essay on 'Princess Hyacintha' had indeed been used as an introduction to *Landet som icke är* since, together with the extensive knowledge of contemporary psychological and critical theory it shows ES to have had as early as 1917, the poem's consciously analytical and self-critical approach to ES's own work might have gone a long way to offset the subsequent popular image of her as an entirely instinctive writer tossed about by 'tuberculosis euphoria' and even schizophrenia.

NB: In the letters translated here, ES's own style and punctuation have been preserved as far as possible. Underlinings are preserved rather than italicised. Comments by the editor are inserted in square brackets [ ]. Each letter has two numbers, the first its number in the present volume and the second its number in 'SS2' (the 1996 Swedish language edition of the letters, full details of which are included in the Bibliography). The first sixty-two letters in the present edition were written to HO.

1919

LETTER 1/90

1 ES seldom if ever dated her letters, but in most cases the postmark date has survived on envelope or postcard as HO points out in her Introduction. Postmark dates are given in square brackets. No date survives for letter 1/90 but it cannot have been written earlier than 11 January 1919, the day HO's review of *The September Lyre* appeared in *Dagens Press*.

2 A reference to the devil in Maria Lagorio's cover design for *The September Lyre*. In a letter to her publisher's literary adviser Runar Schildt (24 December 1918, SS2 Letter No. 88) ES comments, 'The little figure is stylish and suits the book quite well. But it was not my intention to underline the words "as light and merry as armed devils"; the underlining has crept maliciously into the text. I wish you a merry Christmas.' Runar Schildt (1888-1925) was a cousin of the publisher Holger Schildt (1889-1964). ES met Runar Schildt during her visit to Helsinki in 1917 and he came forward in her defence during the *September Lyre* feud early in 1919. Today Runar Schildt is mainly remembered as one of the finest Finland-Swedish writers of short stories.

3 About half a page has been cut off at this point.

4 The title and first two lines of this poem, lost with the section cut off the letter, have here been restored.

5 SS2 (1996) reads 'ett häng' while HO (1955) reads 'ett bärg', neither of which seems to make sense. I have followed the text as published in SS1 which reads 'ett berg' and implies a misspelling by ES (no uncommon phenomenon in her Swedish). The same word also appears to have been misspelt in a number of other places in the letters. This and most of the other poems ES sent HO with this letter were soon to be published in ES's next collection *Rosenaltaret* (*The Rose Altar*, 1919).

6 Georg Christoph Lichtenberg (1742-1799), German naturalist, mathematician and writer. The 'philosopher's house' is supposedly an allusion to a snail-shell in Lichtenberg.

7 'I approached everyone but reached no one', possibly an allusion to the title of *Also sprach Zarathustra: Ein Buch für Alle und Niemanden* (Thus Spoke Zarathustra, a Book for Everyone and No One, 1883-5). The German philosopher and poet Friedrich Nietzsche (1844 -1900) was a dominating influence in ES's first two collections of poems.

COMMENTARY ON LETTER 1/90

1   This almost certainly refers to HO's difficult relationship with her father, a clergyman of reasonably liberal views but unpredictable and neurotic temperament. See Olof Enckell, *Den unga Hagar Olsson*, pp. 20-21.

LETTER 2/91

1   ES regarded Hemmer and Grotenfelt as prospective allies even though they were followers of an older and more conservative tradition of writing. Both HO and Elmer Diktonius violently attacked Hemmer in particular for his conservatism. Grotenfelt was one of the few reviewers to write perceptively and enthusiastically about ES's first two collections of poems, *Dikter* (Poems, 1916) and *The September Lyre* (1918).

2   'Igor Severyanin' was the pseudonym of Igor Vassilyevich Lotarev (1887-1941 or 1942), a leading figure in the St Petersburg 'ego-futurist' movement; ES had once heard him give a recitation at Raivola. The Moscow futurists, whose most prominent representative was Vladimir Mayakovsky, called themselves 'cubo-futurists'. The original futurists in Italy had set out to glorify the advent of the new industrial age of fast transport, factories and urban masses, but the Russian futurists were more interested in liberating the word from its 'traditional subservience to meaning', replacing this with new meaning derived from the word's graphic and phonetic characteristics. Thus, for them, the sign became more important than its object, and outward form and sensory texture more important than communicative value. This 'creative distortion' linked literary futurism to cubism and surrealism in the visual arts. See Victor Ehrlich, *Russian Formalism*, 4th edition, The Hague, 1980, pp. 44-47. For a more detailed discussion of ego-futurism and Severyanin, see Markov, especially pp. 61-101.

3   St Petersburg's fashionable and excellent 'Die deutsche Hauptschule zu Sankt-Petri' (St Peter's German High School), where the language of instruction was German. This was preferred by ES's parents to the Swedish-language school which also existed in St Petersburg. German became the language ES spoke most fluently, and nearly all her earliest poems were written in German.

4   'Pneumothorax is the pressure of air in the pleural cavity...An artificial pneumothorax can readily be induced by inserting a hollow needle through the chest wall; this was formerly used as a method of resting the lung in the treatment of pulmonary tuberculosis,' *The Oxford Companion to Medicine*, 1986, p. 1112.

5   This was the larger of the two wooden houses the Södergrans owned in the same grounds. They had closed it up for economic reasons in 1916 and were now living in the smaller of the two.

6   The famous 'bohemian' evening at the Börs restaurant in Helsinki in 1917.

7   *The Story of Gösta Berling* (1891), first and most famous novel by the Swedish writer and Nobel Prize winner Selma Lagerlöf (1858-1940).

8   *Hufvudstadsbladet.*

9   Runar Schildt.

10   Here, towards the end of this long letter, ES uses for the first time in writing to HO the informal Swedish word for 'you', indicating an assumption of close friendship. While writing the letter she may have become conscious of the growing clash between her polite formal pronouns and her intimate subject-matter.

11   'fit to travel'.

COMMENTARY ON LETTER 2/91

1   HO was writing in 1955.

2   Hjalmar Procopé (1868-1927), Arvid Mörne (1876-1946) and Bertel Gripenberg (1878-1947) were leading poets of the previous generation. Procopé was one of the literary figures ES called on during her 1917 visit to Helsinki. When in 1915, still unpublished, she had shown Mörne some of her poems written in 1912-14 he had remarked: 'Can't you see for yourself how fine your poems are?' (See Letter 61/172, note 6 for the less positive 1915 reaction of Gunnar Castrén.) Sven Lidman (1882-1960) was a novelist from Sweden.

3   It appeared in *Hufvudstadsbladet* on 23 January, and was a reply to Jumbo's attack on ES in the same paper.

4   A leading Stockholm daily.

5   'Jumbo' had brought the neurologist and psychiatrist Harald Fabritius (1877-1946) into the feud to add weight to his contention that ES was mentally disturbed. However, this ploy backfired when Fabritius in his article 'Miss Edith Södergran: Prophetess or Swindler?', published in *Dagens Press* on 25 January 1919, credited her with an unusual capacity for associative thought and a very individual imagination.

LETTER 3/92

1   ES may be referring to a letter written to the publisher Schildt on 30 November 1916 by three women asking him for a written assurance that their good friend 'frk Sörensen' is not the author of ES's first book *Dikter*. ES may have heard about this letter from HO but it is impossible to say how HO herself can have got to know about it.

2   'The obscurity in which the gods hide us'.

LETTER 4/93

1   ES here withdraws the grammatical intimacy begun towards the end of letter 2/91 by reverting to the more formal and in this context chillier Swedish word for 'you'.

2   But here she returns to the friendlier and less formal 'you'.

COMMENTARY ON LETTER 4/93

1   Pär Lagerkvist (1891-1974), Swedish poet, novelist and dramatist.

LETTER 5/94

1   *The September Lyre* 'feud'.

LETTER 6/95

1   'unfortunate letter'.

2   Presumably a reference to one of ES's two letters to *Dagens Press* about *The September Lyre*.

COMMENTARY ON LETTERS 5/94 AND 6/95

1   The actual words HO uses are 'de ahrimanska elementen'. Originally a Zoroastrian concept, Ahriman is the force of materialism in the philosophy of Rudolf Steiner, who later came to have an enormous influence on ES. On Ahriman, see also Letter 47/146, note 4.

2   The writer Ragnar Rudolf Eklund (1895-1946), better known as R. R. Eklund, was engaged to HO from 1917 to 1920. He should not be confused with the painter and writer Ragnar Ekelund (1892-1960), as already mentioned in note 10 to HO's Introduction.

3   Published later in 1919.

LETTER 7/96

1   Or, 'I want to see in my sister a mermaid to hold me captive for many

years; I want to contemplate the god in her'. The original is ambiguous, no doubt unintentionally.

2   The 'Hyacintha' of the poem is ES in her function as poet. See HO's Introduction, note 13.

COMMENTARY ON LETTER 7/96

1   The official Swedish-language student newspaper of Helsinki University.

2   Local Swedish-language newspaper in Vaasa (in Swedish 'Vasa'), principal town of Ostrobothnia on the west coast of central Finland, one of the main Swedish-speaking areas in the country.

LETTER 9/98

1   'Prana' is the 'air of life' in Hindu and Buddhist religious philosophy. ES's use of the word is probably evidence of the influence of Nietzsche.

2   'A shooting up of weeds'.

COMMENTARY ON LETTERS 8/97 AND 9/98

1   Gustaf Fröding (1860-1911), Swedish poet.

2   This is the sentence ES had taken as a direct message from HO to herself.

LETTER 10/99

1   The word 'tower' apears neither in the relevant chapter nor anywhere else in HO's narrative prose-poem *Kvinnan och nåden* (Woman and Grace) nor in R. R. Eklund's collection of prose-poems *Jordaltaret* (The Earth Altar), both of which were published by Schildt later in 1919.

2   From *The Earth Altar* (p. 43), where Eklund speaks of the first morning of Creation which 'drips its dew on exhausted senses'.

3   ES, HO and R. R. Eklund.

4   The first parliamentary elections after Finland's declaration of independence (December 1917) were held in March 1919.

5   The cat ES calls 'Nonno' in Letter 6/95. See note 2 to HO's Commentary on this letter, and the text to which it refers.

6   Akademiska Bokhandeln (The Academic Bookshop, in Finnish 'Akateeminen Kirjakauppa'), still one of Helsinki's two leading bookshops.

7   The 'unwritten' letter is mentioned again in Letter 100.

COMMENTARY ON LETTER 10/99

1   Under the title 'Pathétique, a Chapter from a Work in Progress'.

2   'Multiple naming' has been seen by psychologists as an index of affection: the more names you give a person or animal, the more you love them. See R. Brown and M. Ford, 'Address in American English', *Journal of Abnormal and Social Psychology*, vol 62 (1961), reprinted in John Laver and Sandy Hutcheson (eds), *Communication in Face to Face Interaction*, Harmondsworth: Penguin, 1972, pp. 128-145, especially p. 136. Some commentators seem to have taken the multiple names as evidence that ES had a close relationship with more than one cat during 1919-23, the period in which these letters were written. It is true that photographs taken by ES often show two or more cats, but none of these photographs was taken after 1917. In any case, it seems to me that Letter 6/95 and HO's commentary on it make it quite clear that there was only one cat.

3   A reference to the end of letter 5/94.

4   Max Hanemann lived from 1881 to 1945. Artur Eklund (1880-1927) made his name as a philosopher of sport. Here is the final sentence of his 'gruesome' obituary of ES which filled a whole front-page column of *Svenska Pressen*, as *Dagens Press* had now become, on 28 June 1923: 'Yet her highly-strung will gave but an illusion of strength, and the most she achieved was to be a human soul standing outside the front door of life, longing and dreaming and strewing a few handfuls of the flowers of poesy before stepping back once again into a world of which she had perhaps preserved a few dimly charming memories.'

LETTER 11/100

1   'T.f.' is an abbreviation for 'tillförordnad' (Swedish for 'acting'), used when work is being temporarily done by a stand-in. HO published nothing in *Dagens Press* between 5 and 19 March 1919.

2   In Nietzsche the term Dionysiac denotes the powerful reaction of spontaneity, instinct and nature against reason, utilitarianism and philistinism. Dionysiac art expresses the fundamental urge not to conform.

3   St Petersburg. The catastrophic situation in the city was described in a report in *Dagens Press* on 19 March ('The Latest News from St Petersburg'). There was a massive shortage of food: 'The Bolsheviks distribute little more than 200 grams of bread a day to manual workers and little more than 100 to Bolshevik officials. The rest of the population get nothing at all unless they can find something on the black market.' Epidemics spread: typhus, smallpox and typhoid fever affected so many that the hospitals hadn't room

to take them all in. The city's inhabitants were paralysed by general stagnation and gloom.

4   Hagar.

LETTER 12/101

1   Possibly San Mommé, near Pistoia and not far from Florence in Tuscany. ES and her mother visited Milan and Florence in 1913, but we have no details of their itinerary.

2   Ellen Key (1849-1926), Swedish writer who promoted the emancipation of women and children; ES admired her work.

3   *Die Morgenröte* (Dawn or Dawn of Day, 1881); *Menschliches, Allzumenschliches* (Human, All Too Human, 1878); *Die Geburt der Tragödie aus dem geiste der Musik* (The Birth of Tragedy from the Spirit of Music, 1872). SS2 points out that although Nietzsche started a work with the title *The Will to Power* he never finished it; the book of that title published under his name in 1906 was assembled by his sister, Elisabeth Förster-Nietzsche, who distorted the text after his death in 1900. A version of Nietzsche's work in progress with that title has been translated into English by Walter Kaufmann and R. J. Hollingdale (*The Will to Power*, London: Weidenfeld, 1968). Probably several of the works by Nietzsche that ES names in her letter did reach her through HO, but there is no way of knowing which.

COMMENTARY ON LETTERS 11/100 AND 12/101

1   ES may have persuaded herself that Ellen Key had - at least figuratively - been Nietzsche's 'maitresse'. Key was deeply influenced by Nietzsche's writings and many of her own works bear traces of his thought.

LETTER 13/103

1   The second numeral is non-consecutive here and elsewhere in this book because SS2 contains a good many letters written by ES to people other than Hagar Olsson and Elmer Diktonius. Most of these are of no special interest in the present context.

2   The 'Spanish' flu epidemic which started in Europe in 1918 is said to rank with the Black Death as the severest outbreak of disease yet known. Up to twenty million people died world-wide and fifty times as many contracted the disease. Ten months after this (January 1920) ES did become seriously ill with 'Spanish' flu, no light thing in her weak state of health; see Letter 33/127, note 1 and Letter 34/129.

3   Selma Lagerlöf. HO had never met her and had no interest in calling on her, but ES admired Lagerlöf so much that she sent her copies of her own volumes of poems with personal dedications. See letter 28/121, note 2.

COMMENTARY ON LETTER 13/103

1   In *Dagens Press*.

2   August Strindberg (1849-1912), Swedish dramatist, novelist, short story writer, poet, painter and pamphleteer.

LETTER 14/104

1   The manuscript of ES's new collection of poems *Rosenaltaret* (The Rose Altar). SS2 claims ES hoped HO would pass it on to the publisher, Schildt, after editing it. But surely internal evidence in letters 13/103 and 14/104 makes it clear that ES was very anxious to have the manuscript back again as quickly as possible if HO was too busy to look through it, and to know what HO might suggest leaving out if she did have time to look through it. There is no evidence in these letters that ES wanted HO to pass the poems on directly to Schildt.

2   Stockholm.

LETTER 15/105

1   Park in central Stockholm where the world's first open-air museum was opened in 1891.

2   In Dostoevsky's novel *Crime and Punishment* (1866; part IV, chapter 4) Sonya reads from the Bible to Raskolnikov about the raising of Lazarus from the dead (John 11 and 12). Schoolfield comments (1984, p. 96), 'With some perversity, Edith Södergran chooses a major "Christian" passage in *Crime and Punishment* in order to make her anti-Christian point. What she means is that she wants Hagar to listen to the poem with the same intensity as Raskolnikoff listened to Sonja's reading of John 11: "he knew... that she herself was most anxious to read to *him*, and to him alone, and to make sure that he *heard*, heard it now." Shortly, of course, Edith Södergran would read the Gospels with a devotion equalling Sonja's own.'

3   Quoted from the poem 'Gudorna skall komma...' (The Gods shall come) in *The Rose Altar* (1919).

4   See Letter 1/90, note 7.

5   SS2 comments baldly 'Engelsmännen bombar Kronstadt' (The British bomb Kronstadt). The British and their allies supplied the White Russian

forces with money, equipment and instructors but never declared war on the Bolsheviks or bombed Kronstadt, the Russian naval base on Kotlin island very near the Finnish coast and Raivola. The British Prime Minister, Lloyd George, was strongly opposed to official intervention in the Russian civil war and stated in January 1919: 'the mere idea of crushing Bolshevism by military force is pure madness'.

6   ES admired the German poet Johan Wolfgang von Goethe (1749-1832) and read many of his works at various times in her life, copying out quotations. Anthroposophists (followers of Rudolf Steiner, see Letter 29/122, notes 7 to 9) considered Goethe an 'initiate', and many of Steiner's writings were strongly influenced by Goethe's nature mysticism.

7   'Every poem is written on a particular occasion'. ES may be interpreting Goethe to mean that all poems result from a specific spontaneous impulse, so that 'spontaneous' poetry is nothing new.

8   This poem was left out of *The Rose Altar* and first published in Tideström's edition of ES's *Collected Poems* (1949).

9   It is impossible to discover now what alteration HO suggested for this poem; the only manuscript version still in existence was copied out in pencil by HO.

10   There is no surviving poem with this title but the phrase can be found in the poem 'Letters from my sister' which was mentioned earlier in this letter.

LETTER 16/106

1   The manuscript of *The Rose Altar* has not survived so it is impossible now to establish exactly which poems ES originally included in it. No existing poem has the title 'Eros' but ES may be referring to some other Eros-related poem since she is inconsistent in her use of titles for her own poems. The most likely candidate among the surviving poems is 'Till Eros' (To Eros), printed posthumously in *Landet som icke är* (1925; The Land That Is Not). Five other Eros-related poems (listed in SS2, p. 120) were printed the following year (1920) in *The Shadow of the Future*, but ES is probably not referring to any of these since she passed them for publication not long afterwards. She may also be referring to the lost poem 'Eros och skönheten' (Eros and Beauty) which Schildt had also excluded from the printed version of *The Rose Altar*.

2   'Pansartåget' (The Armoured Train) was also included in the original manuscript of *The September Lyre* but was nonetheless omitted from the

published collection and did not appear in print until Tideström's *Collected Poems* (1949). McDuff, in his English translation of ES's poems (1984), restores this and some other poems to *The September Lyre*.

3   No poem with this title - 'Evening Mood' in English - survives but ES may have been referring to 'Aftonvandring' (Evening Walk) which was included in the manuscript for *The September Lyre* but left out of the printed version.

4   No poem with the title 'Blå rök' (Blue Smoke) survives, but this may be a reference to the poem 'Verktygets klagan' (The Tool's Complaint) which begins 'Life sank before me in blue smoke' and was published in *The Rose Altar*.

5   Mentioned in ES's previous letter (15/105).

LETTER 17/109

1   R. R. Eklund's *The Earth Altar* (1919).

2   Perhaps some political event relating to the end of the First World War.

3   The books ES mentioned in Letter 12/101.

4   See HO's Commentary on Letter 19/112.

5   Finlands Svenska Författareförening; its official English name today is 'The Society of Swedish Authors in Finland'. It was founded on 11 January 1919 and a large number of Finland-Swedish writers were invited to join.

LETTER 18/111

1   As already mentioned (note 8 to HO's Introduction), 'Jumbo' (Gustaf Johansson) was a journalist of reactionary stamp. On 4 May 1919 he mocked HO (in her 'Rachel' persona, see HO's commentary on Letter 16/106) in *Hufvudstadsbladet* for remarks she had made about the Eve of 1 May (Walpurgisnacht), which is traditionally celebrated in Finland, especially by young people. 'Jumbo' sneered: 'I've been a bit curious to know how little Rachel was feeling the morning after. I mean of course the little charmer (I don't know her personally) who writes a column in *Dagens Press*. I can't help wondering what on earth she can have been up to the night before... I really mustn't withhold this little gem from any of my readers who may have missed it. It ends: "Let us go out tonight among the howling packs of trolls and strike bargains for our souls"... not that I'm any great believer in the existence of tiny female souls, especially after reading Rachel's little piece.' 'Jumbo' had of course attacked ES during the *September Lyre* 'feud'.

2   Baron Carl-Gustaf von Mannerheim (1867-1951) served in the Russian

army 1889-1917, commanded the victorious 'White' guard in the Finnish civil war of 1918, and became Regent of Finland 1918-19 (the original intention had been for independent Finland to become a monarchy). Later he led Finland's defence against the Soviet Union in the wars of 1939-40 and 1941-44 before finishing his career as President of the Republic 1944-46.

3   Perhaps a reference to Ellen Key and Selma Lagerlöf, mentioned by ES in Letters 12/101 and 13/103.

LETTER 19/112

1   A reference to the poem 'Var bo gudarna' (Where do the gods live).

COMMENTARY ON LETTER 19/112

1   HO quotes the entire poem in her essay 'Diktaren som skapade sig själv' ('The Poet Who Created Herself'); see Appendix, page 169. The poem was first published in *The Rose Altar* (1919) as 'Stormen' (The Storm).

LETTER 20/113

1   HO was also on the Karelian isthmus, about 100 km (as the crow flies) north of Raivola at her family home in the village of Räisälä, the country parish where her father Karl Sixtus Olsson (1855-1937) had been pastor since 1906. On the kind of life she led when staying there with her parents see her commentary on Letter 26/119.

LETTER 21/114

1   R. R. Eklund.

2   In *The Earth Altar*.

LETTER 22/115

1 During this period of unrest in Russia residents and visitors to the frontier district on the Finnish side of the border could not travel without a special pass issued by the Finnish military authorities.

COMMENTARY ON LETTER 22/115

1   i.e. the Finnish military authorities.

LETTER 23/116

1   Probably Major-General Carl Gustaf (Gösta) Theslöf (1872-1939), active in the capture of Viipuri during the 1918 Finnish civil war.

2   A village on the Viipuri-St Petersburg railway just before Raivola. ES

always uses its Swedish name 'Nykyrka'.

3   Gustaf Bernhard Kasper Holmström (1869-1932), civil administrator at Raivola from 1918 to 1922.

LETTER 24/117

1   Illegible word.

2   But two months later she will complain, 'I'd rather not have Lagorio's apes on the cover this time' (Letter 46/145).

LETTER 26/119

1   The Raivola civil defence corps had no home of its own until 1932. Before this date it rented various villas including the Södergrans' larger house, which had already briefly served as a billet in April 1918 when White troops captured Raivola in the civil war.

2   Possibly the letter mentioned previously in Letters 10/99 and 11/100.

3   'back on the rails'.

LETTER 27/120

1   Street in Viipuri, in Swedish 'Alexandersgatan'.

2   The local defence commandant at Raivola at this time was a 22-year-old infantry captain, Hugo Einari Suoranta.

3   'Alfa' was probably the offices of a Swedish firm in Aleksanterinkatu, Viipuri.

LETTER 28/121

1   ES's new book *The Rose Altar*. HO was at this time on holiday in the Åland Islands, not far from Stockholm.

2   Selma Lagerlöf. There are copies of *The Rose Altar* and *The Shadow of the Future* in her library at Mårbacka, Sweden. In the former ES has written 'To Selma Lagerlöf as a mark of my delight in the saga of sagas. Edith Södergran' (the 'saga of sagas' being of course Lagerlöf's famous novel *The Story* [or Saga] *of Gösta Berling*). ES presumably sent Lagerlöf *The Shadow of the Future* late in 1920, and her dedication reads, 'A Christmas greeting to Selma Lagerlöf from Edith Södergran'.

3   Severyanin went into political exile in Estonia in January 1919 and stayed there until his death in 1941 or 1942. It is not known whether Severyanin's copy was ever sent off or reached him; ES probably did not know he had gone into exile.

4   The copy of *The Rose Altar* for the Swedish poet Vilhelm Ekelund (1880-1949) was not posted till 3 February 1920 (see Letter 34/129). The dedication reads 'To Vilhelm Ekelund with thanks from Edith Södergran. A greeting from young Finland.'

5   What Schoolfield (1984, p. 109) calls 'intense and self-engendered eroticism'.

6   See HO's commentary on this letter, note 1.

7   Goethe's play *Torquato Tasso* (final version 1789), whose subject is the Italian Renaissance poet's unrequited love for Duchess Leonora of Ferrara.

8   Råtte and Totti (and Nonno, Råttikus, etc.) were one and the same cat. On multiple naming, see Commentary on Letter 10/99, note 2.

9   The 'will to power', an essential quality of the Nietzschean Superman.

10   The American writer Edgar Allan Poe (1809-49).

11   There were (and are) 100 pence in a Finnish mark.

12   Presumably for the large Södergran villa which they were hoping to sell.

13   Helena Södergran wrote in a manuscript memoir note about her daughter that Edith was 'related as an artist to Arnold Böcklin'. Böcklin (1827-1901) was with Ferdinand Hodler (see Letter 29/122, note 8) the leading Swiss painter of the nineteenth century. He spent much of his life in Italy and his later work, often sombre and mystical, is considered to be among the most distinguished symbolist painting done outside France. His morbid imagery also appealed to the surrealists. The Swedish painter and etcher Anders Zorn (1860-1920) was criticized as early as the 1880s for the photographic exactitude of his work. He was a cosmopolitan figure (based in London 1882-85), a society portrait painter who painted several Presidents of the United States but is apparently now most admired for his unashamedly voluptuous nudes. ES had one of these on a postcard she later sent HO (see Letter 74/187, note 1).

14   Refers to Arvid Mörne's review of *The Rose Altar* (see HO's Commentary below).

15   Written by Helena Södergran.

16   ES added this note on the back of the page.

COMMENTARY ON LETTER 28/121

1   Karl Bruhn (1894-1948) was editor of the local Vaasa newspaper *Vasabladet* from 1918 to 1925, and later for many years Professor of Education at Helsinki University. He produced a linguistically pedantic

review of *The Rose Altar* in *Vasabladet* on 13 June 1919 under the heading 'Homegrown Literary Experiments' and this was later reprinted with most of its word-count statistics omitted in the 16 July number of *Nya Argus*. In the *Vasabladet* version he described 'I mörkret' (In the Darkness), one of the so-called sister-poems, as 'floating, ethereal poetry'.

2   Though politically part of Finland, the Åland Islands ('Ahvenanmaa' in Finnish) are nearer to the Swedish coast than to mainland Finland and are even now almost exclusively Swedish-speaking.

3   Neither can HO or the note in SS2. The 'prosaic object' that everyone is too modest to name can only have been a chamber pot (the SS2 editor privately holds the same view). ES's word 'drabant' has the basic meaning 'guardsman' while it also carries a phonetic hint of 'drabbas' (to be stricken). It is probably an example of ES's love of humorous private wordplay rather in the manner of James Joyce; she obviously assumed HO would understand what she meant and was surprised when her mother didn't.

LETTER 29/122

1   HO's prose-poem *Woman and Grace*, which came out in autumn 1919.

2   ES is here quoting word for word from the penultimate aphorism in her collection *Brokiga iakttagelser* (Motley Observations, 1919). She sent the manuscripts of both this and *The Shadow of the Future* to her publisher during this month, November 1919. Schildt decided to publish the aphorisms separately (never ES's intention) for Christmas 1919 and held the poems back until the following year.

3   This may be 'Älvdrottningens spira' (The Elf-Queen's Sceptre), printed in *The Shadow of the Future*, the only surviving poem from this period in which ES uses the word 'ring' in the sense of something precious you wear on your finger. She sent the manuscript to the publisher a few days after writing this letter.

4   The Freie Hochschule für Geisteswissenschaft (School of Spiritual Science), headquarters of the Anthroposophical Society. The original Goetheanum, planned by Rudolf Steiner and others, was a wooden building completed in 1914 but burned down during the night of New Year's Eve 1922-23 at the instigation of the Roman Catholic priest of the neighbouring village, Arlesheim. ES mentions the event in Letter 98/213. The present (concrete) Goetheanum was not opened until 1928.

5   Rudolf Steiner (1861-1925), Austrian-born philosopher, natural scientist, educationist and Goethe-scholar. He lectured in Finland (including

a talk on the deeper meaning of the national epic *Kalevala*) by invitation in 1912 and 1913 shortly after breaking with theosophy and founding his own movement, which he called 'anthroposophy'. Anthroposophy is a philosophy (or revelation, depending on one's point of view) based on the premise that the human intellect is capable of contacting spiritual worlds. The first of Steiner's books ES read was *Die geistige Führung des Menschen und der Menschheit* (The Spiritual Guidance of Mankind, 1911), in a Swedish translation first published in 1913.

6   Steiner believed that human beings consist of an ego, an astral body (as do animals), an ethereal body (as do animals and plants) and a physical body (as do animals, plants and minerals). The ethereal body is the life body: on death the ethereal body leaves the physical body of the organism, which then decays. Without an astral body there can be no consciousness. It is the task of the ego to transform the astral body so that a 'spiritual eye' can develop.

7   Steiner, many of whose writings were strongly influenced by Goethe's nature mysticism, believed Goethe had access to occult knowledge, but 'initiate' is not a word anthroposophists would use, since anthroposophy has no creed or party line.

8   Ferdinand Hodler (1853-1918) and Arnold Böcklin (see Letter 28/121, note 13) were the leading Swiss painters at the turn of the century. About 1890 Hodler turned from naturalism to symbolism and became a forerunner of expressionism. Like Rudolf Steiner, Hodler was influenced by the Rosicrucians. He was officially disgraced in Germany for signing a protest against the German bombardment of Rheims cathedral in 1914. Contrast Pierre Drieu la Rochelle's view of this event (Letters 32/126, note 8 and 87/201, note 1).

9   Giotto di Bondone 1266/7 or 1276-1337, Florentine painter, sculptor and architect, generally regarded with Cimabue as a founder of modern painting.

COMMENTARY TO LETTER 29/122

1   *Wie erlangt man Erkenntnisse der höherer Welten?* (1909). The titles in English of its two volumes are *The Way of Initiation, or How to Obtain Knowledge of the Higher Worlds* and *Initiation and its Results*.

2   Translation by McDuff, 1984, pp. 171-172.

3   As they also do in SS1 (1990).

4   Olof Enckell (1900-89), novelist and critic, Professor of Swedish Literature at Helsinki University (1950-67), brother of the modernist poet and critic Rabbe Enckell. Olof Enckell was a pioneer in the field of Finland-

Swedish modernist studies, notably in his books *Den unga Hagar Olsson* (1949) and *Den unge Diktonius* (The Young Diktonius, 1946).

5   HO is of course writing in 1955.

6   Muralt himself suffered from lung tuberculosis. He died suddenly in 1917 and according to the Södergran's Davos acquaintance Elise Bogs, the poem 'Trädet i skogen' (The Tree in the Forest) in *The September Lyre* is a reaction to his death. For ES's description of him written in English as an exercise at Davos see Introduction, note 3.

LETTER 30/123

1   This was Elsa Kataja (1892-1969), a friend of HO's who was working as a dentist in Viipuri. ES often refers to her as 'Kanerva', apparently confusing 'Kataja' with another Finnish surname. See Commentary on Letter 75/188, note 1.

2   ES appears to have heard about a review written in Finnish by one Rafael Forsman under the title 'Edith Södergran, *The Rose Altar*' in the Finnish-language periodical *Aika* (No. 10, 1919). In it Forsman does not compare ES to anyone of the name of Eklund or Ekelund. But it is followed in the same number by a review, also written by Forsman, of R. R. Eklund's *The Earth Altar*, which compares R.R.E.'s prose poems with ES's poems: 'If the rhythm of [R.R.E.'s] style were not so slow-moving and ethereal one could construct free verse similar to ES's from his sentences. But Eklund's temperament is not so laconically concentrated as Södergran's nor so subjective.'

3   ES jotted down several quotes from the Belgian symbolist poet and dramatist Maurice Maeterlinck (1862-1949) in a notebook dating from her early years.

LETTER 31/124

1   The cat was killed by next-door neighbours.

2   *Die Geheimwissenschaft in Umriss* (An Outline of Occult Science, later known as Occult Science, an Outline, 3rd edn 1910).

3   Steiner worked as a researcher at the Goethe archive in Weimar from 1888 to 1897. During this time he took over preparation of *Goethes naturwissenschaftliche Schriften* (Goethe's Writings on Natural Science, 1884-97), which he edited with a commentary.

4   About 1881 Steiner 'met an initiated master' who had an important influence on his progress towards anthroposophy. This is believed to have been Goethe.

5   SS2 here prints 'arms' before 'hands' to indicate that in the original manuscript letter the new word was written over the crossed-out one rather than after it. I have preferred what seems to me a more natural reading order. The same thing happens in three or four other places in the present selection of letters.

6   In late January 1920 ES was forced to remind Schildt he had not sent the advance he had promised for her book of aphorisms.

7   This was the Rafael Forsman review mentioned in Letter 30/123, note 2.

8   The Swedish writer Anna-Lenah Elgström (1884-1968) was active in the women's and peace movements and was one of the founders in Sweden of 'Save the Children'. HO had known her since 1918, and in September 1922 published two poems written by her in traditional style in the second number of the new review *Ultra*. An article in Finnish in *Ultra* 4 describes Elgström as 'the poet of heroism'.

9   Hjalmar Procopé, whom ES had met in Helsinki in 1917, and who had later come to her defence in the September Lyre 'feud'; see HO's Commentary on Letter 2/91.

10   'Bellicism' was a literary trend in France that glorified war, a deliberate counterblast to pacifism. See Letter 32/126, note 8, and Letter 87/201, note 1.

COMMENTARY ON LETTER 31/124

1   Alias Rafael Forsman (Letter 30/123, note 2). 'Koskimies' is the direct Finnish translation of 'Forsman'. In nineteenth-century Finland many Finnish-speakers took Swedish surnames, which they hoped would help make them more upwardly mobile among the largely Swedish-speaking bourgeoisie of the time. But in the first decades of newly independent Finland (the twenties and thirties) this was no longer the case; it was now more fashionable to have a Finnish surname and some families even deliberately switched languages from Swedish to Finnish.

1920

LETTER 32/126

1   Properly 'Angelus Silesius', pseudonym of Johann Scheffler (1624-77), German hymn-writer and mystic.

2   Johannes Eckehart, also known as 'Meister Eckhart' (c1260-c1327), German theologian and mystic philosopher.

3   ES is unlikely to have known that Steiner met Nietzsche in 1889 during his time at Weimar and was so interested in him that he wrote a book about him: *Friedrich Nietzsche. Ein Kämpfer gegen seine Zeit* (Friedrich Nietzsche, a Fighter for Freedom, 1895) plus a number of lesser writings. However, Steiner later (about 1900) distanced himself from Nietzsche.

4   It is not clear what ES means by this, though Steiner's writings were influenced by Rosicrucian thought.

5   The Södergrans' nextdoor neighbours at Raivola were the industrialist Ilya Galkin (1847-1923) and his large family. ES suspected that one or other of the Galkins' nine children had shot her cat. She had earlier been on friendly terms with at least two of the children, whose native language was Russian.

6   Ragnar Ekelund, not R. R. Eklund.

7   HO's book *Woman and Grace*.

8   On 29 November 1919 *Dagens Press* printed an article that had originally appeared in the German newspaper *Berliner Tageblatt* about the French writers Pierre Drieu la Rochelle and Joachim Gasquet and their glorification of war. The German writer of the article, Victor Aubertin, assumes the two are young and pours scorn on them. He quotes a 'hymn' by Gasquet: 'Hate is glorious; and, my God, how beautiful is war; war is sacred, it is the brother of Jesus Christ.' Aubertin notes that the more up-to-date Drieu would be happy to replace the ruins of Rheims cathedral with a futurist building of iron and cement. But the ultimate insult is that the 'bellicists' presume to congratulate Germany on starting the war and destroying the cathedral. There is no evidence that 'bellicism' was a widespread movement: Aubertin's report is based on just two collections of poems, Gasquet's *Les hymnes* and Drieu's *Interrogation*. In some quarters in France the experience of the 1914-18 war, so much of it fought on French territory, had reinforced the influence of Nietzsche: life must be lived at full intensity, the only way to tap the deepest sources of power and energy in human nature and inspire heroism and new moral values. Imbued with a sense of the decadence of contemporary society, Pierre Drieu la Rochelle (1893-1945), later best known as a novelist, short-story writer, essayist and journalist, was attracted first to communism and later to fascism; at this time he was dreaming of political renewal and a united Europe, and to this extent he would have been on the same wavelength as ES, although she was never happy with the idea of physical violence (see, for example, her comment to ED in Letter 64/175 about lashing out with an axe). Joachim Gasquet (1873-1921), twenty years Drieu's senior, was principally a poet and playwright. See also Letter 87/201, note 1.

9   See Letter 29/122, note 4.

10   Arnulf Øverland (1889-1968), Norwegian poet, left-wing polemicist and man of letters.

11   The Finnish and Finland-Swedish painters Tyko Sallinen (1879-1955), Juho Rissanen (1873-1950), Marcus Collin (1882-1966), and Fanny Churberg (1845-92) had all studied in Paris and been influenced to varying degrees by impressionism, expressionism and the trend towards modernism. Churberg, admired particularly as a landscape painter, had been ahead of her time in Finland. The other three (like, for example, the composer Sibelius) produced modernist nationalist work at a time when Finland was desperate to shake off Russia and find her own identity. Collin and Sallinen were the pioneers in this field and Sallinen its outstanding exponent, specialising in harsh Karelian landscapes populated by unsophisticated peasants. His work had recently attracted attention at much-discussed exhibitions in Stockholm, Copenhagen and the United States (see articles in *Dagens Press* on 9 October and 23 December 1919), and in 1923 he would illustrate HO and ED's presentation of the work of young Finland-Swedish poets in the periodical *Frihet.*

COMMENTARY ON LETTER 32/126

1   Dagmar von Schantz (1864-1936) had moved to Raivola in 1919 with her elderly mother. She had heard Steiner lecture in Munich and made notes on some of his unpublished lectures. ES also had contact with another anthroposophist, the Helsinki physical training instructor Sigrid Fontell (1887-1953), who from 1918 often visited friends in Raivola.

LETTER 33/127

1   The section between square brackets was written by Helena Södergran. A week earlier, on 20 January, she had written to tell HO: 'Edith is very ill with Spanish flu and asks me to say hello to you and hopes you will think of her; she's been waiting for news.'

LETTER 34/129

1   'Proco' is Hjalmar Procopé. Neither the book intended for him nor any letter that may have accompanied it have survived. Vilhelm Ekelund (1880-1949) was a well-known Swedish poet, essayist and writer of aphorisms.

2   HO had been suffering from a cold for about two months.

3   The payment due for *Motley Observations.*

4   *Dagens Press.* HO was of course on the paper's staff.

5   The 'higher worlds' are perceived by the 'spiritual eye', according to Steiner. See Letter 29/122, note 6.

COMMENTARY ON LETTER 34/129

1   Frans Eemil Sillanpää (1888 -1964), Finnish novelist, winner of Nobel Prize for Literature in 1939. *Hurskas kurjuus* is the original Finnish title of the novel he published in 1919, and which HO was translating into Swedish as *Det fromma eländet*. The literal meaning of the Finnish title is 'pious poverty' or 'devout destitution'. An English translation by Alex Matson was published in 1938 under the title *Meek Heritage*.

LETTER 35/131

1   It is not known who robbed HO and of what.

2   It is not clear what ES means by this. Incidentally, she opens but forgets to close the brackets, a fairly common occurrence in the characteristic headlong rush of her letter-writng.

3   Else Lasker-Schüler (1869 -1945), German neo-romantic expressionist poet of Christian Jewish origin, lived in Jerusalem from 1937. ES had obviously read HO's article about her in *Dagens Press* (28 February 1920). Several critics have commented on Lasker-Schüler's influence on ES (on which see SS2 p. 163, note 11).

4   *Woman and Grace*, p. 19.

LETTER 36/132

1   Finnish for 'timber company'.

2   Ilya Galkin (see Letter 32/126, note 5) owned a sawmill close to the Södergrans' land. In connection with this he had built a water-run power station which also supplied not only Raivola but parts of Terijoki with electricity. Just before the turn of the century he had enlarged a dam across the outlet of Lake Onkamo for the benefit of his power station. Those who owned land along the shore were now suing for compensation, alleging damage to their property caused by the raised level of the water. It was also claimed that in having the dam enlarged Galkin had worked from plans not approved by the authorities. The case went in Galkin's favour as the plaintiffs failed to prove that the enlarged dam was causing material damage to the environment. See also Letter 37/134 .

3   The Anthroposophical Society was founded in 1913 while the first Goetheanum was being built at Dornach; Steiner acted as adviser and teacher to its members but was never a member himself. It was re-founded as the

General Anthroposophical Society in 1923, with Steiner as president. The Finnish Anthroposophical Society was established as early as 1913 (it will be remembered that Steiner visited Finland in 1912 and 1913). ES may have first come into contact with anthroposophy during her time in Switzerland in 1912-14.

4   See Letter 23/116, note 3.

5   R. R. Eklund.

6   Dagmar von Schantz.

7   Presumably she had now seen some of Tyko Sallinen's work in reproduction; three months earlier (Letter 32/126) she had written that she did not know his paintings.

8   Erich Ludendorff (1865-1937), Prussian general, responsible to a large extent for Germany's military policy and strategy in the later years of the First World War. A political reactionary, he eventually joined the Nazi party.

9   My translation of this poem is based on McDuff's (1984, p. 175) but I have preserved the punctuation and line-division of the Swedish version in ES's letter.

10   'Karma' is an essential element in Steiner's teaching. It may be defined as what we inherit from previous lives as raw material for our present lives; transformed, this becomes the basis for future lives.

11   Annie Besant (1847-1933), leading British theosophist. Her close associate the British Anglican clergyman Charles Webster Leadbeater (1847-1934) was a prolific theosophical author. Reincarnation was an important doctrine in theosophy, as in anthroposophy.

12   Error for 'irrlichtelieren', German for 'flitting about'.

13   *Die Pforte der Einweihung, Ein Rosenkreuzermysterium* (The Portal of Initiation, a Rosicrucian Mystery, 1910). The first of four mystery plays written in verse by Steiner. Today they are performed at the Goetheanum in Dornach and elsewhere, including performances in English in Britain and the United States. The English titles of the other three are *The Soul's Probation*, *The Guardian of the Threshold*, and *The Soul's Awakening*.

COMMENTARY ON LETTER 36/132

1   HO was buried in 1978 with the sister-ring on her finger.

2   French dramatist and poet (1868-1955).

3   During ES's 1912-14 sanatorium period in Switzerland.

LETTER 37/134

1   Barbra (sic) Ring (1870-1955), Norwegian novelist, cultural historian and children's writer.

LETTER 38/136

1   *Die Prüfung der Seele* (1911). Mystery play intended as a prologue to Steiner's first play *The Portal of Initiation*. On the mystery plays in general see Letter 36/132, note 13.

2   It is not clear why ES thought Steiner would come to Stockholm at this time. He had already lectured there four times between 1908 and 1913, and had also visited Helsinki on the last two occasions (April 1912 and May-June 1913).

3   Steiner describes his threefold system in *Die Kernpunkte der sozialen Frage in den Lebensnotwendigkeiten der Gegenwart und Zukunft* (The Threefold Commonwealth, 1919; an earlier English title is Threefold State - the True Aspect of the Social Question). Anthroposophists consider society to consist of three mutually autonomous parts which co-operate with one another: government, economic life and cultural life. Government should not have authority over the other two but be equal in status to them. The more closely the three parts are woven together the more totalitarian a state will be, so the ideal is a social system in which the three elements function entirely independently of one another. A 'Movement for a Threefold Social Order' (or 'Threefold Commonwealth') was founded in 1916. This Movement included members unconnected with the Anthroposophical Movement. In the 1920 edition of the Finnish 'Who's Who' (*Vem och vad*, published by Schildts) ES stated that in the 'narrower sense' her political allegiance was to the Swedish People's Party of Finland (which represented the interests of Finland-Swedes) but in a 'higher sense' to the Movement for a Threefold Social Order.

4   Short for 'Helsingfors'.

5   Probably a reference to Dagmar von Schantz (see Commentary on Letter 32/126, note 1).

6   'Edith Södergran has embraced Christianity, which recently she had so much despised, and has now decided to abandon poetry for its sake' (Schoolfield 1984, p. 119).

7   Alexander Tunzelman von Adlerflug (1879-1946), later lieutenant-general.

COMMENTARY ON LETTER 38/136

1   Hjalmar Branting (1860-1925), Swedish journalist and statesman. A liberal socialist, he became Prime Minister in Sweden's first Social Democratic government (1920).

2   The owner of the Waldorf-Astoria cigarette factory in Stuttgart gave Steiner the necessary financial backing to found a school on anthroposophical principles in 1919 for the children of his employees.

LETTER 39/137

1   Swiss-German for 'was ist?' (How's life?)

2   At this time the German mark was already losing value as a result of the printing of too much paper money during the 1914-18 war, but its spectacular final collapse did not occur until 1923.

LETTER 41/140

1   As she often did, ES was writing to HO on a picture-postcard saved from her days in Switzerland before the war. Filisur is near Davos.

COMMENTARY ON LETTER 41/140

1   HO's ill-health during this period probably had a psychological basis. She was caught up in a conflict of loyalty between ES and her close friend Kylli Siegberg, daughter of the Helsinki family where she had lodged for many years. Both were making considerable emotional demands on her for attention. A year later this problem was to became even more acute - see Commentary on Letters 55/163 and 56/164, note 2. Another reason for HO's reluctance to spend more time at Raivola was the fear of catching tuberculosis from ES, who longed for closer physical (not necessarily sexual) contact between them. A hypochondriac at the best of times, HO was adept at developing convenient psychosomatic illnesses in times of stress.

LETTER 42/141

1   See Letter 29/122, note 5.

2   See Letter 31/124, note 2.

3   See Commentary to Letter 29/122, note 1.

4   *Theosophie. Einführung in übersinnliche Welterkenntnis und Menschenbestimmung* (Theosophy: an Introduction to the Supersensible Knowledge of the World and the Destination of Man, 1904).

5   *Aus der Akasha-Cronik* (The Submerged Continents of Atlantis and Lemuria, their History and Civilisation. Being Chapters from the Akashic Records, 1904, 1908).

6   On Steiner's mystery plays see Letter 36/132, note 13.

7   On the Threefold Commonwealth see Letter 38/136, note 3.

8   The Anthroposophical Society.

9   See Letter 36/132, note 11. *The Hidden Side of Things* was first published in India in 1913 in two volumes and reprinted in 1919. ES gives its title in English, so presumably she may have read it in English. In 1912-13 she had of course studied English in Switzerland with an Australian teacher (for an example of her writing in English see Introduction, note 3) and in the library of the Davos-Dorf sanatorium she had had a chance to read English books but no British or American modernist writers.

10   A plane had recently been circling over a trade fair being held in Helsinki. On 26 June 1920 ES had written to her 'aunt' Jenny Barcker (1856-1927, a family friend since childhood): 'Now you must be having the great fair there in Helsinki' (SS2 Letter 139). In fact this event opened on 28 June and lasted a week. It had been designed to draw international attention to the achievements in trade and industry of newly independent Finland. On 28 June *Dagens Press* devoted a whole page to a description of the opening ceremonies.

11   On anthroposophical reincarnation or 'rebirth' theory see Letter 36/132, note 10 and, for a full account, Ahern, pp. 104-6.

12   Dagmar von Schantz.

13   Johan Vilhelm (John) Sonck (1865-1941), a district medical officer in the province of Viipuri and military medical officer for Raivola, also a leading theosophist and vegetarian. ES's autograph album contains an undated quotation from the Bhagavad Ghita in his handwriting.

14   Rudolf Steiner, *Die Evolution vom Gesichtspunkte des Wahrhaftigen* (5 lectures given in Berlin Oct-Dec 1911; *The Inner Realities of Evolution*. Earlier English title *Evolution in the Aspect of Realities*).

15   Rudolf Steiner: Drei Gedichte und Vortrag (Three poems and a Lecture, 1915. These are satirical verses; an English translation has been published in Rudolf Steiner; *Twelve Moods*, Mercury Press, Spring Valley, USA, 1984).

LETTER 43/142
1   Siuntio - in Swedish Sjundeå - is a town 40 km west of Helsinki with many Swedish-speaking inhabitants.

COMMENTARY ON LETTER 43/142
1   Axel Lille (1848-1921), journalist and deputy in the Finnish Diet

during Russian rule. SS2 (p. 184, note 1) suggests that since Lille published nothing on the Movement for a Threefold State (or 'Threefold Commonwealth') before 27 August, ES must have read some article published elsewhere. Holmström makes the point (1993, p. 33) that HO was much more interested in Steiner's political theories than in his mystical ideas.

LETTER 44/143

1   Enclosed with this letter was a visiting card on which ES had written 'I have received with thanks 2,100 Finnish marks through Hagar Olsson'.

2   *Drei Vorträge über Volkspädagogik* (1919; Three Lectures on Adult Education. An English translation of these lectures is contained in, *Education as a Force for Social Change*, Anthroposophic Press, Hudson 1997).

3   Rudolf Steiner.

4   German; 'farsorge' is an error for 'vorsorge' or 'fürsorge'. ES is asking whether there is anyone to take care of the inmates of the lunatic asylum which is our world.

5   Hugo Stinnes (1870-1924), German financier and parliamentarian, owner of an industrial empire. ES will refer to him again more than two years later in Letter 80/192. Her mention of him here may be deliberately humorous as Stinnes was a symbol for money and business success. ES is not likely to have known that his industrial empire had ramifications within the publishing world.

6   On Hjalmar Branting see Commentary on Letter 38/136, note 1.

7   Henri Barbusse (1873-1935), French writer and journalist. His novel *Clarté* (Light, 1918), influenced by his experiences as a volunteer in the First World War, led to the foundation in several countries of groups promoting pacifism and social and political revolution. In 1919 he founded the Clarté Movement which published a journal also called *Clarté* (the Swedish edition first appeared in 1924) that dealt with political, cultural and ideological questions; he described himself as an ardent pacifist and communist. His idea of a worldwide organisation of intellectuals appealed to ES who in her letters to HO wrote repeatedly of her dream of bringing together artists from all over the world. Plans to found a Clarté movement in Finland soon attracted the interest of HO, ES and Elmer Diktonius (who had met Barbusse). When after ES's death Stella Arvidson, active in the Clarté organisation in Lund (Sweden), wrote in the spring of 1925 to ED and HO to ask them to promote the movement and its journal in Finland, HO immediately saw an opportunity to get ES's work more widely known and

wrote an article about her which *Clarté* published (Holmström 1993, pp. 93ff).

8   See note 2 above.

9   Hermann Bahr (1863-1934), Austrian dramatist, novelist and critic, author of the manifesto *Expressionismus* (1916; Expressionism), which HO had reviewed in *Dagens Press* three months earlier. Hans Thoma (1839-1924), popular German landscape painter, influenced by Arnold Böcklin (see Letter 28/121, note 13). Probably Hugo von Habermann (1849-1929), German portrait-painter favouring an impressionist style, and Marie Eugenie delle Grazie (1864-1931), Austrian writer and close friend of Rudolf Steiner. ES names these four because they had signed an appeal, 'An das deutsche Volk und an die Kulturwelt', made by Steiner in 1919 to the German people and the world of culture in general.

10   Bjørnstjerne Bjørnson (1832-1910), Norwegian novelist, playwright and poet. His play *Kongen* (The King) first appeared in 1877.

11   Goethe's drama *Prometheus* was never completed, but remained a 'magnificent fragment' first printed in 1773.

12   The money she had received from the Society of Authors. See note 1 above.

LETTER 45/144
1   The Raivola postmark is illegible, but this postcard must have been posted at Raivola a couple of days before it was postmarked again in Helsinki. See note on HO's commentary below.

2   Steiner's third play was *Der Hüter der Schwelle, Seelenvorgänge in szenischen Bildern* (The Guardian of the Threshold, a Spiritual Process in Scenic Images, 1912).

COMMENTARY ON LETTER 45/144
1   I.e. HO leaves Helsingfors for Raivola before 7 September. Before she gets to Raivola, ES (perhaps on September 5) sends postcard 45/144 to Räisälä, thinking HO must still be there. The card is forwarded by HO's family from Räisälä to Helsingfors, reaching its destination on 7 September, by which time HO was probably already with ES at Raivola. HO cannot have left Raivola any later than 10 September for her return journey to Helsingfors. ES may have written Letter 46/145 later on the day that HO left.

LETTER 46/145

1   Dagmar von Schantz.

2   HO's dentist Axel Aspelund (1868-1932), active in the anthroposophical movement.

3   The Anthroposophical Society.

4   Hans Ruin (1891-1980), essayist, critic and editor of the liberal cultural and political monthly review *Nya Argus*. Ruin was one of those ES sought out on her famous visit to Helsinki in late September and early October 1917, when she met a number of Finland-Swedish and Finnish writers and critics (for a list see SS2 Letter 83, note 3); Ruin wrote in her autograph book at the time: 'The desire to think the impossible and attempt the fantastic comes naturally to her'.

5   There seems to be no evidence of any Threefold Commonwealth meeting at Jena (in eastern Germany). But on 9 September 1920 *Dagens Press* advertised 'Anthroposophical Academy Courses' to be held at the Goetheanum in Dornach from 26 September to 16 October; this was in connection with the formal opening of the Goetheanum which, as we shall see, HO would attend with Aspelund.

6   Walter Hasenclever (1890-1940), German expressionist dramatist, writer of film-scripts (including *Anna Christie* for Greta Garbo, 1930) and lyric poet.

7   *The Shadow of the Future.*

8   Holger Schildt.

9   Elsa Kataja; see Commentary on Letter 75/188, note 1.

10   Edvin Rautell (1862-1935), journalist; from 1914 to 1928 editorial secretary and editor-in-chief of *Dagens Press* (known from 1922 as *Svenska Pressen*). The serial was *Mrs Balfame* (1916) by the prolific American popular novelist Gertrude Atherton (1857-1948). Its serialisation in *Dagens Press* began on 30 April 1920.

COMMENTARY ON LETTER 46/145

1   Printed in *Dagens Press* on 9 October 1920.

2   There are two apes on the cover of *The Rose Altar* (1919) and the 'devil' on the cover of *The September Lyre* (1918) is also ape-like; see Letter 1/90, note 2.

LETTER 47/146

1   The original of this letter has been lost; date as given in Olsson (1955).

2   Finnish for 'the letting agreement shall become null and void if the

house is sold'. In December 1920 Helena Södergran reported to Jenny Barcker (SS2, Letter 152) that she and Edith had been renting out the large house or villa to the defence corps since October. Most of the troops were from Swedish-speaking areas in Ostrobothnia on the Finnish west coast. For a previous occasion when troops were billeted in the Södergran villa see HO's Introduction, note 6.

3   *Matthew* 5,3.

4   Ahriman, prince of darkness. In anthroposophy Ahriman represents materialism, i.e. the force which induces human beings to become cold and cynical and to despise spiritual values; in other words, Ahriman is the will and the intellect.

COMMENTARY ON LETTER 47/146

1   Marie Steiner, née von Sievers (1867-1948), actress; married Rudolf Steiner in 1914 as his second wife.

2   Bengt Harald (Harry) Lille (1884-1920), engineer. See Commentary Letter 43/142, note 1 for more on his father.

LETTER 48/150

1   ES has now received HO's Swedish translation of Frans Eemil Sillanpää's Finnish novel *Hurskas kurjuus*. See Letter 34/129, note 1.

2   '[but is] gripping and full of life'.

3   *Matthew* 15,13.

4   Rudolf Steiner, *Die tieferen Geheimnisse des Menschheitswerdens im Lichte der Evangelien* (Some Deeper Secrets of Human Development in the Light of the Gospels, 1909); *Das Johannes-Evangelium* (The Gospel of St John, 1908); *Das Lukas-Evangelium* (The Gospel of St Luke, 1909); *Das Matthäus-Evangelium* (The Gospel of St Matthew, 1910); *Exkurse in das Gebiet des Markus-Evangeliums* (Background to the Gospel of St Mark, 1910-11, earlier known in English as Excursus on the Gospel According to St Mark); and *Das Markus-Evangelium* (The Gospel of St Mark, 1912).

1921

LETTER 49/154

1   The uncorrected shorthand reports of Steiner's lectures were intended to be confidential for members. They were not published openly until the

refounding of the (General) Anthroposophical Society in 1923.

2   A subsection of the Baltic commission of the American Red Cross was set up in Viipuri in 1919. Some 2,000 Karelians benefited from the distribution of food, principally flour and canned milk.

3   On 28 January 1921 *Dagens Press* published an article by R. R. Eklund under this title, a discussion of Professor Knut Tallqvist's essay-collection *Konungen med Guds nåde* (1921; King by the Grace of God), a study of the insignia of ruling powers. Eklund wrote that the book would incur 'the repugnance of every true democrat'.

4   *Veckans krönika* (a weekly family magazine), 1920, No. 51.

5   Written by Helena Södergran.

LETTER 50/156

1   The Bolshevik Baltic fleet (the Soviet Union did not come into being until July 1923) was based at Kronstadt on Kotlin Island outside Petrograd (St Petersburg). A revolt was started there on 28 February 1921 by sailors who had no serious quarrel with the Bolsheviks' aspirations of 1917 but merely wanted to emphasize that there had been a discrepancy between what the leadership of the Communist Party had promised and what it had fulfilled. The sailors claimed that democratic principles had been ignored by a privileged, self-appointed elite. Added to this they had suffered badly during the winter of 1920-21 when their food had been poor and their barracks unheated. Between August 1920 and March 1921 about half Kronstadt's 4,000 communists left the Party. The general view was that the sailors of Kronstadt were the conscience of the revolution, but the leaders of the Communist Party saw them as a threat to Party authority. On 8 March Trotsky, as chairman of the revolutionary council, ordered 25,000 soldiers faithful to the regime to attack the 15,000 rebels in Kronstadt. The rebels held their positions until 17 March, when the troops faithful to the regime were doubled in number and a new offensive began. The sailors were running out of food, ammunition and fuel and had little alternative but to surrender. About 6,500 persons from Kronstadt, both military and civilian, fled across the frozen sea to Finland. See also Letter 52/158, note 2.

2   Runar Schildt.

3   Schildts paid an advance of 700 Finnish marks for *The Shadow of the Future*.

4   In a letter to Gunnar Tideström, dated 28 July 1946, Sigrid Fontell stated that Sonck arranged joint meetings for theosophists, anthroposophists

and others in Raivola, his purpose being to unite the various groups; she commented that the meetings were 'private and of a markedly local character'.

5   It seems that no Jewish incarnation of Steiner is known to anthroposophists.

6   Because it was taking so long to finish. Hence no doubt the unfinished sentence in the previous line; ES had perhaps forgotten how she meant to continue it when she returned to go on with the letter after a break.

7   Nostradamus was Michel de NostreDame (1503-66), astrologer, seer and private physician to King Charles IX of France.

LETTER 51/157

1   I.e. Good Friday.

2   Under the title 'The Destruction of the West, an Epoch-making European book', HO had published two articles in *Dagens Press* (23 and 24 March 1921) discussing *Untergang des Abendlandes* (The Decline of the West, 2 vols, 1918-22), in which the German philosopher Oswald Spengler (1880-1936) predicted the eclipse of Western civilisation.

3   'My God, I'm lazy'.

LETTER 52/158

1   For a list of Steiner's writings on the gospels see Letter 48/150, note 3.

2   During 17-18 March some 6,500 refugees from the Kronstadt naval base crossed the frozen sea and landed at Terijoki. They were settled in several refugee camps. The largest of these, not far from Raivola at Ino near Uusikirkko, contained 3,584 men, 10 women and 3 children. A small camp at Raivola contained 168 persons who were moved to Ino at the end of April. The Ino camp continued till the end of June when the refugees were moved to various places including Turkinsaari outside Viipuri, whence a large number returned to Russia. In general, the Soviet government granted the rank and file an amnesty but the leaders were put on trial. Altogether about 3,940 men, 50 women and 80 children were interned in the fortified camp at Ino, which was administered by the Finnish authorities helped by the American Red Cross, which provided food and other necessities.

3   Vladimir Bogoyavlensky (1877-?1950), parish priest to the Raivola Orthodox congregation from 1911 to 1924. The Orthodox church in Raivola was next door to the Södergran home and had been built in 1881 to replace an earlier wooden structure which had become rotten.

LETTER 53/159

1   'Don't take it amiss, dear child'.

2   This is difficult, and also relates to ES's poem 'O himmelska klarhet' (O heavenly clarity), written over a year later in September 1922 and eventually published in *Landet som icke är* (The Land That Is Not). Schoolfield (1984, p. 124) has a long note on the subject. The problem lies with the New Testament text of II *Corinthians* 3,10, where the Greek word δοξα (doxa) is translated as 'klarhet' (clarity) in Swedish and as 'glory' in English versions. The context is the superiority of the truth as revealed by Christ over the truth of the Old Testament, and the English King James Bible has: 'For even that which was made glorious had no glory in this respect, by reason of the glory that excelleth. For if that which was done away with was glorious, much more that which remaineth is glorious.' The Swedish term 'klarhet' also has overtones of 'enlightenment', and ES relates it to Christ's teaching that we must become like little children before we are fit to enter the kingdom of heaven.

COMMENTARY ON LETTER 53/159

1   From Helsinki.

LETTER 55/163

1   Anna-Lenah Elgström.

LETTER 56/164

1   Max Wolffhügel (1880-1963), German artist, teacher at the first Waldorf school which was founded in 1919 for the children of workers at the Waldorf-Astoria cigarette factory in Stuttgart. See also Commentary on Letter 38/136, note 2.

2   'Too late!'

3   After the end of the First World War Steiner's lecturing activities were dominated by the social question. The basis of the 'Movement for a Threefold Commonwealth' was set out in *Kernpunkte der sozialen Frage* (The Threefold Commonwealth); its aim was to better the terrible social conditions left by the war. However, Steiner withdrew from the Movement and called off the official campaign when he was strongly attacked by both communists and the budding Nazi movement. Attempts to assassinate him were made by 'nationalist circles' in Munich and Eberfeld in May 1922.

4   The sculpture is at the Goetheanum. Ahern (pp. 16-17) describes it: 'a large carving of three sinewy, striving forms, two demons and "the

representative of humanity", who has the upper hand. One demon, Lucifer, represents passion and fantasy (as opposed to imaginative truth); the other, given the Zoroastrian name of Ahriman, is the force of hardening, especially when it takes the form of dried-up intellectualism. The sculpture, partly chiselled by Steiner himself, expresses the need for self-knowledge so that the two demons can be transcended.'

5   On Mannerheim see Letter 18/111, note 2.

6   'Military hospital' (Finnish).

7   See Letter 49/154, note 1.

8   *Von Jesus zu Christus* (From Jesus to Christ) was originally a series of ten lectures given by Steiner at Karlsruhe in 1911.

9   Perhaps the Frenchwoman already mentioned in Letter 42/141 in connection with Sonck. 'Pborg' is short for 'St Petersburg'.

COMMENTARY ON LETTERS 55/163 AND 56/164

1   HO was operated on at the district hospital in Viipuri on 5 June 1921 and returned there later in the summer following complications.

2   HO is not altogether candid here. She had suffered from a conflict of loyalty between ES and her Helsinki friend Kylli Siegberg as early as July 1920 (see Commentary on Letter 41/140, note 1). At the end of May 1921 she travelled to Räisälä to spend the whole summer with her parents at the manse, and she was joined there a few days later by Kylli Siegberg. But the summer holiday they had planned to share took an unexpected change of direction when HO was rushed to Viipuri for an emergency appendectomy during the night of 4-5 June. Kylli Siegberg went with her and stayed faithfully at her side at Viipuri and Räisälä during a long convalescence (interrupted by several relapses) of more than two months, towards the end of which the two friends decided to share a flat in the capital. It was not until early September that HO was well enough to return to work in Helsinki. It was in this context that HO, on her way back to Helsinki, suffered the 'nervous tension' at the prospect of seeing ES that she describes in her Commentary to Letter 56/164 and paid the lightning visit of a few hours to Raivola that so annoyed ES (Letter 58/167).

LETTER 57/165

1   The post office at Raivola was near the railway station.

2   Miina was of course the Södergran's elderly new maid, who had replaced the boy-struck young incendiarist Aino. See Letter 49/154.

LETTER 58/167

1   HO arrived and left the same day, hence ES's irritation.

2   The surgeon Marta Helena Nobel-Oleinikoff (1881-1973).

3   Hjalmar Procopé.

LETTER 59/170

1   On Herr Bogs see Commentary to Letter 36/132.

2   Published in Erik Grotenfelt, *Det röda vinets barn* (Child of the Red Wine, 1915).

3   Published in 1913. But ES never translated anything by Arvid Mörne.

4   From Jarl Hemmer's *Pelaren* (The Pillar, 1916).

5   ES never translated anything by Runar Schildt.

6   On Bertel Gripenberg and Hjalmar Procopé ('Proco') see Commentary on Letter 2/91, note 2; and on Ragnar Ekelund, HO's Introduction, note 10. Jacob Tegengren (1875-1956), and Mikael Lybeck (1864-1925) were also Finland-Swedish poets of the older generation. Gripenberg had come to ES's defence during the *September Lyre* 'feud' with a piece attacking 'Jumbo' (*Hufvudstadsbladet*, 23 January 1919).

7   Emil Hasselblatt (1874-1954), university librarian, critic and journalist, was at this time vice-chairman of the Society of Swedish Authors in Finland.

COMMENTARY ON LETTER 59/170

1   A fair copy of ES's German translation of *Woman and Grace* survives, given by Helena Södergran to HO after ES's death.

1922

LETTER 60/171

1   HO (1955) gives the date as 6 January.

2   HO and her mother stayed at the Hospiz Hotel during their time in Viipuri.

3   Probably Friedrich Israel's *Gedichte aus Finnland*, (Poems from Finland, 1920), which HO had reviewed in *Dagens Press* on 12 June 1920. ES also refers to this anthology in Letter 69/181.

COMMENTARY ON LETTER 60/171

1   Diktonius' first collection of poems and aphorisms *Min dikt* (My

Poem) was published in Stockholm in autumn 1921 by the small and short-lived communist-orientated firm Lyrik. HO was planning to review the book.

2   On Ruin see Letter 46/145, note 3.

3   The 'dangerous article' was HO's review of *My Poem*, which appeared in *Nya Argus* under the title 'Radikal dikt' (Radical Poem) in mid-March 1922. The article also contained the first publication in Swedish of the full text - it had already been printed elsewhere in French - of what was to become Diktonius' perhaps best-known poem, 'Jaguaren' (The Jaguar).

LETTER 61/172

1   This may have been Erik Kihlman's *Ur Finlands svenska lyrik* (Selected Finland-Swedish Poetry, 1923), but this was being published by Schildt and not Bonniers who published no anthology of Finland-Swedish poetry during this period. In 1924 Bonniers were to publish Sten Selander's anthology *Ung lyrik* (Young Lyricists), but this contains the work of poets from Sweden only.

2   Emil Zilliacus (1878-1961), writer and academic.

3   The suggested alterations concern ES's translation into German of HO's *Woman and Grace*. I have only attempted English translations of the German alternatives where this seems useful.

4   But German *does* have a word for Swedish 'skär': 'jungfräulich' (corresponding to Swedish 'jungfrulig'), which ES must have known. Perhaps she felt it did not fit the context.

5   ES may be referring to her translation of Friedrich Adler's poem 'Beethoven', about to be published in *Nya Argus* 4, 15 April 1922.

6   Gunnar Castrén (1878-1959), later successively Professor of the Literature of Finland and Professor of Literature in Swedish at Helsinki University, was at this time a member of the editorial board of *Nya Argus*. When in 1915, before any of her work had been published, ES showed Castrén some of her poems and asked his opinion of them, he told her she had all too uncritically followed German expressionist models, and that he believed there could be little future for her work in Finland. But later he was to write very positively about it, as for example in a signed leader in the Stockholm daily *Svenska Dagbladet* on 11 September 1928. She had of course also approached Arvid Mörne with her poems in 1915; for his more encouraging response see Commentary on Letter 2/91, note 2.

LETTER 62/173

1   A collection of poems by Arvid Mörne (1913).

2   *Woman and Grace.*

LETTER 63/174

1   The first letter in ES's series to ED, in private hands until 1991.

2   On 18 March 1922 ED left Helsinki for Raivola where he stayed a couple of days. On 23 March he described his impressions of ES in a letter to his friend and former music-teacher, the composer Erkki Melartin: 'It's already a couple of days since I last saw her, but I still feel something out of the ordinary vibrating around me. She's herself, just that, no one else is anything like her. Despite her weakness (hunger and poverty) more of a "superperson" than anyone else I've seen. She hardly has a body at all, just a soulful, glorious face. A human face. And how she can smile - this sick woman. Utterly radiant. I'm still warm from it, I always will be.' (Quoted in Enckell, *Den Unge Diktonius*, 1946 p. 180)

3   'Aimless tramp' (Finnish).

4   ES had probably read some review in the press of the memoirs of the former German Chancellor Otto von Bismarck (1815-98), the third part of which came out in Swedish translation in 1921 as *Kejsaren och jag* (The Kaiser and I).

LETTER 64/175

1   This undated letter must have been written on 4 April since ES states that she is writing on her 30th birthday.

2   This may refer to the translated poems later sent to ED with letters 66/177 and 67/178.

3   ED had sent ES his first book *My Poem* which contains aphorisms as well as poems. ES is referring here to two of the aphorisms: 'Those artists are not fit to be alive who live so long before their time that they hear neither their own screams nor the screams of the millions of other human bodies condemned to the same hell as they are' and 'I write because I am weak. Better to go out into the world and lash out around oneself with an axe'.

4   Perhaps the 'bellicists' Joachim Gasquet and Pierre Drieu la Rochelle, already mentioned in Letter 32/126 and, in Drieu la Rochelle's case, also in Letter 63/174. If so, ES clearly did not realise that Gasquet was not only not young but already dead.

5   A reference to HO's trip to Switzerland for the opening of Steiner's Goetheanum in the autumn of 1920; see HO's commentaries on Letters 46/145 and 47/146.

6   The familiar form 'du' was apparently (his letters to ES do not survive) not acceptable to ED, as even at the very end of her life ES continued to use the formal style in writing to him. He seems not to have responded when she suggested near the end of her first letter to him (63/174) 'You can write to me as freely and unconventionally as you like.' It is as if he felt a need to keep her at arm's length despite his sympathy with her unconventional approach to poetry, the aggressive directness of his own writing, and his strongly left-wing political views and apparently violent desire to smash all the old conventions. Or perhaps it was simply that she was a woman, and he felt ill at ease with women's uninhibited expression of emotion. Or it could simply have been that he felt awed by this 'superperson' whom he considered the greatest poet of his generation. Contrast this with the use of familiar and unfamiliar forms of address between ES and HO, where ES only reverts to stiffness and formal language when offended and angry (Letter 2/91, note 10 and Letter 4/93 notes 1 and 2).

7   Miina was the Södergrans' home help. Denis Peck was an elderly Estonian eccentric who lodged for a short time before his death in January 1914 in the Södergrans' 'little house', which was where they were now living themselves. ES quotes Miina's words in Finnish.

8   Carl Jonas Love Almqvist (1793-1866), Swedish poet, novelist and dramatist. *Drottningens juvelsmycke* (The Queen's Jewel, 1834) is a semi-historical romance set in Sweden at the time of the assassination of King Gustav III in 1792. ES may have been identifying with its androgynous central character, Tintomara.

LETTER 65/176

1   *Min dikt* (My Poem).

2   David Lloyd George (1863-1945), British Prime Minister 1916-22. Observing famine with 'unfeeling detachment' may perhaps refer to his attitude or supposed attitude to Russia, which was stricken by famine in 1921, and/or to his part in determining the severity of the war reparations inflicted on a near-destitute Germany (agreed at £6,600 million in April 1921). ES's knowledge of current affairs must have been mostly based on reports in *Dagens Press*.

3   A 'daughter of Abraham' was afflicted by 'a spirit of infirmity' for eighteen years until healed by Jesus (*Luke* 13, 10-17).

LETTER 66/177

1   Though undated, this letter clearly follows 65/176, at the end of which

ES asked ED if he could introduce her to Barbusse. She enclosed with the present letter her translations into German of Diktonius' poems 'Liv' (Life) and 'Jaguaren' I-IV (The Jaguar, parts I-IV), together with her own as yet unpublished poem 'O himmelska klarhet' (O Heavenly Clarity).

2   Diktonius' collection *My Poem* contains no fewer than three texts in which the painter Vincent van Gogh (1853-90) is mentioned. Two of these can be classed as aphorisms from their form and length. The third, which comes in the final section of the book 'Några hårda sånger' (A Few Harsh Songs), is clearly the poem ES is referring to. It begins with the words 'Stenar talar, köttet skriker, / lyktstolper vrider sig av livshunger...' ('Stones speak, flesh screams, / lampposts writhe in hunger for life...'). A variant of this poem was to appear in *Ultra* 5 (14 November 1922), p. 74, as 'Vincent van Gogh, a Hymn by Elmer Diktonius'. It is also possible ES may be referring to Diktonius' poem 'Vanitas hav' (Sea of Vanity) from the sequence 'Havet och berget' (The Sea and the Mountain), about to be published in Diktonius' second collection *Hårda sånger* (Harsh Songs), published in June 1922.

3   I.e. Barbusse's novel *Clarté* (1918). On Barbusse see Letter 44/143, note 7.

4   Meaning obscure.

5   HO had been admitted to a sanatorium near Helsinki with 'nervous tension' accompanied by fever, a circumstance ES can hardly have been aware of.

LETTER 67/178

1   This letter was recorded by ED who kept a list of letters sent to him but it apparently consisted of nothing but ES's German translations of ED's poems 'Sova?' (Sleep?), 'Vad jag är smutsig' (How dirty I am), 'Människor bygger städer' (Humans build cities) and 'Evigt lever jag' (I live for ever), all from *My Poem*, 1921.

LETTER 68/179

1   ED was in contact with Barbusse and put forward a proposal to found a branch of his organisation Clarté (see Letter 44/143, note 7) in Finland. Nothing ever came of this.

2   ES enclosed with this letter her German translations of ED's poems 'Jag ser den heliga askan' (I see the holy ashes), 'Min själ har tvättats ren av tårar' (My soul has been washed clean by tears), 'En vilopunkt' (A Point of

Rest) and 'En glittrande ringorm' (A glittering ringed snake), all to be published in *Harsh Songs*.

3   ES's German translation of HO's *Woman and Grace*.

4   ED was planning to return to England following his long stay there from March to October 1921. But among other things the preparatory work necessary before the launch of the new review *Ultra* made it necessary for him to stay in Helsinki (see Commentary on Letter 77/190, note 1).

LETTER 69/181

1   Unless some letters have been lost this is ES's first letter to HO for nearly three months.

2   From *Woman and Grace*.

3   Ragnar Ekelund, who of course should not be confused with Ragnar Rudolf Eklund (R.R.E.) or the Swedish poet Vilhelm Ekelund.

4   Herr Bogs.

5   This was Friedrich Israel's anthology of Finland-Swedish and Finnish poetry in German translation, published by Schildts and already mentioned in, note 3 to Letter 60/171. It contained poems by Runeberg, Topelius, Stenbäck, Wecksell, Tavaststjerna, Leino, Gunnar von Numers, Lybeck, Greta Langenskjöld, Hemmer, Per Hallström, V. A. Koskenniemi and Israel himself.

LETTER 70/183

1   A reference to line 11 of ED's poem 'Liv' (Life, in German 'Leben'); ES's German translation was enclosed with Letter 66/177.

2   *Matthew* 10, 37.

3   Possibly the fifth poem in the sequence 'Rast' (Rest) in *Harsh Songs*. It is often unclear which of ED's poems ES is talking about in her letters to him since he often leaves his poems without titles while rather than quote the first line she mentions what for her is the subject of the poem, in this case 'cars'. Cars are not mentioned in any other poem in *My Poem* and *Harsh Songs*. ES sent her German version of this poem to ED with Letter 72/185.

4   The first poem in the sequence 'Levandet' (Living) in *Harsh Songs*.

5   'so charming, so delightful'.

6   Untitled prose poems in R. R. Eklund's short collection *The Earth Altar*. The first lines of the relevant pieces are: 'Ute på slätten står ett ensamt träd' (Out on the plain stands a solitary tree), 'Vad är slätten?' (What is the

plain?), 'En stor och fruktansvärd hed är tystnaden' (Silence is a great and terrible heath), 'I en skum vrå inne i stugan hänger en kniv' (In a dim corner inside the cottage hangs a knife), 'Se drömmaren' (See the dreamer) and 'Skapare, givare, vederkvickare och upprättare' (Creator, giver, restorer and rehabilitator). For a taste of R. R. Eklund's poetic prose in a quotation from the last-named piece, see Commentary to Letter 10/99.

LETTER 71/184

1   ED may have been heading for the Tyynelä boarding-house near Oitti, about 60 km north of Helsinki (Enckell 1946, p. 175).

2   It is not clear which poem ES means.

LETTER 72/185

1   Enclosing ES's German translations of the first poem in ED's sequence 'Stora och lilla jag' (Big and Little Me), and the fifth poem in his sequence 'Rast' (Rest).

2   A reference to the episode in HO's *Woman and Grace* in which Elkanah's woman meets the Messenger in the Garden of Gethsemane (1919 edition, p. 37).

3   *Harsh Songs*, which came out the same month (June) as the letter appears to have been written.

4   The enclosed translations of poems by ED.

LETTER 73/186

1   HO (1955) prints the second paragraph before the first. The two paragraphs were written on different sides of a postcard and it's anybody's guess which was written first. I have followed the order in SS2, which starts with the paragraph written on the front beside the address.

2   ES had probably borrowed books through HO from the private collection of the lecturer Artur Siegberg, her Helsinki landlord for many years and the father of her close friend Kylli.

3   On 'Kataja' see Commentary on Letter 75/188, note 1

4   An allusion to Verlaine's 'Art poétique' (The Art of Poetry).

LETTER 74/187

1   This letter (actually a picture postcard) was omitted by HO from her 1955 edition. The picture is a highly erotic painting by Anders Zorn showing a windswept nude leaning against a rock at the side of a lake or by the sea.

On Zorn see Letter 28/121, note 13.

LETTER 75/188

1   There is no Raivola postmark. SS2, presumably in error, gives the place it was sent from as Terijoki. But it was the recipient HO who was at Terijoki (c/o Fru Tchaikovsky - the address is given in SS2), and all the evidence suggests that ES was as usual at Raivola.

COMMENTARY ON LETTER 75/188

1   The Kanerva/Kataja story is characteristic. To begin with ES feels warmly towards Kataja as a stranger who has taken the trouble to come and see her to bring greetings from HO, the person constantly in her thoughts (this was around 25 November 1919 - Kataja was working as a dentist in Viipuri 1919-20). Then she becomes an object of jealousy, a bogey-woman, someone ES feels must be standing between her and HO, distracting HO's attention from her, someone no doubt more glamorous and worldly than herself and with much more to offer HO. ES's hostility comes through indirectly in her insistence on not learning Kataja's proper name but continuing for some time to call her 'Kanerva', probably to begin with an innocent mistake. Cut off from the world, ES's vivid imagination works overtime on people she seldom sees or has never even met: HO must have forgotten or betrayed her, Ellen Key must have been Nietzsche's mistress, Anna-Lenah Elgström must be a saint, Steiner either a saint or a devil, etc., etc. HO's commentary often draws attention to this quality in ES. On 14 June 1922 Kataja visits Raivola and ES discovers from her that HO, starting her summer holiday, has left Helsinki for Räisälä en route for the seaside at Terijoki without telling her (ES). ES tries to take control by sending HO Kataja's Terijoki address (perhaps HO knew it already) on 17 June and beginning to arrange for HO to stay either there or at another Terijoki boarding-house. By 9 July ES realises that HO has made her own arrangements for Terijoki and is overcome by irrational jealousy of Kataja. Commenting indignantly some 30 years later on ES's attitude, HO remarks that Kataja was 'presumably at Räisälä at the time' but gives no reason for this. Perhaps Kataja, though the same age as ES and HO, was an Olsson family friend. Incidentally, SS2 implies she was married, listing in the index (p. 308) 'Kataja (Kanerva), Elsa née Paatola', though ES in Letter 74/187 is clearly unaware of this.

LETTER 76/189

1   Fru Laubmann was obviously the person ES had decided HO should lodge with in Raivola, and 'twenty-five a day' is of course not cigarettes but the price in Finnish marks Fru Laubmann would charge.

COMMENTARY ON LETTER 76/189

1   Raoul af Hällström (1899-1975), actor, theatre director and journalist, on *Ultra*'s editorial board for its first four numbers.

2   Lauri Haarla (1890-1944), Finnish poet, dramatist and writer of historical novels, completed the editorial board with HO and af Hällström.

COMMENTARY ON LETTER 77/190

1   Lauri A. Salava (1894-1955), ED's brother-in-law and a friend since school days, was a bookdealer and occasional poet. According to Johan Wrede ('Tidskriften *Ultra*', in P. O. Barck *et al* (eds), *Festskrift till Olof Enckell* 12.3, 1970, Helsingfors, 1970), ED had returned from continental Europe to Finland with the idea of establishing a little magazine which would open 'the windows of Finland to Europe'; Manne Stenbeck ('Ett icke ointeressant dokument' in *Ord och bild* 69 (1960) p. 312), believes he may have been inspired by Ivan Goll's large anthology *Les cinq continents* (see Commentary on Letter 80/192). ED and Salava called their new bilingual Finnish/Swedish review *Ultra: Kirjallistaiteellinen aikakauslehti / Tidskrift för ny konst och litteratur* (Ultra: Journal for New Art and Literature), and recruited HO to the editorial board to take care of the Swedish-language side. Haarla was the Finnish-language specialist and the 23-year-old af Hällström was supposed to provide contact with 'youth'. Salava also founded the related short-lived publishing house Daimon (see Commentary on Letter 79/191). It is not clear how *Ultra* and Daimon were financed, but it was rumoured (no concrete evidence has been found) that ED's old friend O. W. Kuusinen, now a powerful figure in the Russian-led Comintern (Communist International), may have been behind it. If so, as HO implies, its backers would doubtless have been disppointed by its lack of political content. One reason for this may have been that ED's new romance with his future first wife Meri Marttinen not only took him away from Helsinki but perhaps distracted him from *Ultra*; see Letter 85/199, note 3.

LETTER 78/222

1   Undated fragment of a letter omitted from Olsson 1955. SS2 places it in May or early June 1923, but I believe internal evidence makes September 1922 a more likely date. ES is still talking of translating and it was around this time that she began writing her major late poems about the moon and death. She still hasn't seen *Ultra* and though what she says about Diktonius' poems is obscure it relates naturally to her letter of 31 August (77/190). Finally, though tired she is still energetically engaged with such worldly matters as financial problems caused by the troops billeted in the big house

(they had been there since October 1920; on this see Letter 47/146, note 2). The tone of her letters in the spring of 1923 is quite different.

LETTER 79/191

1   Söderströms and Schildts dominated the world of Swedish-language publishing in Finland then as now.

2   The books Franz Fromme published between 1917 and 1942 suggest a considerable interest in questions of independence and national identity among Europe's 'smaller' nations such as Belgium and Ireland. I have found no evidence that Fromme wrote on Finland, but in 1938 he published in Berlin his translation of a book by Fredrik Böök from Swedish into German as *Das reiche und das arme Schweden* (Sweden Rich and Poor). Major-General Count Rüdiger von der Golz (1865-1946) commanded the German expeditionary force, or 'Baltic division' as it was called, which captured Helsinki for the Whites on 13 April 1913 during the Finnish civil war (see also Letter 105/219, note 2). The German philosopher Rudolf Eucken (1846-1926) won the Nobel Prize for Literature in 1908; not long after ES's death he came to Finland and gave two lectures on the world political situation (reported in *Hufvudstadsbladet*, 19 and 20 October 1923).

3   Raoul af Hällström.

COMMENTARY ON LETTER 79/191

1   *Vilande dag* (1922; Resting Day). Daimon soon collapsed for economic reasons. On Gunnar Björling see Letter 90/204, note 5.

LETTER 80/192

1   Edmond Fleg (1874-1963), French-Jewish poet, playwright, novelist and religious writer. It has not been possible to establish which French journal ES is referring to; it had presumably been sent to ES by HO. ES's translation into Swedish of Fleg's poem 'Panthéon' appeared in *Ultra* 5 (14 November 1922), p. 75.

2   'Synoptic Poem on Three Planes' (or 'Levels'). This was presumably briefly quoted or merely referred to in the French journal. It seems likely to have been the work of Nicolas Beauduin (1883-?), French poet, dramatist and writer of 'mysteries', who published among other things *Signes doubles; poèmes sur 3 plans* (Double Signs: Poems on Three Planes, 1921) and *Sabbat; poème synoptique sur plusiers plans* (Sabbath: Synoptic Poem on Several Planes, 1922). ES mentions Beauduin with approval in Letter 89/203.

3   I.e. 'after the big event [of sending off the manuscript of the book]', lit. 'after the festival' (Latin).

4   'Månen' (The Moon) was published in *Ultra* 4 (31 October 1922) p. 53, and after ES's death in *The Land That Is Not* (1925).

5   'Captivity' and 'Churchyard Fantasy' were both published in *The Land That Is Not*.

6   The Swedish word 'jägare' means not only 'huntsman' but 'light infantryman', and at this time it would have suggested the German-trained Finnish volunteers who formed the core of the White army in the 1918 civil war, one of whom was clearly living in Raivola with his wife; 'krigare' is a more general word. The poem has no political overtones.

COMMENTARY ON LETTER 80/192

1   Ivan (also spelt Yvan or Iwan) Goll was the pseudonym of Isaac Lang (1891-1950), Jewish Franco-German poet, dramatist, novelist and essayist. Born in Alsace, he led a peripatetic life and wrote in French, German and English. Mainly known for his expressionist and (later) surrealist lyric poetry. Worked with the composer Kurt Weill in the mid-1920s. See Letter 89/203, note 4 on his wife and collaborator Claire Goll.

2   Lidia Stahl had also done the French translation of ED's 'The Jaguar'. He mentions in a letter to HO (3 October 1922) that he has sent some of ES's poems to Stahl for translation into French. Stahl forwarded these translations to Goll who, according to ED, took the view that they were 'too short to represent ES adequately in the anthology, but apart from that he liked them a hell of a lot'. Lidia Stahl (1872-1939) was a colourful figure on the international revolutionary circuit. Though no longer in her first youth, she had seduced ED's political mentor O. W. Kuusinen who then lost her to the American journalist John Reed; Reed's wife Louise Bryant cattily reported that this 'middle-aged woman' had headed the Kronstadt Soviet for more than six months in 1918 (Louise Bryant: *Six Red Months in Russia*, New York, 1918, p. 162). Late in 1920 ED sought out what he called 'this dangerous woman' in Paris, and it was through her that he met such figures as Henri Barbusse (Letter 44/143, note 7) and Ivan Goll. Schoolfield (1985, p. 216) observes that 'although the story of Diktonius' passage into major languages began brilliantly enough' (with Lidia Stahl's French rendering of 'The Jaguar'), 'he has not fared well since.'

3   In *Ultra* 4, 31 October 1922, p. 53.

LETTER 81/193

1   The final lines of 'Churchyard Fantasy'. The poem was not published in *Ultra*.

2   ES's translations into Swedish as 'Ouverture' (Overture) and 'Insjöballad' (Inland Lake Ballad) of two of the Russian ego-futurist Igor Severyanin's poems were published in *Ultra* 2 (30 September 1922), p. 20 and 7-8 (20 December 1922), p.108. She also translated two other of his poems as 'Valentina' and 'Den trettonde' (The thirteenth) but *Ultra* did not publish these, perhaps because they clashed with its radical political line. For Severyanin and Russian futurism see Letter 2/91, note 2.

3   See Letter 80/192, note 2.

4   This refers to Severyanin's 'Overture'.

LETTER 82/195

1   There are no notices of payment of any kind for 1922 in the Society's archives.

2   On Hasselblatt see Letter 59/170, note 7. There are no letters from ES among the Hasselblatt papers.

3   This may be a reference to the photograph (original now lost) used as a model for Albert Gebhard's drawing of ES in *Ultra* 4 (31 October 1922), p. 51. The photograph itself was used on a leaflet advertising Schildts' Christmas List for 1918.

COMMENTARY ON LETTER 82/195

1   Throughout her life HO made a practice of retiring to sanatoria and nursing homes when stressed or exhausted. Her view of them was much more positive than ES's.

LETTER 83/196

1   'Pauli' has not been identified.

2   German publishing house with socialist leanings directed by Ernst Rowohlt. The firm is still active today but its archive was destroyed during the Second World War and no material concerning ES's anthology project survives. It took ES some time to learn to spell Rowohlt's name accurately.

3   Printed in *Ultra* 7-8 (20 December 1922), p. 115 and in a fuller version in SS1 (1990) p. 196.

4   Added by Helena Södergran. I have omitted two brief sections of biographical and bibliographical information she gives on the German-Jewish proto-expressionist poet Alfred Mombert (1872-1942) who is mentioned neither in ES's letters nor in HO's commentary. She comments that she and ES have not been able to get hold of any collection of his poems. Mombert was influenced by Nietzsche, and ES had been familiar with his

poems for many years, but perhaps only through anthologies.

LETTER 84/198

1   Published in *Harsh Songs*, 1922.

2   A reference to the poem 'Det finnes ingen som har tid i världen' (There is no one who has time in the world), published in *The Land That Is Not* (1925). The manuscript is lost but a copy typed by ED has been discovered.

3   'Stallions' alludes to an aphorism in ED's *My Poem* about the bitterness felt by conventional people confronted with 'wild stallions' galloping in freedom.

4   Presumably a reference to the Treaty of Versailles which formally ended the First World War and led to great economic hardship in Germany. It was signed by the Allies and Germany in June 1919 and ratified in July 1920.

LETTER 85/199

1   ES's article on Severyanin appeared in *Ultra* 5 (14 November 1922), p. 72.

2   Altogether six of ES's poems were published in *Ultra* if we include a collection of aphorisms. The complete is: 'Min barndoms träd' (My Childhood's Trees) in no 3 (15 October 1922), p. 47; 'Zigenerskan' (The Gypsy Woman'), 'Hemkomst' (Homecoming) and 'Månen' (The Moon) in No. 4 (31 October 1922), pp. 51 & 53; 'Novembermorgon' (November Morning) and 'Tankar om naturen' (Thoughts about Nature, aphorisms) in No. 7-8 (20 December 1922), pp. 108 & 115. As already mentioned in note 3 to Letter 83/196, 'Thoughts about Nature' was published in a fuller version long after ES's death. The other poems were first collected posthumously in *The Land That Is Not*.

3   ED was staying near Jyväskylä in central Finland at a farm which belonged to the parents of the 23-year-old Finnish singer Meri Marttinen who a year later would become his first wife. This romance may not only have distracted him from *Ultra*, but may also explain his slowness and inefficiency in sending ES suitable poems for the anthology. In any case, he probably did not have all his poems with him in the country.

4   ED's article, 'Edith Södergran. Kritisk hyllning.' (ES, a Critical Appreciation) appeared in *Ultra* 4, 31 October 1922, pp. 52-53.

COMMENTARY ON LETTER 85/199

1   The copy of the Severyanin caricature ES sent HO survive and is reproduced in SS2., p. 256. Anyone interested in what he 'really' looked like will find a 1912 photo-portrait in Markov, between pages 176 and 177.

LETTER 86/200

1   The poet Jarl Hemmer; see HO's Introduction, note 6.

2   A reference to ES's Swedish translation of Edmond Fleg's poem 'Panthéon'.

COMMENTARY TO LETTER 86/200

1   This fuss about the placing of ES's poem on the page seems a little exaggerated. Each page of *Ultra* contained two well-spaced columns of large print, so that nothing was very much 'to one side', though equally nothing could be slap in the middle.

2   The title of the piece Bogs sent was 'Sind Bücher teuer?' (Are Books Dear?).

LETTER 87/201

1   See Letter 32/126, note 8. *Dagens Press* for 29 November 1919 contained an article 'Bellicists' by Victor Aubertin which had previously appeared in Germany in *Berliner Tageblatt*. This presented two French poetry collections which glorified war, Pierre Drieu la Rochelle's *Interrogation* (1917) and Joachim Gasquet's *Les hymnes* (1919). In Aubertin's opinion Drieu la Rochelle's work had a 'more modern tint' than Gasquet's (hardly surprising since, apparently unknown to Aubertin, Drieu was the younger by twenty years), while Drieu loved 'the muddle and mess of slaughter because it seems to correspond to the style of his school'. Among other things, Drieu had delighted in the damage done by the Germans to Rheims cathedral (in contrast to the Swiss painter Hodler, see Letter 29/122, note 8) . Presumably ES did not know it, but Gasquet had died in 1921; his last book, published in the year of his death, bore the challenging title *Il y a une volupté dans la douleur*. The French 'bellicist' movement - if movement it ever was - may have appealed to ES but seems to have left little mark on posterity.

2   A reference to ES's Swedish translation of Severyanin's poem 'Valentina', not published in *Ultra* but still extant in manuscript, and published together with the original by Jänicke (1984).

COMMENTARY TO LETTER 87/201

1   A more basic reason for HO's hostility to Hemmer is that though no older than herself he personified the conservatism that characterised established Finland-Swedish literary circles at the time. Many years later Hans Ruin remembered how two days after the 1917 evening at the Börs

restaurant Hemmer described ES as 'highly strung and eccentric', and said that in his opinion she 'needed a man'. *Ultra* 6 contains a review by ED sharply critical of Hemmer's latest collection of poems *Väntan* (Expectation, 1922); it was not so much that ED was hostile to Hemmer as a person as that he wanted to pillory him because other critics had singled him (Hemmer) out as the one really promising figure among Finland's younger writers. HO probably shared ED's views on this.

LETTER 88/202

1   ES enclosed a letter from Ernst Rowohlt Verlag, dated 17 October 1922 and addressed to the firm of Bogs & Voigt; this had been forwarded to her (ES) by Bogs in Germany together with a press cutting revealing that as a publisher Rowohlt had been fined for blasphemy.

2   On the 23 October ES and her mother wrote separate letters to HO. Helena Södergran was replying to HO's private letter to her suggesting that ES might benefit from a stay in a sanatorium (see Commentary to Letter 82/195). This letter from Helena Södergran to HO is included in Olsson 1955 but not in SS2):

I cannot but be deeply moved by all the warmth and goodwill that pervade your letter. But please don't take it amiss if your well-meant advice, which would certainly be ideal for many other people, is not followed.

Let me explain. Edith has been ill since the late autumn of 1908, and as soon as her illness was diagnosed she entered Nummela sanatorium where she was treated for two years (including periods when she came home) without notable improvement. It was only in Switzerland, where Dr Muralt administered artificial pneumothorax, that any progress was made in fighting the disease. Rest in bed, better nourishment and fresh air were the basis of her treatment there as at Nummela, and we continue the same here too to the best of our ability. Nummela is the best sanatorium in Finland but she never felt comfortable there, and feeling comfortable is one of the most important things with this disease. Bonsdorff himself found that she knew how to look after herself and he is a man who knows what he is talking about. Her treatment by doctors ended with the travel difficulties that followed the outbreak of war, but here at home she has never for a single day neglected to follow the necessary regimen; she has lived year after year with care and caution, and care and caution are not to be lost sight of in a sanatorium either. What has had the most negative effect on her health has been our economic distress with all its large and small consequences. Staying in a sanatorium would not be able to alter any of that would it.

Being in a sanatorium would be even more depressing for her since she would not feel comfortable there and in fact would <u>loathe</u> it. - So now you will understand, Hagar, that I neither will nor can put any pressure on her to move in the direction you have proposed.

Her great concern at the moment is the fate of the anthology and she would happily use her grant for that if it should be necessary, but difficulties have come up. in that respect as must be clear from her letters I believe. She has now been busy with translations and the like for a year and the fact that it isn't leading anywhere is having a depressing effect.

But even if the grant can't be used towards the publication of the anthology it will certainly give her considerable relief and improve the quality of care she can receive, and for this I beg to convey my most heartfelt thanks.

With my warmest regards

H.Södergran

And please don't think it obstinacy or caprice on her part that she won't go into a sanatorium - we have spent far too long in them not to be aware what they are, especially here in the Nordic countries! One sees far too much grief in them.

But we must <u>keep this knowledge to ourselves,</u> Hagar - because it is possible for young people in the first stages of tuberculosis to find help in a sanatorium and the dark side must be hidden from them.

[Dr Axel von Bonsdorff (1869-1945) was director of Nummela sanatorium (now Röykkä hospital) in the Nurmijärvi district north of Helsinki, which incidentally is the part of Finland where ED's family owned the farm on which he spent childhood summer holidays.]

LETTER 89/203

1   This refers to ED's poem 'Rachel' in Harsh Songs, in which the 25-year-old poet describes his erotic feelings for 6-year-old Rachel (the real-life Rachel was a daughter of ED's hostess in Cornwall, Eva Hubback; see Letter 93/207, note 2).

2   'Books of verse'.

3   'Let alone "Young Swedish Lyric Poets in Finland"'; the full German expression would be 'geschweige denn', 'då' being Swedish for 'then'.

4   'Nicolas Beauduon' is clearly a spelling error for Nicolas Beauduin, on whom see Letter 80/192, note 2. René Ghil was the pseudonym of René

Guilbert (1862-1925), French poet and literary theorist. Claire Goll (1890/1-1977) was born Klara Aischmann in Germany and married Ivan Goll (see Commentary on Letter 80/192, note 1) in 1921; together they produced memorable lyric poetry. Like her husband, she was Jewish and wrote in German, French and English. It is not known whether ES ever read much of Beauduin, Ghil and Claire Goll. They are not mentioned in *Ultra*, but ED may have sent her clippings about them containing brief quotations from their work. Incidentally, it is interesting that in one way or another ES came into contact with the work of so many Jewish writers from abroad: Claire Goll, Ivan Goll, Alfred Mombert, Edmond Fleg, Else Lasker-Schüler and perhaps others. It may be that Jews were more likely to have the kind of cosmopolitan outlook the St Petersburg-educated ES found refreshing in contrast to the stuffy literary establishment in Finland - a country with an extremely small Jewish population.

LETTER 90/204

1   The drawing of ES based on Albert Gebhard's photograph; see Letter 81/195, note 3 and the illustrations in SS2, pp.251 and 263.

2   Postcard from Rowohlt to Bogs & Voigt dated 1 November 1922, forwarded by Bogs to ES together with a cutting about Rowohlt's three months' imprisonment.

3   The poem is 'Undret' (The Miracle), first published posthumously in *The Land That Is Not*. ES may have submitted it to *Ultra*'s editorial board but it never appeared in *Ultra*.

4   ED mentions ES's dog Martti in his article about her in *Ultra* 4.

5   The important modernist poet Gunnar Björling (1887-1960) had a poem of homage to ES in *Ultra* 4. Although older than ES, HO and ED, he was not yet widely known; his first collection of poems *Vilande Dag* (Resting Day) having just appeared (on HO's initiative) from the short-lived Daimon press.

6   Both versions of the line mean 'I own a palazzo twelve stories high' but 'uti' is an archaic word commonly used for rhythmic reasons in older Swedish verse.

7   'I shall tune my harp, my harp's golden strings'.

8   Another example of ES's habit of opening brackets and forgetting to close them.

9   This last sentence has been jotted in pencil on the envelope.

LETTER 91/205

1   ED's article about her in *Ultra* 4.

2   It is not clear what this refers to.

3   Gustaf Fröding (1860-1911), Swedish poet, previously referred to in HO's Commentary on Letters 8/97 and 9/98.

4   Published in *The Shadow of the Future* (1920).

5   Poem by ED, published in *My Poem* (1921).

6   In a letter to HO dated 3 October 1922 ED had called Severyanin's poem 'Overture' 'decadent trash' though he liked ES's Swedish translation of it. See also Letter 81/193, note 2.

LETTER 93/207

1   ED's latest collection of poems *Hårda sånger (*Harsh Songs*)*.

2   The sequence of poems in *Harsh Songs* entitled 'Havet och berget' (The Sea and the Mountain) contains several that relate to Cornwall. In August-October 1921 ED had spent seven weeks there at St Merryn near Padstow as a guest of the British economist, educationist and champion of women's rights Eva Hubback (1886-1949), and had been much impressed by the violence of the Atlantic.

3   In *Harsh Songs*.

4   At this point five and a half lines have been completely obliterated with black ink.

5   On Ivan Goll, who corresponded with ED, see Commentary on Letter 80/192, note 1. The 'pyjama-drama' was presumably something by Ivan Goll. ES makes the same comment about not understanding the exotic as she does when faced with Claire Goll's work in Letter 89/203.

6   There is a hymn to Vincent van Gogh by ED in *Ultra* 5, 14 November 1922. See also Letter 66/177, note 2.

LETTER 94/208

1   First published posthumously in *The Land That Is Not*.

2   Arvid Mörne reviewed ED's *Harsh Songs* in *Svenska Pressen* on 30 September 1922. His review of R. R. Eklund's *The Earth Altar* had appeared in *Dagens Press* on 20 May 1919; see Letter 21/114 and HO's commentary on that letter. *Svenska Pressen* was a new Swedish-language evening daily formed in 1922 by the almagamation of two Helsinki Swedish-language papers, *Dagens Press* and *Svenska Tidningen*.

3   Erik Kihlman's anthology *Ur Finlands svenska lyrik* would appear in 1923. It contains nothing by HO, Eklund or ED, but 14 poems by ES.

LETTER 95/209

1   'November Morning' was printed in *Ultra* 7-8 (20 December 1922), p. 108 and posthumously in *The Land That Is Not*.

LETTER 96/210

1   The envelope has been turned inside out and re-used. On the inside is typewritten 'To the Author Edith Södergran Raivola' with a Jyväskylä postmark dated 21 October 1922, suggesting that the envelope had once contained a letter to ES from ED.

2   A reference to ES's hostility towards Gunnar Castrén. See Letter 61/172, note 6.

3   In 1923 the two illustrated family magazines *Veckans krönika* and *Allas Journal* amalgamated, and the resulting illustrated family magazine was simply known as A.

4   Possibly one of these two poems was 'Undret' (The Miracle), mentioned in Letter 90/204 (and see 90/204 note 3) and first published in *The Land That Is Not*. This is the only extant poem by ES in which the word 'nun' appears; if there was another it is lost.

5   When she had begun translating poems by Drieu la Rochelle which had been sent her by HO.

6   See Letter 94/208, note 3.

LETTER 97/211

1   *Ultra*'s last number was 7-8, 20 Dec 1922. Its fate was sealed by economic difficulties and quarrels between members of the editorial board.

2   Presumably a reference to possible ice at sea and winter weather generally.

3   ED's review of Hemmer's *Väntan* (Waiting) in *Ultra* 6, 30 November 1922, p. 92, castigates him as the representative of a bourgeois conservative literary tradition. An unsigned contribution to *Ultra* 2, 30 September 1922, p. 30, headed 'Ultra-krönika' (*Ultra* Review), asks why Hemmer has been awarded the so-called Åkerlund prize in Sweden. See also Letter 87/201 and HO's commentary on it.

4   The art dealer Gösta Stenman (1888-1947) had run the Stenman Gallery in Helsinki since 1913. On 28 December 1922 a notice in *Svenska*

Pressen announced briefly that the directors of the Stenman Gallery had decided not to exhibit a collection of Austrian art partly because the quality of the works in it 'was not what they had been led to expect', and that the exhibition could be seen in the hall of the German school in Helsinki instead.

5   Common abbreviation of 'Helsingfors'.

1923

LETTER 98/212

1   ED was now sleeping in an alcove in his mother's flat in Helsinki. Flats and houses of the period often had such an alcove in the kitchen intended as a place for the maid to sleep, as of course was also the case with the Södergran's home at Raivola. In country farmhouses the whole family might sleep on benches around the kitchen for warmth.

2   A week earlier she had told HO that the manuscript had been sent off 'on 28 November precisely'.

3   'Glimtar ur van Goghs brev' (Glimpses into van Gogh's Letters), selected and translated by ED, *Ultra* 7-8, 20 December 1922, pp. 125f.

4   See Letter 64/175, note 7 on the 'hermit' Denis Peck.

5   The Hotel Ruskola was about half a kilometre from Raivola railway station. It was also quite normal for visitors to Raivola to rent rooms in private homes.

6   ED did not join the Society of Swedish Authors in Finland until 1925.

LETTER 99/213

1   The Goetheanum in Dornach burned down on the the night of 31 December 1922. See Letter 29/122, note 4.

2   'the cultural ties'.

3   Following this final rebuff ES burned the manuscript of the anthology. After her death Helena Södergran reported to ED (4 August 1923): 'Last winter Edith burned the two exercise books that contained the anthology before my eyes. She kissed them and laid them on the fire. She sacrificed them to God "I should have trusted in Him and not in this".'

4   Perhaps the 'rival' who bit Martti a couple of months earlier (Letter 91/205).

5   'fit to work'.

6   In the poem 'Undret' (The Miracle). See Letter 90/204, note 3 and Letter 97/211. The posthumously published version in *The Land That Is Not*

has 'dräkten' ('habit', 'dress') rather than 'doken/doket' ('headdress', 'wimple').

7   This could be a reference to plans by HO and ED to start a new periodical following the collapse of *Ultra*. This new periodical is discussed in a letter from HO to ED dated 29 December 1922; it was to have been called *Independence*.

LETTER 100/214
1   Rakel Kansanen-Toivola (1888-1949). See HO's commentary on Letter 102/216.

LETTER 101/215
1   'visitors from Helsinki' (Finnish).

LETTER 102/216
1   In Olsson 1955 HO regarded this undated text as a continuation of 101/215, whereas SS2 judges it to be a separate letter, posted to HO between 8 and 16 March 1923 together with the book-cover featuring an embroidered picture of a 'marchioness' with a goose (see SS2, p.279).

2   'suitable for exhibition in an art gallery'.

3   See Letter 88/202, note 2 where Helena Södergran's reply to HO's letter is reproduced in full.

4   The mention of Halila had alarmed ES as it was the name of a sanatorium.

COMMENTARY ON LETTER 102/216
1   The Finnish painter Tyko Sallinen; see Letter 32/126, note 11.

2   I.e. the Finnish delegation.

3   The lines that provoked Hemmer's scorn come at the end of the poem:
> With one leap
> the jaguar hurls himself over
> the tops of the firs -
> the stars exult as he roars! -
> one lightning leap through the air
> then deep as an arrow into the earth's breast.

LETTER 103/217
1   The writer Hjalmar Procopé; see Commentary on Letter 2/91, note 2.

2   Forest was being cleared to increase the acreage of arable land in the Raivola area.

3   With her beloved cat dead ES is beginning to give multiple names to her dog Martti (on multiple names see Commentary on Letter 10/99, note 2). The Finnish word 'rakki' means 'cur'.

LETTER 104/218

1   ES's picture postcard features a portrait of the French film director and actor Max Linder (1883-1925, real name Gabriel Maximilien Leuville).

LETTER 105/219

1   In the periodical *Frihet* No 2, 1923; reprinted in ED's *Meningar* (Opinions, 1957), pp. 208-213.

2   During May 1923 the fifth anniversary of the victory of the Whites in the Finnish civil war was celebrated in Viipuri and the Karelian isthmus. Many so-called 'monuments to freedom' were unveiled in various places. On Mannerheim see Letter 18/111, note 2. The lawyer and politician Pehr Evind Svinhufvud (1861-1944) had been speaker of the Finnish Diet during Russian rule 1907-12 before being banished to Siberia by the Russian government in 1914-17. After Finland's unilateral declaration of independence late in 1917 he became head of the country's provisional government, and in 1918 led the victorious White administration during the Finnish civil war with Mannerheim as commander-in-chief. Temporary Regent of Finland 1918 (followed by Mannerheim 1918-19), he ended his active career as President of the Republic 1931-37.

3   The Goetheanum at Dornach. See Letter 29/122, note 4.

LETTER 106/220

1   See HO's Commentary on Letter 102/216.

2   Also known as Lake Geneva.

3   On 19 April 1923 *Hufvudstadsbladet* carried an announcement of grants to writers from the Society of Swedish Authors in Finland. HO got 5,000 Finnish marks and ED 4,000.

4   Harry Blomberg (1893-1950), Swedish writer and editor, contributor to *Ultra*, corresponded with ES but her letters to him have been lost. On 15 December 1922 Blomberg had written to ED: 'I sent my book to Södergran but have heard nothing from her. Is she ill or indifferent? I hope the latter'. The book was probably his latest collection of poems *Landkänning* (Landfall), which HO reviewed in the final number of *Ultra*.

LETTER 107/221

1   ED's collection of aphorisms *Brödet och elden* (The Bread and the Fire) came out in autumn 1923.

LETTER 108/223

1   Posted by Helena Södergran after ES's death. The date must be wrong since John the Baptist's Day (Midsummer Day) is always 24 June. It has been claimed that this letter also contained on a separate piece of paper two poems in German by unknown authors written out in very weak handwriting in pencil reinforced by ink, but there is no proof of this. See footnote in SS2 pp. 286-7. On the other hand she did write out two poems in German on the day she died, but these are now thought to be one by Steiner ('Geister eurer Seelen') and the other a translation by ES of part of a poem by R. R. Eklund.

2   *Nya Argus* 6, 15 June 1923, contains on p. 94 'Två mjuka dikter' (Two Gentle Poems) by ED.

3   A return for all the many views of Switzerland ES had sent HO over the years. The scene made a deep impression on HO: many years later she told a new friend, Nadja Martinoff: 'I suddenly saw before me the beautiful narcissi up in the mountains at Les Avants in Switzerland, with the glistening peaks of the Alps as a backdrop, and I thought, we'll go walking there one day' (letter dated July 1945).

HAGAR OLSSON TO ELMER DIKTONIUS, 2 JULY 1923

1   As quoted in Holmström 1993, pp. 72-73.

2   Eric Olsoni (1893-1973), theatre critic, editor and bookdealer.

HELENA SÖDERGRAN TO HAGAR OLSSON, 8 JULY 1923

1   As quoted in Olsson 1955 (1973 edn, pp. 168-9).

2   Närpes, an almost entirely Swedish-speaking district in west central Finland, is where ES's father was born. Perniö (in Swedish 'Bjärnå') and Nauvo (in Swedish 'Nagu') are in south-west Finland.

3   ES seems to have made her peace with Steiner at the very end. Apparently she not only wrote out one of his poems on the last day of her life (see Letter 108/223, note 1) but asked that the anthroposophist Dagmar von Schantz (once dismissed as 'vulgar' in a letter to HO) should conduct her burial service. This, however, was not permitted by law.

4   On the 3,000 Finnish marks see HO's Commentary to Letters 101/215 and 102/216.

HELENA SÖDERGRAN TO HAGAR OLSSON, 8 AUGUST 1923

1   Excerpt from letter reproduced in full in Olsson 1955 (1973 edn, pp. 169-70).

LETTER 109/224

1   ES's handwriting is so unclear that even Helena Södergran seems to have difficulty reading it in places since she did not ink over every word. I follow SS2 in reading 'hjärteblod' (heart's blood). Olsson 1955 reads 'hjärtebarn' (heart's child). The original is clearly reproduced in SS2, p.287.

APPENDIX

1   Some years earlier, reviewing a selection of ES's poems edited by Jarl Hemmer, HO had written: 'In reading her poems, one should at least let them remain what they were for her - reality. To her imagination and reality were one and the same, as they are for a child. Her relationship. with animals, with trees, with things in general was formed by imagination, her whole vision of the world was touched with magic. This is the explanation for her quite exceptional faith in the power of art. This faith was naive, in the deepest and most fundamental meaning of the word. To describe it as Hemmer does as "a desperate need to assert her own importance" and "hubris" is to trivialise it', *Svenska Pressen*, 2 November 1929.

2   HO was writing in September 1940, during the uneasy peace which followed the 'Winter War' (see Introduction, note 1). Finland had not in fact lost the whole of Karelia.

3   Russians would call them 'dachas' and they are certainly not 'villas' in any south-European sense but large wooden houses more elaborately decorated than would be the case further west even in Finland. The Karelian isthmus was of course the hinterland of St Petersburg when Finland was under Russian rule from 1809 to 1917.

4   In the later 1930s the resort of Kuokkala, near Raivola, became a favourite holiday destination for Finland-Swedish and Swedish poets, Diktonius among them, and they would make a pilgrimage to Raivola where Helena Södergran was still living.

5   At the time of writing in late 1940 HO did not yet know that little was left of these 'expressively beautiful trees'. When Finnish troops returned to Raivola during the 1941-44 'Continuation War' with the Soviet Union they found a scene of desolation. As one of those who had known Raivola in the Kuokkala days reported: 'The church is gone, not a trace of it. Our [troops] set fire to it during the Winter War. Where it stood there is a large garage now...The gravestone no longer exists. Quite disappeared. Probably the Russians carried it away somewhere...The Södergran garden is partly a horse-pasture, and partly a luxuriant thicket of blooming roses and bushes. Most of the big trees are burned or damaged. The house went up in flames at the same time as the church...' (Sven Grönvall to Elmer Diktonius, 23 June 1943; quoted and translated by Schoolfield, 1984 p. 25).

6   See Letter 2/91, note 3.

7   See Letter 64/175, note 8.

8   Presumably a reference to the ego-futurists (see Letter 2/91, note 2; in the same letter ES accuses Severyanin of being 'obsessed with the boudoir').

9   1940-41.

10   HO gives two excerpts from 'Fragment' here. The complete poem was first published in *The September Lyre*, 1918.

11   On pneumothorax see Letter 2/91, note 4.

12   On Peck see Letter 64/175, note 7.

13   In Finland most first names, whether names of saints or not, are allotted their own day of the year, and a person's name-day is as important as their birthday.

14   An allusion to the poem 'O mina solbrandsfärgade toppar' (O My Sunflame-Coloured Peaks) in *The September Lyre*.

15   From the poem 'Jorden blev förvandlad till en askhög' (The earth has been turned to a heap of ashes) in *The Rose Altar*, 1919.

16   The Second World War, and particularly the uneasy peace in Finland after the 'Winter War' of 1939-40.

17   This is the complete poem, first published in *The Rose Altar*.

18   ES quoted the last three of these lines in her first letter to HO (Letter 1/90); the full twenty lines of the poem 'Var bo gudarna...' (Where do the gods live) first appeared in *The Rose Altar*.

19   From the poem 'Lidandets kalk' (The Cup of Suffering) which was among those enclosed with ES's first letter to HO (1/90). It was first published in *The Rose Altar*.

20   From the poem 'Besvärjelsen' (The Invocation), published in *The Rose Altar*.

21   HO quotes the whole letter under its title 'Individual Art' in the Introduction to her 1955 edition of ES's letters (see pages 24-25).

22   'Homecoming' first appeared in *Ultra* (see Letter 85/199, note 2), and all three poems were published in the posthumous collection *The Land That Is Not*, 1925.

23   Materialistic. On Ahriman see Letter 47/146, note 4.

24   From the poem 'O Heavenly Clarity', written in September 1922. See note 22 above, and on the word 'clarity' (klarhet) see Letter 53/159, note 2.

25   This was a short collection of aphorisms (25 lines in all) apparently written in September 1922. The first seventeen lines, which do not include the comment on religion and nature quoted here by HO, were printed in

Ultra 7-8 (20 December 1922), p. 115; the rest remained unpublished until much later. The complete set appears in SS1 pp. 196-197.

26   Letter 47/146.

27   Letter 48/150.

28   Whitsunday falls between May 10 and June 13, depending on the date of Easter.

29   This can only have been Martti, perhaps an 'official' name for him recalling ES's days in Switzerland. 'Martti' is Finnish for 'Martin'.

FURTHER READING

For a fuller list in all languages and for a list of sources of unpublished material, see SS2, pp. 294-304. Schoolfield (1984) also contains a comprehensive bibliography.

Abbreviations:
SS   Edith Södergran, *Samlade Skrifter* (Collected Works of Edith Södergran)
SLSF   Svenska litteratursällskapet i Finland (Swedish Literature Association in Finland)
FSLH   *Finlands svenska litteraturhistoria* (The History of Swedish Literature in Finland)

In English (all or in part)

Ahern, Geoffrey. *Sun at Midnight: the Rudolf Steiner Movement and the Western Esoteric Tradition.* The Aquarian Press, Wellingborough (England), 1984. Written by a non-anthroposophist.

Bradbury, Malcolm and James McFarlane (eds). *Modernism 1890-1930.* Penguin Books, Middlesex (England), 1974, and later editions from other publishers. Hardly mentions ES but is an excellent general guide to the concept of modernism.

Allwood, Martin (translator, in collaboration with Cate Ewing and Robert Lyng). *The Collected Poems of Edith Södergran.* Mullsjö, 1980.

Broomans, Petra, Adriaan van der Hoeven, and Jytte Kronig (eds). *Edith Södergran, A Changing Image, Looking for a New Perspective on the Work of a Finnish Avant-garde Poet.* University of Groningen (Netherlands), 1993.

Espmark, Kjell. 'The Translation of the Soul: A Principal Feature in Finland-Swedish Modernism', *Scandinavica* 15 (1976), pp. 5-27.

Goodrich, Austin. *Study in Sisu: Finland's Fight for Independence.* Ballantine Books, New York, 1960.

Gustafsson, Lars. 'The Enigmatic Particles in the Nucleus,' in Gustafsson, *Forays into Swedish Poetry* (trans. Robert T. Rovinsky). University of Texas Press, Austin and London, 1979, pp. 100-105.

Hannula, J.O. *Finland's War of Independence.* Faber, London, 1939.

Hartgrove, J.Dane. 'The Kronstadt Uprising of 1921', in *The Modern Encyclopedia of Russian and Soviet History*, ed. Joseph L.Wieczynski, vol 18, Academic International Press, 1980.

Jones, Glyn W. and M. A. Branch (eds) *Edith Södergran, Nine Essays on her Life and Work.* University of London with the Finnish Literature Society, London, 1992.

Katchadourian, Stina (translator). *Love and Solitude: Selected Poems 1916-1923*. Fjord Press, San Francisco, 1981. (Contains 31 Södergran poems in English with facing Swedish texts)

McDuff, David (translator). *Edith Södergran: Complete Poems*. Bloodaxe Books, Newcastle-upon-Tyne, 1984. Contains a useful general introduction, clear literal translations of the poems and an extensive range of photographs taken during ES's lifetime.

Markov, Vladimir. *Russian Futurism, A History*. University of California Press, Berkeley and Los Angeles, 1968.

Puntila, L.A., trans. David Miller. *The Political History of Finland 1809-1966*. Otava, Helsinki, 1974.

Schoolfield, George C. *Edith Södergran: Modernist Poet in Finland*. Greenwood Press, Westport (Connecticut) and London, 1984. A comprehensive survey of her life and work.

Schoolfield, George C. *Elmer Diktonius*. Greenwood Press, Westport (Connecticut) and London, 1985. Similar in approach and range to the same author's *Edith Södergran*.

Schoolfield, George C. and Laurie Thompson (eds). *Two Women Writers from Finland: Edith Södergran and Hagar Olsson*. (Papers given at a Symposium at Yale University October 21-23 1993), Lockharton Press, Edinburgh, 1995. (This contains seven papers in English, seven in Swedish, one in Danish, and one in German. The papers on Södergran are predominantly in English, those on Olsson predominantly in Swedish.)

Shepherd, A. P. *A Scientist of the Invisible*. Hodder & Stoughton, London, 1971. An introduction to Rudolf Steiner and anthroposophy by a committed believer.

Wrede, Johan. 'The Birth of Finland-Swedish Modernism,' *Scandinavica* 15 (1976), pp. 145-165.

In Swedish or Other Languages

Edith Södergrans dikter, med inledning av Hagar Olsson. Holger Schildt, Helsingfors, 1941.

Enckell, Olof. *Den unge Diktonius*. Holger Schildt, Helsingfors, 1946.

Enckell, Olof. *Den unga Hagar Olsson*. SLSF, Helsingfors, 1949.

Enckell, Olof. *Esteticism och nietzscheanism i Edith Södergrans lyrik*. SLSF, Helsingfors, 1949.

Fages, Loup de. *Edith Södergran*. Debresse, Paris 1970. A French view.

Holmström, Roger. *Hagar Olsson och den öppna horisonten, Liv och diktning 1920-1945*. Schildts, Helsingfors, 1993.

Holmström, Roger. *Hagar Olsson och den växande melankolin, Liv och*

239

diktning 1945-1978. Schildts, Helsingfors, 1995.

Jänicke, Gisbert. *Edith Södergran diktare på två språk.* SLSF, Helsingfors, 1984. Written in Swedish, a German view of a poet who always claimed her best language was German. Also contains texts of her translations from French and Russian.

Olsson, Hagar. *Ediths brev.* Holger Schildt, Helsingfors/Bonniers, Stockholm 1955. Reprinted 1973 and 1990.

Olsson, Hagar. *Tidig prosa.* Schildts, Helsingfors, 1963. Contains HO's first three books *Lars Thorman och döden* (1916), *Själarnas ansikten* (1917) and *Kvinnan och nåden* (1919), with an introduction 'Ett stycke liv' by Jörn Donner.

Rahikainen, Agneta (utgivare). *Som en eld över askan: Edith Södergrans fotografier.* SLSF/Akademiska bokhandeln, Helsingfors, 1993. Photographs taken by ES reproduced in large format with apposite quotations from her writings.

Ström, Eva. *Edith Södergran.* Natur och Kultur, Stockholm, 1994. A basic introduction in Swedish.

Södergran, Edith. *Brev* (*Samlade skrifter* 2, utgivna av Agneta Rahikainen). SLSF, Helsingfors, 1996 (=SS2). The standard edition of the letters. Very extensively annotated and with a wide range of relevant pictorial illustrations of all kinds.

Södergran, Edith. *Dikter och aforismer* (*Samlade skrifter* 1, redigerade av Holger Lillqvist). SLSF, Helsingfors, 1990 (=SS1). The standard edition of the poetry.

Tideström, Gunnar. *Edith Södergran.* Holger Schildt, Helsingfors/ Wahlström & Widstrand, Stockholm, 1949. The pioneering study.

Witt-Brattström, Ebba. *Ediths jag: Edith Södergran och modernismens födelse.* Norstedts, Stockholm, 1997. A feminist view, critical of Tideström's male-orientated approach.

Wrede, Johan. 'Tidskriften Ultra,' in *Festskrift till Olof Enckell 1970*, SLSF, Helsingfors, 1970.

Zilliacus, Clas. 'Avantgardet i öster - finlandssvensk modernism', in Lönnroth, Lars and Sven Delblanc (utgivarna). *Den svenska litteraturen*, 5 (1989), reprinted as 3 (1999), pp. 149-176. Bonniers, Stockholm. Written from a Swedish point of view.

Zilliacus, Clas (ed.). *Finlands svenska litteraturhistoria II: 1900-talet.* SLSF, Helsingfors/Atlantis, Stockholm, 2000. Places Finland-Swedish modernism in the context of the rest of the century's Finland-Swedish literature. Also contains a thumbnail career sketch and full work-list for each writer as well as a comprehensive bibliography of secondary sources.

www.ingramcontent.com/pod-product-compliance
Lightning Source LLC
Chambersburg PA
CBHW052033020726
47501CB00004B/1384